Readings
and Resources
in Youth Ministry

Readings and Resources in Youth Ministry

Edited by Michael Warren

Saint Mary's Press
Christian Brothers Publications
Winona, Minnesota

This book is for Bro. Paul Feeney, CFX,
whose teaching on nonviolence and social justice
has influenced so many young people
and inspired so many others
to take up that educational challenge.

The publishing team for this book included Robert P. Stamschror, development
editor; Barbara Allaire and Mary Kraemer, manuscript editors; Lynn Dahdal, production editor; Cindi Ramm, cover designer; and Mary Kraemer, indexer.

The acknowledgments continue on page 254.

Printed in the United States of America

Printing: 6 5 4 3 2 1
Year: 1993 92 91 90 89 88 87

ISBN 0-88489-178-X

Contributors

Msgr. Thomas Cahalane is a pastor and the ecumenical officer for the Diocese of Tucson, Arizona.

Nancy Hennessy Cooney is the director of Ministry Watch, located in Milwaukee, Wisconsin. Ministry Watch is a computerized system for the nationwide recruitment of professionals in ministry.

Richard Costello is the director of development for the Diocese of Norwich, Connecticut.

Craig Dykstra, PhD, is the Thomas W. Synnott Professor of Christian Education at Princeton Theological Seminary in Princeton, New Jersey.

Jeffrey Johnson is the coordinator of youth ministry for the Archdiocese of Saint Paul–Minneapolis, Minnesota.

Rev. Don Kimball is the program director for Cornerstone Media, located in Santa Rosa, California.

Gisela Konopka, DSW, is professor emeritus at the University of Minnesota, Saint Paul. She served in the School of Social Work and the Center for Youth Development and Research.

Merton P. Strommen is the founder and longtime director of the Search Institute in Minneapolis, Minnesota.

Michael Warren is an associate professor of religious education in catechetical ministry in the Department of Theology at Saint John's University, Jamaica, New York.

Young Life Board of Trustees is headquartered in Colorado Springs, Colorado. Young Life is a Christian, nondenominational, youth ministry organization.

Tom Zanzig is a consultant and an author at Saint Mary's Press in Winona, Minnesota.

Contents

Part B: Doing Youth Ministry

Part C: Envisioning the Future of Youth Ministry

Introduction

Over the past fifteen years or so, youth ministry has emerged in the Roman Catholic Church in the United States as a fresh and lively form of pastoral work. Using a new language of ministry and a more integrated vision of young people, their needs, and their place in the Church, Catholics have sought to inform one another about the principles of youth ministry and its possibilities. One of the first needs of this emerging field was for a literature that would give those interested a verbal repertoire with which to talk about and think about youth ministry.

Of course, among Protestant Churches, youth ministry had long had an important place by the time Catholics finally came to use the category. Catholics exploring youth ministry found great help in Protestant writing and continue to do so. However, Catholics needed to develop their own literature, and I myself have worked to develop some of that literature. Thus, I was disappointed when a few years ago, two books about youth ministry I had edited were allowed to go out of print. They were *Youth Ministry: A Book of Readings* and *Resources for Youth Ministry.* Because I thought the books were useful, especially to those who were just coming to understand youth ministry, I sought to have them reprinted. However, my attempts were in vain.

It was a casual conversation with Robert Smith, FSC, of Saint Mary's Press that finally led to the present book, which combines material from the two earlier collections. At the time of that conversation we were working on publishing *Sourcebook for Modern Catechetics,* and Bob encouraged me to pursue with Saint Mary's Press the reissue of the pertinent material from the youth ministry books. There were inevitable delays, but now the book appears in a form that I hope will be a valuable resource to those in youth ministry, especially those training others for youth ministry.

The difficulty I have found in re-editing this book is that my own thinking has gone beyond the material in the earlier books. However, I recognize that persons being introduced to the field of youth ministry will need access to the kind of basic thinking found in those books. Also that material forms a valuable record of the progress of youth ministry thinking in the United States.

Readers familiar with the two earlier books will recognize new material here, particularly the essays of Tom Zanzig and Craig Dykstra. These are precisely the kinds of material I would have included in the original books, had they been available at that time. Also, I have included my own recent reflections on the current state of youth ministry, which were given to the first national convocation on youth ministry in Canada. The ideas offered there are an attempt to redirect youth ministry in general toward a greater awareness of social reality, including issues of social justice. Youth ministry in the United States has still to decide whether it conceives of itself as offering young people a "haven in a heartless world" or the "option for the poor" and for solidarity with victims. If this book records some of the contributions of the past, that decision about the direction and priorities of our work with young people sets forth the challenge of the future in youth ministry.

In addition to the usual editing of the new essays in this collection, all the reprints (except the essays by Strommen and Konopka and the statement of the Young Life Board of Trustees) have been edited to use inclusive language, to modernize punctuation, and to create a consistent style in spelling, capitalization, and endnotes throughout the book.

Part A:

Thinking
About Youth Ministry

Essay 1

Evangelization of Youth

Michael Warren

The term evangelization *currently is being used in many different senses. The following article attempts to trace the development of evangelization theory and then apply it to youth ministry. The theory of evangelization developed by missionaries like Alfonso Nebreda does not simplify our ministry in any way. What it does do is put it on a firm foundation. The following ideas might profitably be discussed by parish councils and ministry teams to explore the total community context of a parish's ministry to youth.*

This essay is reprinted from Youth Ministry: A Book of Readings, *ed. Michael Warren (New York: Paulist Press, 1977), pages 47–57.*

Is this the best of times or the worst of times for leading young people to Christian faith? Some would say it is the worst of times, and to back up their position they would point to the statistics recently issued by the Department of Education of the United States Catholic Conference. Entitled "Where Are the 6.6 Million?" this report presents some discomforting data. According to these figures, the number of Catholics of high school age receiving no formal religious education has risen from almost 1.5 million, or 36.5 percent, in 1965 to more than 3 million, or 61.4 percent, in 1974. "Worst-of-timers" would also point out that in every diocese of the country there are parishes that have simply, and usually quietly, shut down their programs of adolescent catechesis. For these parishes the situation is so hopeless as not to be worth the effort. But, for anyone to whom the above assertions are questionable, we now have *proof* in the form of the following "Greelization":

> The NORC research would indicate that the various forms of non-parochial school religious instruction which have become popular in the Catholic Church in the last ten years are not an adequate substitute for parochial schools. In most cases they seem to have practically no effect at all. (Andrew Greeley, "Is the Church Declining?" *Origins* [8 April 1976], p. 672)

Yet some others are claiming that it is the best of times for working with young people. I myself know many people working with youth, including those working in programs that supposedly "have practically no effect at all," who are finding considerable personal satisfaction in their efforts and who claim that a whole renewed ministry to youth is emerging in the U.S. Catholic Church. More and more dioceses now have programs for training and employing young people in their early twenties as full-time youth ministers. In this country, youth retreats have never been used so widely or so well as they currently are. Some bishops will point out that in their dioceses no other area of ministry is showing the degree of creativity or the radical efforts that characterize ministry to youth.

What seems to have happened, if one may be allowed to interpret the current situation, is that work with Catholic youth, especially outside of Catholic schools, had indeed reached a sort of crisis of limits, an absolute low point. However, this crisis was the start of new life. When we reach a crisis point in anything—from personal life to social and political life—we are forced to reexamine fundamental principles and priorities. We are forced to search out the essential. In a crisis everything else becomes a luxury. Where ministry to youth is succeeding, it is operating from well-based fundamental principles of ministry.

In fact, one of the most valuable aspects of the current renewal of youth ministry may well be that it is uncovering principles of ministry applicable to dealing with other age-groups. Radical ministry to youth, for example, has long since ceased operating on any person's *fiat,* including those of parents and pastors. Young people come together because they want to, not because they have to. They have been searched out and sounded out and invited out and then welcomed in. The day is not long off when the initiatives of youth ministers in going out to meet young people in parks, around their public schools, and at their other hangouts will be a model for a radical ministry to adults who are alienated from their religion. Parish ministry in the future will lose much of its present character of sedentary availability and move closer to the sort of outreach ministry to which Jesus commissioned his first disciples. Youth ministers are helping us uncover the true task of ministry, as not so much one of dealing with assembled communities, but as one of being assemblers of the community. The task of assembling the community is basically the task of evangelization.

The new dynamism of renewed ministries in the Catholic Church, including ministry to youth, was foreshadowed almost a quarter century ago in Europe. In fact, the situation out of which the word *evangelization* grew twenty-five years ago is strikingly similar to that out of which contemporary youth ministry is growing. Understanding this similarity will be helpful in understanding other relationships between youth ministry and evangelization.

After World War II, Europe seemed to be in a desperate situation as regards the Christian Churches, including the Catholic Church. Catholic missionaries being trained in France to spread the Gospel in mission lands came to see that many "Christians" in Europe had been baptized and instructed but had never come to conversion to the Way of Jesus. Europe itself was as much a mission territory as the so-called pagan lands. The religious affiliation of the nonconverted Christians had been socially induced but never personally ratified. In fact, Alfonso Nebreda came to see that it was easier to lead to Christ a Japanese who knew little of the Gospel than it was to lead a French Catholic who reacted to the same message with a stifled yawn.

These missionaries, under the direction of their teacher, Dominican theologian Piere André Liégé, began to distinguish between catechesis and evangelization. Catechesis was a process of leading both communities and individual members of the faithful (i.e., of the faith-filled) to maturity of faith. Catechesis, then, dealt with those who had already been converted to Jesus. The preconversion process of proclaiming the Gospel and leading people to faith in Jesus demanded a new term and a more radical frame of mind. For the new term, Liégé suggested the word *evangelization,* that is, "gospelling" or even "good-newsing." Evangelization demanded a missionary attitude. Indeed those who studied with Liégé, even if like Pierre Babin they remained in France, maintained a pastoral attitude that was basically a missionary one. It is no wonder, then, that so many of the statements on current youth ministry echo so many of the concerns of Liégé's Evangelization School of more than two decades ago.

What, then, are these concerns on which youth ministry in this country is based and that are so close to the concerns of evangelization? Because of the limitations of space, I will examine two that are of key importance: concern for clear witness and concern for indigenization.

One of the preoccupations of literature dealing with evangelization is a concern with signs and ultimately with the sign of witness. At a time when the Church in Europe seemed to be dying because many persons were Christian in name only, such a concern with witness was needed. The personal lives of men and women showed few signs of fidelity to the Gospel of Jesus. Thus the Roman Catholic Church and the other Christian Churches were found to be severely lacking in credibility. As groups of persons supposedly committed to Jesus' Way, their personal and corporate lives were not believable.

Far from being limited to European catechists in the 1950s, this preoccupation with the lived life of a community as a key source of its credibility characterized the earliest Christian communities in the Christian Testament. Scholars point out that the word used for proclaiming the Gospel among the first disciples of Jesus was *kerussein* or "to preach." Once communities were more solidly established, another word began to be used. It seems that when the Churches secured a foothold in society, the "gospelling" of individual preachers was not of itself sufficient. The churches themselves had to be signs of the Good News. The new word was *matturein,* meaning "to witness."

Thus the later Johannine writings prefer the word *witness,* suggesting a more communitarian dimension of the task of proclaiming the Gospel. By the time of John, those to whom the Gospel had been preached had become established as communities of believers, and their task was one of taking care that their corporate life be a clear sign. In the context of John, then, *witness* suggests a corporate form of preaching. The community's life of communion and fellowship was to be a powerful word, making believable their commitment to the Gospel.

In a quick overview of the literature of contemporary youth ministry, one finds much attention to the importance of communitarian witness. Those working with the young point again and again to the importance for young people of a fellowship of adult believers whose corporate life reflects the Gospel in deed and not just in word. Personal and corporate credibility is a powerful positive force in the lives of the young. On the other hand, parish life that is a mere going-through-the-paces and where the Gospel has been domesticated, if not caged, seems to many young people astonishingly incredible.

Admittedly this is a difficult issue to face, since it suggests that the evangelization of young people cannot succeed fully without a more Gospel-centered life on the part of whole parishes. Moreover, all will admit that such a reconversion process is not an easy one to effect, even if all could agree on the new orientation that would be called for. Many youth ministers will claim they are simply trying to do the possible in forming smaller fellowship groups comprised of a majority of young people and a minority of adults struggling to deepen their own commitment to Jesus and his Way. One can find these groups on youth retreat weekends and in Sunday youth liturgies attended by large numbers of young people in Catholic high school and college chapels.

Those directing such community-centered programs are aware that a future problem will be finding adult communities, especially parishes, that these young people can eventually join. Many of these leaders will apologize for what is an apparent alienation from parish life by claiming they are attempting not the ideal but more an expedient called for by the times. However, they can take heart that their efforts seem to be following the lines elaborated by the recent apostolic exhortation of Pope Paul VI, *On Evangelization in the Modern World.* By trying to establish core groups of believers to which others can affiliate more or less closely, leaders are undertaking an effective evangelization of young people.

> Above all the Gospel must be proclaimed by witness. Take a Christian or a handful of Christians who, in the midst of their own community, show their capacity for understanding and acceptance, their sharing of life and destiny with other people, their solidarity with the efforts of all for whatever is noble and good. Let us suppose that, in addition, they radiate in an altogether simple and

unaffected way their faith in values that go beyond current values, and their hope in something that is not seen and that one would not dare to imagine. Through this wordless witness these Christians stir up irresistible questions in the hearts of those who see how they live: Why are they like this? Why do they live in this way? What or who is it that inspires them? Why are they in our midst? Such a witness is already a silent proclamation of the Good News and a very powerful and effective one. Here we have an initial act of evangelization. (No. 21)

One could theorize that the eventual conversion of many nominally Christian adults will take place by means of the witness of these smaller communities-within-communities, which seem to have such an influence now in the lives of the young.

For all ages it is true that adherence to the Gospel cannot remain abstract and unincarnated, but it must at some point become embodied and concretized by a visible entry into a community of believers.

Another concern of youth ministry that is closely connected with evangelization is indigenization. Although many persons ministering to youth are unfamiliar with the somewhat awkward term *indigenization,* the meaning behind this word guides much of the best thinking in youth ministry today. Thus a brief examination of indigenization is in order here.

For many decades now, much of the so-called new catechetics could be summed up in the word *adaptation.* The Word of God is a word for human persons and must be proclaimed in such a way that it connects with a person's own life. Following this insight through to its logical conclusions has triggered vast changes in the way the ministry of the Word is undertaken. Catechists have taken keen interest in the various social sciences, as one step in uncovering the mentalities of those to whom they wish to proclaim the Gospel. Stages of psychological development got special attention, in an attempt to help others grow in their understanding of the Christian message. Catechists questioned many practices taken for granted in the past, particularly the practice of having children memorize theological propositions they could not possibly understand and could very probably misunderstand. In a sense, then, adaptation looks at the matter of communicating the Gospel from the point of view of the communicator. Adaptation is the task of the communicator, who must take pains to tailor the Gospel to particular mentalities.

Indigenization, however, has moved the question of adaptation to a new depth, to a new level of seriousness. This term suggests that the Good News can and must come to grow in the life of a people. The Gospel is meant for all soils. It is meant to be a native flower wherever it is sown. Whereas adaptation suggests a transplant, that is, something living in nonnative soil, indigenization suggests the process by which Christianity takes root totally in the unique soil and atmosphere of a particular culture or mentality. Whereas adaptation is done by those who proclaim the Gospel, indigenization can only be encouraged by ministers of the Word, with the actual process happening among the people.

The strongest recent pressure for indigenization has come from India, struggling to find, at the end of a long period of colonial rule and of aping Western customs, the forms of Christian living natural to the Gospel in their culture. Indian catechetical leaders realize that many Indians will not be able to recognize the gospel call except in Indian dress. For many theologians, a prime analogue of indigenization is the Incarnation. Indigenization is much more in line with the Incarnation than is adaptation. Jesus came as a native. As exegete Raymond Brown is so fond of saying, "He was a Galilean Jew of the first third of the first century." If Jesus came as a native, then the Good News is meant to go native wherever it goes.

In youth ministry, the Gospel-gone-native can be seen in many developments, one of the chief being the new sense of ministry taking root among young people themselves. Where once young people showed in response to the Gospel a desire for apostolic action of various kinds, today's young people in addition are asking to exercise a direct ministry in the Church. In some dioceses, college graduates are being trained as youth ministers and are assuming full-time positions ministering either to their peers or to those just younger. Young people of high school age are now serving as leaders on retreat teams. In some cases, the adults who direct them recognize them as the most effective members of these teams. In some places, teens are now training to develop the skills for various peer ministries, including peer counseling.

Another form of indigenization in youth ministry is youth liturgies. Matteo Ricci, the Jesuit who was refused permission to allow the seventeenth-century Chinese to develop their own native forms of Christian worship, would be pleased at the reverent and appropriate liturgical forms being developed by young people. These forms are expressive of the entire mentality of young people. For instance, these liturgies use a variety of strategies to allow each person to have his or her own say in response to the scriptural readings. Such responsiveness is important to young people groping to discover their own word of faith. Subgroups work to prepare appropriate mime, dance, and musical responses within the Eucharist. Black and Hispanic teens are finding ways to express both their own youth culture and their ethnic riches in worship. Our national liturgical scene is being enriched by these efforts.

Such developments are threatening to parish leaders who wonder if the young will ever return to parish assemblies from these more "native" liturgies. The more accurate question might be whether parish assemblies will welcome some of the native riches of young people and in this way allow them the influence they are denied in most parishes. Youth ministry today is enfranchising young people, giving them a vote and a say and a task and a ministry.

Although young people need the sort of intergenerational contact available in parish life, one wonders if they will ever get it unless parishes on their own part are willing to seek out and recognize the gifts of the young.

Again, this aspect of youth ministry is summed up in another passage from Pope Paul's exhortation:

> The Gospel, and therefore evangelization, are certainly not identified with culture, and they are independent in regard to all cultures. Nevertheless, the Kingdom which the Gospel proclaims is lived by men who are profoundly linked to a culture, and the building up of the Kingdom cannot avoid borrowing the elements of human culture or cultures. Though independent of cultures, the Gospel and evangelization are not necessarily incompatible with them; rather they are capable of permeating them all without becoming subject to any one of them.
>
> The split between the Gospel and culture is without a doubt the drama of our time, just as it was of other times. Therefore every effort must be made to ensure a full evangelization of culture, or more correctly of cultures. (No. 20)

Pope Paul, summing up reflections of the catechetical community on evangelization over twenty years, has affirmed something that good youth ministers have been putting into practice for many years now. Before one can speak to a particular culture, one must know it, be familiar with it. One must attend to it, in the sense of paying attention to it and spending time trying to understand it. Youth ministry does not wish to affirm every aspect of youth culture, but it is serious about understanding all aspects. Youth ministers worthy of their calling listen to young people, listen to their music, attend the movies they find significant, read their magazines and their novels. Such ministers to youth are constantly preparing themselves for speaking out of youth culture and not at it.

One can hope that youth ministry will continue to grow in the coming years and that many will continue to select it as an area of specialized ministry. One can also hope that some of those who have had success in youth ministry will begin giving more attention to an area of ministry long neglected and in desperate need of full-time specialists. That area is ministry to the young adult.

For many years now there has been in the United States a network of persons ministering to young adults—but only if they happened to be on college campuses. Our bias in the Catholic Church has been toward those in schools and colleges, a bias that seems to lurk unconsciously in Greeley's latest assertions about contemporary Catholic life in the United States. Yet there are many thousands of Catholic young people who elect not to go to college but who move into various kinds of employment, working in offices and department stores or in service garages and short-order kitchens.

These young people have religious needs like everyone else, but somehow they seem to have disappeared from our parish assemblies, especially in the big cities. There is little hard data on those aged eighteen to twenty-five and their attitudes toward the established Churches, possibly because it is difficult to locate these young people. They seem to disappear into their jobs and their singles apartments and their scattered hangouts. The Churches are not going to find them neatly assembled together on college campuses. If there is going to be ministry to young adults, if we are going to find out what their religious and other human needs are, these persons must be sought out through the hard work of dedicated ministers.

Ministry to young adults will have to find these young people where they are. In cities like New York that ministry will involve attention to the various watering places where this group comes together on weekends, night spots with names like "The Brass Onion," "Shenanigans," "The Players," and so forth. If one could make projections from what is currently going on in youth ministry, the key to young adult ministry will lie in calling young adults to minister to their own peers. After all, they know the places, the people, and the problems. They also have the maturity for serious ministry.

Outcomes of these initiatives are still unclear. Serious attention to this neglected area will not happen overnight. Whatever happens will, like youth ministry, follow sound principles of evangelization, such as witness and indigenization. Ministers to young adults will have the joy of learning by doing. May they find joy in small accomplishments.

Youth Evangelization—
Ten Years Later

Michael Warren

When reviewing all the material to be included in this book, I knew that the one piece I could not publish in its original form without either revision or addition was the essay on the evangelization of youth. Although the earlier essay was written over ten years ago, not long after the publication of Paul VI's *Evangelii Nuntiandi,* I have decided to retain it in this collection because it provides a useful understanding of evangelization. However, my own continuing concern for the evangelization of young people has taken on new emphases, which I wish to explain in this new essay.

In writing the original piece, I saw my task as a youth ministry thinker to be one of encouraging youth ministers to take seriously the task of assembling the community. The Church in the United States had come to the end of a long period in which the local parish could expect young people to assemble themselves as part of the believing community. Up to that time there had been heavy reliance on the Catholic school and the weekly Confraternity of Christian Doctrine (CCD) session to do the work of inviting young people to discipleship. However, young people were no longer showing up for CCD sessions, and teachers in schools reported resistance to classes in religion.

When writing the essay ten years ago, I was trying to highlight and encourage exciting innovations in the outreach to young people alienated from the Church. In many cases these efforts were undertaken by skillful ministers who themselves were not much older than the youth they were reaching. Readers will have noted in my descriptions of these efforts the considerable confidence I placed in the formative power of the liturgy. If anything, my confidence in these realities has grown, though it is now more nuanced. And I am more careful to specify the conditions under which the worshiping community is authentic.

I have grown alarmed at the possibility that a group of Christians could so accommodate itself to a particular culture that discipleship could, chameleon-like, lose its distinctiveness and its sharp challenge to a militarized, consumerist culture. The power of the concocted culture fed by consumerist imagery and by the violent imagery of domination is not easily resisted by young people. They tend to absorb the features of the dominant culture in an unquestioning way and are eager to find their place in that culture. When the Church invites them to enter a religious culture that rejects certain features of the wider culture, the young may well hesitate or balk.

What links these two essays is my underlying concern for the problem of culture. I reaffirm my claim in the previous article that the Gospel always goes native. But in the following pages I wish to stress that it must go native the way Jesus did; that is, he identified with the victims of his society. Whenever this fact is forgotten, aspects of evangelization tend to become muddled, and this is what has happened in North America.

Some people seem to think that evangelization is about getting people back onto the church rolls. One does this, they seem to think, by offering religious pep rallies. Thus they divide the world into the *churched* (those on the church rolls) and the *unchurched*, forgetting the possibility that many who have never been converted could be among the *churched*. They seem to think that being evangelized is about affiliation, like joining a union or a club.

But being evangelized is not about affiliation in the above sense. It is about transformation, that is, about a shift in vision and life structure. Evangelization is a proposal for conversion; catechesis is a kind of therapy needed to maintain conversion. The more one understands the problems of conversion, the less one will speak of evangelization in the language of public relations or of marketing strategies. As we shall see, it is all too possible for those working with youth to fall into these mistaken ways of thinking about evangelization.

Also important in the recent history of evangelization is how the meaning of the word itself has shifted. Originally, the word *evangelization* was used in the very specific relationship to catechesis I have just explained— activity toward conversion. However, in Pope Paul VI's apostolic exhortation on evangelization, *Evangelii Nuntiandi,* issued at the end of 1975, the term was also used as a synonym for the entire ministry of the Word. Up to that point, evangelization had been understood as one of the four dimensions of the ministry of the Word, that is, the Church's ministry to the meanings that bind the community together. Besides evangelization, the other dimensions of that ministry are catechesis, theology, and liturgical preaching.

This shift in the meaning of the word is unfortunate: now a person seeing the term must first determine whether it means the general ministry of the Word or the specific ministry of leading persons to conversion. The specific meaning is the more helpful one because it names a particular activity that needs to be named. In a later apostolic exhortation, *Catechesi Tradendae* (1979), Pope John Paul II also used the term *evangelization* in both the general and the particular senses. Those who speak or write of the evangelization of youth, if they are to be clearly understood, must keep in mind these distinctions and specify which meaning they intend.

Understanding the history and these uses of the term *evangelization* provides a basis for appreciating the place of evangelization in work with young people. In the rest of this essay I will deal first with the Church's message of evangelization and then with its embodiment of the Good News. This approach may shed some light on the question of the evangelization of youth today. The whole question must be placed in the context of the problem of culture, which is where I begin.

Church and Culture

I have already stated my conviction that the Church is not some sort of social club, even though it is clearly a social entity and a gathering of persons who share a vision. What is the difference, then, between the Church and a labor union, which is also a social entity committed to a vision? The difference has to do with the nature of the vision and the kind of commitments involved in belonging. The vision that leads one to stand within the Church is a total life-orienting vision, affecting not just one's labor but all aspects of one's life. In its specific forms, committed religiousness embraces not just generalized values or principles but a way of thinking, feeling, and living. I use the term *committed* here to distinguish between those who belong to the Church as to a kind of social club and those who have been converted to the lived commitments of the *ekklesia*. I want to suggest the difference between the person who stands squarely within the vision and commitments of the *ekklesia* and the person who has drifted there and continues to float there without any footing.

The distinction between standing squarely and floating is an important one for evangelization because evangelization invites persons to something very specific—a changed way of living. In the early Church, no person was admitted to baptism who could not prove to the community not only the intention of living as a Christian but also the clear ability to do so. Evangelization then has two sides: a positive invitation to a certain lifestyle and a call away from behaviors counter to Jesus' Way.

However, in the commodity-oriented culture of economically privileged countries, it is not an easy matter to maintain the specificity of the invitation and of the life structure to which Jesus' Way calls us. The power of the electronic media in these countries is such that the media will subvert gospel commitments unless the commercial culture is actively resisted. An example may help illustrate this problem as it affects the evangelization of youth.

Suppose we approached the evangelization or catechesis of young people in the following way. Instead of proposing to the young what the Church is called to be or supposed to be and then claiming that such is what their own local church actually is, suppose we did a catechesis or evangelization of signs. Suppose we did not ask the young to believe in the Church, that is, to believe beyond what they actually see of the Church's own life. Suppose instead we encouraged them to find a living community that shows by the sign of its own deeds that it follows Jesus' concern for the outcasts, and to then join *that* Church or community.

Suppose our message to youth was this: *Rather than working as a young and powerless person in the Church of your birth to call that community to fidelity to the Jesus of justice, find the community of disciples who are already seeking to be faithful. Find a community that is actively and evidently struggling toward justice, and ask to walk with them in their journey toward fidelity. Find the believable ones and become one of them.*

In the face of this advice, one can ask which parish in a particular area might qualify as worthy to be selected by the young people. A further question is, would a Roman Catholic youth choose a Roman Catholic parish at all?

It is worth noting how a parish can so reduce the scope of the Gospel to the actual lived values of its own particular members, including its leaders, that there is little disparity between the "Gospel" and the life of this community. The community has not changed its own life; instead the community has changed the Gospel. What is offered its people is a puny "Gospel" reduced to a neatly manageable size that is suitable to the parish's own version of Christianity. Such a "Gospel" represents more the socioeconomic values of a particular residential area than the troubling words and deeds of Jesus. Often enough, the commitments of Jesus to the powerless and to society's rejects are quietly put aside in favor of commitments to one's own crowd and its status and privilege.

In our time so much has been written about the Gospel's challenge to culture. But it is ironic how easily culture, especially the commodity-oriented culture of the First World, has tended to subvert the Gospel itself. In *Evangelii Nuntiandi*, Pope Paul VI wrote somewhat optimistically:

> What matters is to evangelize man's culture and cultures (not in a purely decorative way as it were by applying a thin veneer, but in a vital way, in depth and right to its very roots). . . . Though independent of cultures, the Gospel and evangelization . . . are capable of permeating them all without becoming subject to any one of them. (No. 20)

However, the task of evangelizing culture has not gotten easier in the years since Paul VI wrote those words.

In dealing with young people, one comes to see vividly how difficult it is to propose gospel values such as compassion for the poor, solidarity with the weak, and nonviolent resistance to evil, especially in a culture where images of domination, exploitation, and violence are beamed continually at the young via the electronic media. In such a culture one questions how many young people at all would, as in my earlier example, be even looking to search out a credible community to follow. My point here, however, is that no evangelization is possible without the faithful countercultural Church. Notice how, in the following passage, Paul VI centers the task of evangelizing culture as the work of the *ekklesia,* the tribe of disciples.

> For the Church, evangelizing means bringing the Good News into all the strata of humanity, and through its influence transforming humanity from within and making it new: "Now I am making the whole of creation new." But there is no new humanity if there are not first of all new persons renewed by Baptism and by lives lived according to the Gospel. The purpose of evangelization is therefore precisely this interior change. . . . the Church evangelizes when she seeks to convert . . . both the personal and collective consciences of people, the activities in which they engage, and the lives and concrete milieux which are theirs. (No. 18)

What Paul VI is saying in this passage is that the *ekklesia* reimagines the world and the place of human life in it, but imagines it along the lines of the imagination of Jesus.

The Church's Message to Youth

What is the Church proclaiming, the same Good News preached by Jesus and the Apostles or a message fundamentally subverted by greed and the search for comfort that are at the center of a commodity-oriented culture? Are there renditions of the gospel message that would be unrecognizable in certain of our local communities that are accustomed to congenial, lifestyle-affirming versions? And what versions are offered to our young people in catechetical and other youth programs? Would the following version be one they have ever heard before?

Jesus' death is not some vague metaphysical reality caused by the will of God. Jesus' life did not mysteriously end in crucifixion. In historical fact, Jesus did not encounter death except as caused by others' rage that was sparked by his outspoken concern for the victims of his society. Though his death is often presented as a timeless, ahistorical decision by Jesus to die for all humankind, in reality he died because he challenged the unjust structures of his day. This means that for Jesus his mission, his call, and his very religiousness involved calling for a transformation in how the people of his time dealt with those who had no rights or opportunities in his society—the poor.

If all this is true, it means that the God whom Jesus calls Father is the one who expresses his power in the face of death and reverses that death. God reverses the death of the very one who gave hope to the outcasts. If

Jesus' death as a criminal and a total outcast dashed all the hopes and expectations of the outcasts, his being raised up as a living spirit gave them hope and expectations beyond their wildest dreams. The Resurrection of Jesus is Good News, but especially for the outcasts. For the wretched, the Resurrection is a sign that God regards them as his favored ones. Not only did God send Jesus among them as a gift of hope, but he also saw fit, through raising him up, that Jesus remain among them as a living spirit.

The death of Jesus, however, reveals something else. The God who disclosed himself through the life, death, and Resurrection of Jesus also revealed that his most dramatic epiphany comes at the point of greatest human poverty and weakness. He appears in the outcast, criminalized Jesus, tortured and hung up to die, one who became an expression of human wretchedness.

Unfortunately, as soon as the terms *poverty* and *weakness* are conjoined, we can too easily see the reality they represent not as a social condition but as a philosophical state, an inner condition shared by all persons, rich and poor alike. Indeed, Christian tradition has always accepted as true that human poverty is a condition of all persons regardless of social state, thus universalizing the mystery of Jesus as applicable to every human being.

This tendency to spiritualize and universalize these terms is unfortunate if it blinds us to the historical fact that the epiphany of God actually takes place in the particular one whose physical and social condition is that of an outcast, one who became so by taking the part of the marginalized. If you want to find where God is hidden, the Gospel suggests, look to the infant child of needy parents who were street people (they had no shelter). This is where the power of God shows itself most dramatically but also most typically. The Good News is that the most radical religious hope belongs to the victims of the social order, because God hears their cry.

It is clear that this Good News must be universalized, so as to have meaning for persons of all social conditions in life. Yet, once we forget the actual historical conditions that disclosed the secret of God's presence, we are in danger of misunderstanding the Good News. The crucified one shows us that the poverty and weakness he endured are a consequence of sin, not a natural state. Indeed God wants to reverse sin and its consequences and in Jesus did overcome them. Jesus' death was planned and orchestrated by the forces of evil, not by the will of God. The Good News is that injustice does not have the last word. God takes the side of the victim.

We cannot forget that, in Jesus' preaching, holiness and goodness demand taking the side of the victims. The rich man and his five brothers are excluded from the Kingdom of God because they ignored the beggar Lazarus in his need. As presented to us in the Scriptures, God does indeed hear the cry of the poor and insists that we ourselves hear and respond to it. That cry of distress evokes in history the saving action of God, from the Exodus to the Resurrection. Jesus insists that the cry also evokes similar saving action in us, that the transcendent action of God becomes rooted in everyday life through the loving kindness of ordinary people.

Do young people in North America have much opportunity to encounter this kind of Gospel? As one who examines dozens of renditions of the Gospel offered to youth each year, I judge that few young people ever have access to the above version. Actually it could be quite a disturbing account to many young people, who might be shocked at its literally unheard-of claims. I would be pleased to think that those working with youth might conspire and ask each other, Should we tell them? Is now the right time or should we wait until they are older and can bear it? Will it be too much for them? At least such conspiring would indicate that those working with the young know there is more to the Gospel, that it is shocking, and that it must not be glibly shared.

However, the gospel message in North America tends to be an analogue (though in a religious mode) of the "good news" of the consumer culture, which is about self-love, self-improvement, and respectability. This message tends to avoid those aspects of the Gospel that are inimical to middle- and upper-class culture, especially Jesus' solidarity with victims.

In examining the Church's message, however, one must get beyond the verbal message to the embodied message proclaimed by the life of the community. Jesuit theologian Jon Sobrino suggests that the Church reexamine its understanding of the basic evangelizing message of the Gospel. (See Jon Sobrino, "Evangelization as Mission of the Church" in *The True Church and the Poor* [New York: Orbis, 1984], pp. 253–301.) Sobrino warns us that not every "good news" proclaimed by persons in the Church is the Christian Good News. We can see this truth in the checkered history of the Church, as when the Gospel was used to prop up the civil authority of kings and other rulers. Neither does every manner of spreading the faith do justice to the content of the Gospel. For example, evangelization is not a proclamation of sublime realities without an accompanying effort to make the content of those realities concrete. Without the effective practice of liberation and the building of the Kingdom in specific ways, the preaching of the Good News is empty verbiage. The failure to accompany proclamation with an effective practice of liberation is not just one of many possible faults of the Church. It is rather a failure that denies the Church itself, in its character as a sign of the coming Kingdom. In other words, there is a heretical proclamation of the Church as the zone of speech-without-liberation, rather than as the zone of the practice of liberation. Paul VI makes this point in *Evangelii Nuntiandi:*

> It is . . . primarily by her conduct and by her life that the Church will evangelize the world, in other words, by her living witness of fidelity to the Lord Jesus — the witness of poverty and detachment, of freedom in the face of the powers of this world, in short, the witness of sanctity. (No. 41)

Sobrino reminds us that evangelization, as the proclamation of the Good News in deeds and concrete actions, is the grace and vocation of the Church. The Church exists to evangelize, in the sense of doing deeds that embody the Good News. Such a claim would seem somewhat exaggerated were it not a direct quote from *Evangelii Nuntiandi:* "Evangelizing is in fact the grace and vocation proper to the Church, her deepest identity. She exists in order to evangelize" (no. 14). The Church, then, is the zone where the Kingdom has begun because sharing, justice, and compassion actually happen there. As Jesus and those who joined him in his mission engaged in preaching the coming Kingdom and in being signs that this Kingdom is a present possibility, so too is the Church of our own time to be such a sign.

For most youth ministers, the problem of *doing deeds* that embody the Good News is the sticking point in their attempts to accept the above understanding of the Church's mission and of evangelization. Youth ministers become anxious, not so much about the idea of the social justice agenda, but about the agenda as an outline for a new kind of program of activities in youth ministry.

At the parish and diocesan levels, youth ministry leaders are program oriented and think in terms of specific strategies. I would say that this is their gift. However, I would caution against leaping too quickly to ambitious plans of action. What has to happen first is that the young church in a particular place has to grow to be a different kind of young church. That growth will be a combination of education toward a new way of noticing—a new level of awareness—and tentative first steps of action. In my work of proposing nonviolent peacemaking to youth, I began by studying relevant literature myself. My advice on encouraging action is to expect progress to be gradual, if not actually slow.

Conclusion

Perhaps some people will need specific instances from the literature about youth ministry to convince them that much current writing on the evangelization of youth ignores both the understanding of evangelization suggested here and its concrete implications. Such a detailed review of the literature would conclusively show that contemporary thinking in the field of youth ministry focuses on promoting psychological comfort and in-group affirmation. Even some of the charts purporting to explain graphically the scope of youth ministry pull one's awareness away from the justice dimension of ministry and toward the privatized dimension. However, such a detailed analysis of the literature will have to wait for a later treatment.

In the meanwhile, I would be pleased if all those working with youth in the Church would ponder the significance for their ministries of the following insight of theologian Daniel Maguire:

> In the social order . . . talk of love and friendship can be a prescription for disaster. There [in the social order] justice is the closest one can get to friendship. Justice is incipient love, and *in the political order, it is the only form love takes* [emphasis added]. Privatistic talk of love is at that level unavailing, naive, and ultra-conservative in effect. Ironically, love talk in the socio-political sphere provides an ideological veil for injustice and inures one to the needs of the poor for whom justice is life blood. ("The Primacy of Justice in Moral Theology," *Horizons* 10, no. 1 [1983]: 74)

When the invitation to discipleship given to young people includes the call to justice and an offer of mentorship in discovering the full scope of human relationships, then evangelization will have found its true radical character.

Essay 3

Can the Liturgy Speak to Today's Young People?

Michael Warren

The liturgy and teens. This is a difficult topic. Parents anguish over the topic as they try alternately to cajole and threaten reluctant teens to go to Mass. Teachers in Catholic high schools express concern over the large number of teens who have dropped out of Sunday Eucharist. Pastors stepping out before their Sunday congregations are not slow to notice the absence of most parish teens from the assembly. And if one is put in the position, as this writer has often been, of speaking some sense and some hope to those who would assist young people to take their next steps in Christian faith, one regularly faces the anguished question, "What can we do to get our kids to go to Mass?" What that question is lacking in phrasing and nuance is made up for in its earnestness. The following article is this writer's attempt to talk common sense and the possible, rather than overblown, theory and pious exhortations about the matter of liturgy and teens. Written in response to the question that forms the essay's title, these reflections reveal a conviction that the very question itself is badly put and betrays a misconception about liturgy. In order to make sense of a complex question, then, in the following ideas I approach liturgy from the point of view of expressive human activity, hoping by that approach to show how it relates to young people.

Readers will note how the following reflections actually complement those of the previous two essays on evangelization, which raise questions about the kind of believing community we are talking about. The problem I am highlighting is not just that of the faith of young people but the faith of the assembling community itself.

This essay is reprinted from Resources for Youth Ministry, *ed. Michael Warren (New York: Paulist Press, 1978), pages 225–236; it was originally titled "Can the Liturgy Speak to Today's Teenagers?"*

My thesis is that liturgy is expressive human activity. The original Greek word for liturgy means "the action of the people," a meaning that suggests strongly that the people are expressing something by their action, that their action is expressive action. In its Christian sense, then, liturgy is an action by which a community expresses its attitude about the way it is between God and human beings, but more specifically about the way it is between this group gathered in the Spirit of Jesus and the one Jesus called Father. Quite simply, liturgy is a way of saying something. We have all had experiences where we just had to say something, where what was inside us just had to be expressed. Well, liturgy comes out of a similar thrust. Vatican Council II's *Constitution on the Sacred Liturgy* explicitly adverts to this character of liturgy when it says, "The liturgy is thus the outstanding means by which the faithful can express in their lives, and manifest to others, the mystery of Christ and the real nature of the true Church" (no. 2). In my judgment, it is this expressive character of liturgy that more than anything else helps us understand the various initiatives we must take with regard to Christian worship in particular circumstances.

Now there is an expressive character to all human activity. In fact one could argue that all human interaction falls on an impressive-expressive continuum.[1] One can see this more clearly in the matter of education. A large part of educational activity involves impressing on others concepts, facts, and skills. This is the impressive side of education. People need input; they need to be taught. Realities have to be communicated to them. Educators, however, recognize that impressive activity is not enough in the educational process. It must be completed by expressive activity; that is, the learner must come to express in her or his own way the ideas, facts, or skills that she or he is learning.

In education there are two levels of expressivity. Level one is a low level of expressivity, the one I would call *repetition*. A child, say, is taught the multiplication tables and then is expected to be able to express them, that is, to repeat them. Until that level of expressivity is attained, the child really has not learned the tables. However, the math teacher hopes the child will go a step further and be able to use the multiplication tables creatively in solving actual problems as they arise. In other words, there is a second stage of expressivity that comes when the person is not just repeating what she or he has been told but is actually using the skill or idea in a unique, original, and creative way. Level two, then, is a high level of expressivity, one that I would call *the creative act*. As an English teacher, I always felt that my students would have truly profited by my impressive activity if some of them became themselves creative writers, expressing in original works their imaginative perceptions of human existence. I was happy when in their compositions, which they *had* to write, they showed originality and creativity, but I hoped that some day some of them would begin creating out of their own creative urges, not out of my assignment.

We can see the impressive-expressive continuum clearly in the interaction between mother and child. The mother repeats words endlessly to the child, impressing on the consciousness of the child human speech. And the child responds at first with level-one expressivity. The child repeats or makes efforts to repeat some of the more simple words. Eventually the child has a small repertoire of words she or he can repeat. But true growth or another stage of human activity occurs on that day when the mother lovingly makes a request or gives a command to the child and the child responds with the single word "No!" That response is not simply a repetition but is expressing in an original way the child's own will. The mother may be shocked or dismayed, but we can rejoice that a new level of human expressivity has been reached and that the child is now expressing her or his own self.[2]

One further example: There was a time, not too long removed, when teaching religion to children was centered dominantly (not exclusively, but dominantly) on impressive activities and level-one expressive activities. We were taught the Baltimore Catechism, and we had to know it word for word. So much did we focus on level-one expressivity that our repetitions were encouraged by means of "the tickler," a long slender stick more accurately called a rattan—because it definitely did not tickle. I would say that an accurate though simple explanation of the catechetical renewal throughout the world would be that the focus has moved from level-one expressivity to level-two expressivity. Words that have been impressed on people are to take root in the soil of their own lives and flower as their own special words, expressing in an original and creative way the special meaning of those persons' lives. Parents who still ask, "What does *that* have to do with religion?" may simply not be aware of the importance of level-two expressivity.

If it is clear that there is an expressive character to all of human life and that liturgy is expressive human activity,[3] then we can move to the next point, namely, that adolescence is a highly expressive period of one's life. Expressivity is central in all human life, in all stages of development; yet it has a special urgency in adolescence. There are reasons for the acute expressivity of adolescence but I do not have time to go into them here. Instead let us remind ourselves of the way young people are and of how important expressivity is to them.

Listen to their speech. It has its own adolescent character of exaggeration. If anything, it is overly expressive. Listen to the words they use, especially the adverbs. Most adjectives used by young people employ backup adverbs to give added punch. Thus things are not just good or bad but "really, really good" or "really, really bad." Superlatives abound. It was not a wonderful party; it was the greatest, wildest, craziest party. ("It really was. Was it ever! I mean, I never saw anything like it—really!") Just allow yourself to hear their speech patterns, especially the adjectives and adverbs, and you will soon hear what I mean.

In other senses also, the speech of adolescents shows their acute expressivity. They are constantly checking, at least verbally, to make sure you are understanding what they are expressing. In other words their expressivity is so important to them they are fearful that it is inadequate or not being done properly. Did you ever notice how often young people use terms such as "Do you know what I mean?" Adolescent speech tends to use as spoken punctuation marks certain expressions like "you know" and "right." (New York teens use "you know" most; those from parts of the Boston area use "right" a great deal.) Listen:

> I was working out at Jones Beach, you know, right there in front of Bathhouse 3, you know, and this guy comes up with this girl on his arm, a nice-looking girl in a yellow bikini, know what I mean? And he says to me, he says—and like I say, I'm looking at the girl in the yellow, you know—but otherwise I'm minding my own business or trying to, you know, and. . . .

In speech like this, expressivity is not just being carried on by someone telling a story. Expressivity is an underlying *issue*. Underlying the very story is a way of telling it that suggests that being understood is of key importance for the teller.

Of course, in addition to verbal expressivity, there are other senses in which expressivity is central to young people. Bodily and emotional expressivity are also important, probably because the physical and the emotional are just being discovered as means of expressing the self. Read the poetry and witness the body contact of young people to see what I mean. Talk to teenage athletes of both sexes about what sports mean to them to get an inkling of that one aspect of their bodily expressivity. Any issue of *Seventeen,* a popular magazine for girls, betrays how important it is for girls in our culture to exhibit in their dress and features their self-image.[4] Clothes and music are also aspects of the acute expressivity of adolescence.

Now if this overview of expressivity in young people has any merit, then it explains why catechetical programs for young people are dominated by expressivity. It is the nature of young people to have to discover their own word of faith. The flower of faith cannot be transplanted because it would then be one person's flower of faith, growing in another person's soil. The flower of faith has to grow from seed in each person's special soil and grow as one's own flower.[5] In my experience, catechetical programs that keep young people passive or that are centered on level-one expressivity are doomed to failure. That is why I would say that for every sixty minutes of catechetical activity, forty to fifty minutes should involve significant and free expressive speech on the part of the kids themselves. In fact I would say that the key organ for the catechist dealing with teens is not the big mouth but the big ear. There is an important catechetical task of listening, of evocative listening, the kind of listening that encourages others to come to speech.[6]

Expressivity and Liturgy

What does all this have to do with liturgy? There are many implications for
liturgy in these previous remarks about expressivity. First there is a danger
of tending to think of liturgy as impressive activity rather than as expressive
activity. In fact the very question that forms the title of this article seems
to me to betray this tendency. The question asks, Can the liturgy speak to
young people? Can it say something significant to teens? Yet the liturgy is
not so much saying something *to* somebody as it is allowing people to express something of their lives and values by means of it. Liturgy is a vehicle
for expression. There is a sense in which the liturgy is not making any statement to anybody outside of the liturgical assembly. The liturgy is itself a
statement and is the expressive activity of the assembly. The real question
about young people and the liturgy is, How can the liturgy become a vehicle
for young people to express in their lives the mystery of Christ and the real
nature of the Christian community?

I am saying that liturgy, particularly eucharistic liturgy, is an action expressing the faith of a believing community. Liturgy is an event in which
faith comes to expression. It is also a mode of ritual expression in which
faith becomes an event. Liturgy centers on faith coming to communal expression. Writing of the Eucharist in *Theological Studies,* liturgiologist John
McKenna notes:

> It is normally, ideally, the faith of the Church here and now present, i.e., the
> local assembly, which shares in this realization [of the eucharistic presence of
> Christ]. It may be true that, in the absence of a believing assembly here and
> now, the intention of the minister may supply the *minimum* required of a sacra-
> ment, *viz.,* the faith of the Church at large. This remains, however, the bare
> minimum, and one should build one's theology not on the minimum but on the
> ideal or normal. . . . Thus God freely and sovereignly effects a real presence
> in the Eucharist. He does so, however, through the faith of the Church, since
> this presence involves both Christ present and offering himself to his Church
> and the Church accepting and responding to this offer in faith. Moreover, in-
> volved in this mutual presence is an invitation to each individual in the assembly
> to personally share in this presence and thus have it attain the goal for which
> it was intended.[7]

Thus, for liturgy to become a vehicle for the young people or any people
to express in their lives the mystery of Christ, the liturgy must be the prayer
of a believing assembly. And there I suggest is a problem that is not just
a problem of teens.

To avoid getting into a full critique of liturgical practice in our contemporary parish life, the following reflection must suffice. There was a time
when we were all reminded of the dangers of servile work on Sunday. Ser-

vile work is that form of labor that has its purpose apart from the enrichment of a person's inner life.[8] Nonservile work is any kind of activity that has its end in the activity itself. Artistic activity and even digging in one's yard is nonservile since it is recognized as nourishing one's inner life. To live a fully human life one needs nonservile activities; otherwise one becomes a slave, a drudge. Based on this understanding of servile work, then, I suggest that there is such a thing as servile worship. This is worship that is engaged in out of obligation or routine or out of cultural or family pressures. In worship that is servile the purposes of the act of worship are not in the act itself. Servile work is wrong only when it consumes all of one's life. Servile worship is wrong all the time. In fact it is no worship at all. It is pseudoworship. In some parishes young people's experience of Sunday Mass is more like the scene depicted in the fantasy on page 36 than like the coming together of a true worshiping assembly. "A Sunday Fantasy" ideally should be choreographed and set to music.

My second response to the question is this: Remember that a crucial factor in all worship is what happens before worship. What life context does worship fit into? If worship is expressive activity, then it is expressing a perception of life based on a quality of reflectiveness. In worship we come, in a sense, to waste time on the Lord, to move from our servile world of pressure and work to a place where we can offer thanks to God for his many blessings, including the blessing of communion in the Spirit of Jesus. How does a person come to the point of wanting to offer this kind of worship, not out of servile compulsion but out of the thrust of one's inner life? I presume that such true worship does not occur automatically or mechanically. I have found myself that my eucharistic prayer is as strong as my prayer outside the time of Eucharist. Only when the Sunday Eucharist (or daily Eucharist) is fitting into a context of prayer in my total life do I find that my own personal participation in the eucharistic liturgy has the quality of response it should have. This is my own experience, and from that experience I hypothesize that the need of most adults today is not so much for greater change in liturgical ritual as it is for a spirituality that will enrich daily prayer.

The same is true for young people. We need greater attention to their spirituality, that is, to the manner in which they attend to the presence of God in their total lives. A key contribution to the faith development and eventually to the liturgical development of young people is being made by informal prayer groups and by youth retreats. On a Christian experience weekend, teens are coming to the eucharistic liturgy from a context of grappling with questions of faith, of sharing their own faith perceptions, and of prayer. Liturgy speaks powerfully in that context. Prayer programs are enriching the quality of reflectiveness of young people as well as their spirit of responsiveness to God. If we think about our own past history, who have been the people who have led us to a deeper spirituality? Who were the ones who

A Sunday Fantasy

It was a bright April Easter morning, with a cold blue sky sunning itself waiting to be warmed. And they streamed down the sidewalks to church. They streamed out of the side streets and out of neat houses and down from tenements. And across the park they streamed, all decked in finery. And they nodded and smiled to one another as they streamed. Briskly they came from all directions. Hot coffee and warm buttered rolls and the funnies were beckoning. There were no frogs in the gutters and the locusts were nowhere to be seen.

It was to church they were coming. All knew what would happen: Some would head for the front pews but most would head for the rear. And the middle would be left for the latecomers trying to be casual. And they would all wiggle out of their coats. And they would stuff parcels and purses under the kneelers. Then they would prop themselves bum to knee in prayer of hasty reverence, ending in the half-hidden, hasty sign of the cross of a ball player on the free throw line. No talk would be heard, just heels clacking and shoes shuffling and coughing, the mindless silence.

But not this morning. For the prophet stood at the door, tall and thin, like some lean male witch. And he shook the bony finger in their faces. And his burning eyes pierced their stares and made the frogs and the locusts hop out of nowhere. And this is what he said:

Servile worship is sin. Beware, beware lest you trespass in
the Lord's House.
Today is Sunday. Let there be no servile worship.
It is not allowed on the Lord's Day that you offer servile
worship.
Except you be hungry for the Lord, you may not enter.
Except you be hurrying to the tomb to make sure he is not
there, you must not enter.
Except you come to offer yourself, you must stay out.
Cease your Sunday sin of servile worship.
Better to go to Seidmann's bakery before the rolls run
out.
Better to get an extra Sunday paper and linger over the
real estate ads.
Better hot coffee and a morning nap than to blaspheme
the Lords' House and the Lord's Time and the
Lord's Day.
For you are the Lord's and He wants more than your fifty
minutes and your servile worship.

helped us treasure our moments of more formal worship? The one affects the other.

I find lots of adults who would like to teach things to kids, to do a work of impression on them. I find many more who like to take kids on trips or supervise their sports programs. But I do not find enough adults who are willing to engage in spiritual direction of young people, that is, adults who are willing to own up to their own faith commitment as a means of helping young people begin to own up to or at least to discover theirs.[9]

A third reflection has to do with the liturgy of the Word. If it is true that adolescence is a special time of expressivity, then this insight must guide our approach to the liturgy of the Word. Actually every homily should be highly expressive, in the sense that it should touch the hidden longings present but only dimly recognized in the assembled community. Human speech captivates us when it expresses and brings to the light what we had been feeling or suspecting but could not articulate for ourselves.[10] In that sense, every homily is expressive not just of the preacher but also of the community. To achieve this quality the preacher must know the lives of his people. He must have a feel for them. He has to have allowed the word of God to stir him up. He must have himself moved from darkness into light as regards this particular Word. Unfortunately, instead of moving from darkness to light some homilists only move from silence to speech. Can we attend to the deeper needs, to the hurts and hopes, struggles and strivings of our young people? Can we be in touch with them in such a way that when we speak we do indeed speak not just to their lives but out of their lives? This is one aspect of the liturgy of the Word.

Put a young person with good Christian instincts in an assembly of servile worshipers, and she or he will not want her or his worship to be given in that servile context. Thus my first response to the question, How can liturgy become a vehicle for young people to express in their lives the mystery of Christ? is this: Let them be part of a believing assembly gathered to express their love and gratitude to God for his deed in Jesus Christ. In some parishes, the problem might not be that young people do not want to go to Mass. It might instead be that they find that in fact they cannot worship in an assembly of servile obligation-fillers.

There is another aspect, however. Young people need themselves to discover their own word. They need to listen to one another, to hear the Gospel according to Matthew, Mark, Luke, John, as it has been discovered by Jane or John Doe. They need very much to dialogue about the Gospel. They need to talk it over, talk it out in their own words. Unfortunately we still have not yet caught up with the need of modern human beings to articulate. Even as a college theology teacher I must remind myself again and again of what I keep discovering about young people: "Your words, Mike, are of secondary importance; their words are of primary importance." In reviewing previous classes, I find that what the students seem to remember best are not the things I said but rather the insights they themselves articulated in the class.

Finally, I wish to call your attention to a document published in 1974 by the Sacred Congregation for Divine Worship, a document that I think has hidden in it much common sense about liturgy. The document is called *Directory for Masses with Children.* [11] It is a list of guidelines for liturgical expression suitable for children, but it contains many principles that could and I think must be applied to liturgical expression for many different age levels beyond childhood. Stress in the document is placed on leading persons according to their age, psychological condition, and social situation. This document, it seems to me, opens many doors with regard to introducing young people to a fuller liturgical life that is truly expressive of their relationship with God. Today we need many varieties of eucharistic assemblies in which young people can express their faith: small groups of teens, large assemblies of young people, faith-filled adult communities that teens can affiliate with.

I realize that a myriad of other questions have been ignored here: the proper use of paraeucharistic forms of worship, training youth as leaders of song in worship, the role of youth as preachers of the Word in many current settings such as youth retreats and programs to help younger persons prepare for Confirmation. My thesis here has been that any attempt to assist young people to grow in faith through worship must take into account the specific kind of people they are. My conviction has also been that the Eucharist for us Christians is our special gift. In the act of handing it on to our youth, we receive it back with a new realization of its giftedness. Young people offer us that opportunity.

Notes

1. The ideas contained in the following paragraphs, although not necessarily the terminology, are commonplace in many different works of educational theory. See especially Paulo Freire, *Pedagogy of the Oppressed* (New York: Herder and Herder, 1970), pp. 75–118, and Freire's *Cultural Action for Freedom* (Cambridge: Harvard Educational Review Monograph Series, 1970), pp. 12–14. See also a provocative, brief section of Malcolm Knowles's *The Adult Learner: A Neglected Species* (Houston: Gulf, 1973), pp. 173–175, where he distinguishes between reactive and proactive learning. The role of expressivity in religious functioning is also a commonplace theme in the sociology of religion. A good treatment with much potential application to Christian ritual can be found in Joachim Wach, *The Comparative Study of Religions* (New York: Columbia Univ. Press, 1961), pp. 59–143, esp. pp. 97–120.

2. John Macmurray provides a useful analysis of the interaction between mother and child in *Persons in Relation* (London: Faber and Faber,
1970), pp. 44–63 and *passim*. Macmurray adverts to the character of delight
and of play in the mother-child interaction, a character that suggests the unity
and centrality of the *relationship* between mother and child. It is in affirming the centrality of that bond as a human relationship that the artificial distinctions made here between the impressive and expressive make most sense and
are most useful.

3. Bernard Lonergan's analysis of religious experience and its outcomes
hinges on the key role of expressivity. Although *Method in Theology* (New
York: Herder and Herder, 1972), pp. 108–119 gives little specific attention
to liturgy, Lonergan is speaking of the same reality in discussing the way
community invites expression of the meanings that bind it together. The role
of the community in expressing these meanings is a central issue in Lonergan's
system.

4. Any periodical targeted for various ages and segments of the youth
population can be revealing as to the issues and tasks that are preoccupying
their attention. The marketers pay careful attention to the needs, dreams,
and hopes of those they attempt to influence. Probably too little attention
has been paid to this literature as a source of data about young people relevant to their growth in faith.

5. Gabe Huck in a recent discussion of children's liturgies called forceful
attention to the dangers of speaking of "adapting liturgy" as if liturgy were
something rigid and alien from life, something that had to be artificially
tailored to a person's experience. Actually liturgy is an expression of the life
of the people. When the function of expression is obstructed, then attention
must be paid to correcting the situation. What some might call "adaptation"
of the liturgy is actually an intelligent clearing away of obstacles hindering
persons of any age or culture from coming to ritual expression of Christian
faith. In this sense, then, adaptation is a process of letting liturgy be liturgy.
See Gabe Huck, "Review of Edward Matthews's *Celebrating Mass with
Children,*" *Worship* 51, no. 2 (March 1977): 196–197.

6. What is said here of young people is just as applicable to adults. Adults
need, and in the writer's experience welcome, channels for expressing their
experience of God as much as do teens. Possibly this is one reason why so
many middle-aged and older adults attend Sunday liturgies specifically designed for children and teens.

7. John H. McKenna, "Eucharistic Epiclesis: Myopia or Microcosm?"
Theological Studies 36, no. 2 (1975): 271.

8. Josef Pieper has a provocative section on servile activity in his fine
essay *Leisure: The Basis of Culture* (New York: Mentor-Omega, 1963), pp.
46–55. Rich resources for foundational reflection on liturgy can be found
both here and in Pieper's later work *In Tune with the World: A Theory of
Festivity* (Chicago: Franciscan Herald Press, 1973).

9. In this writer's opinion, far too little writing has been done on the theory and practice of spirituality and spiritual direction for young people. Though some Catholics working in Catholic high schools, colleges, and on youth retreats are in fact developing programs, few have written of these efforts. Two Catholics working and writing on this matter are Mark Link, the author of *You* (Niles, IL: Argus Communication, 1976), and Richard Costello, the director of the Youth Ministry Office in Norwich, Connecticut. At the 1977 Youth Ministry Workshop at Saint John's University, Jamaica, New York, Costello gave a week-long series of lectures entitled "Ministering to the Spiritual Development of Teens." His article "Imaginative Prayer for Teens" appears in the October 1977 issue of *Religion Teacher's Journal;* other material is in process.

10. A statement on this matter worth frequent rereading by those called to preach can be found in Henri Nouwen, *The Wounded Healer,* chap. 2, "Ministry to a Rootless Generation" (New York: Doubleday, 1972), pp. 25–47. Some readers will be more familiar with this chapter in its earlier form as an article entitled "Generation Without Fathers," *Commonweal* 92 (12 June 1970): 287–294. See also the chapter "Preaching: Beyond the Retelling of the Story" in Nouwen's *Creative Ministry* (New York: Doubleday, 1971), pp. 22–40.

11. Sacred Congregation for Divine Worship, *Directory for Masses with Children* (Washington, DC: United States Catholic Conference, 1974).

Youth Ministry: Reflections and Directions

Tom Zanzig

Many people concerned with youth ministry have found Tom Zanzig's comprehensive essay "Youth Ministry: Reflections and Directions" to be particularly helpful. I am pleased to be able to include it in this collection.

I call special attention to his use of the "wedge model," and especially to his warnings about the misunderstanding and misuse of models in general and about the mistake of taking this one model to be the *model. It is important to notice that in his explanation of the model Zanzig attempts to overcome its visual segmenting of aspects of ministry that can never be split off one from the other, for example, evangelization from service, and its apparent, visual diminishing of systematic catechesis in a move toward a committed core group. In this essay, Zanzig continues an important dialogue about evangelization and catechesis, a dialogue so much in its infancy that it must continue long into the future.*

This essay is reprinted from PACE 11 *(Winona, MN: Saint Mary's Press, 1980–81), Special Supplement, by permission of the publisher.*

This article is an attempt to assess in as broad a way as possible the current status of Catholic youth ministry in the United States. I define *youth ministry* as the Church's ministry to, with, by, and for young people from ages fourteen to twenty-five. I want here to share what I feel to be the most fruitful and important developments in the field in the last several years and also to state a number of my concerns about the state of youth ministry as it exists today.

There is a definite need for serious reflection at this time on where youth ministry has come from as well as on where it appears to be headed. In this article I will offer the following:

- a presentation of what I feel to be the most helpful and directive model of youth ministry available today, a model that integrates in a rational way the many varied components and expressions of our ministry to and with young people
- based on that model, a description of the role and responsibilities of the professional youth minister
- some reflections on each of the various components of a total ministry to, with, by, and for youth
- finally, a discussion of the critical question of the relationship between youth ministry and youth catechesis and some suggestions for resolving some of the tensions that now surround that question[1]

A Model of Youth Ministry

The use of models in theological and educational discussion has become the in thing in recent years. This popularity has a rather firm base, however; namely, the fact that models are very helpful tools for understanding; they work. But this is true only when models are properly understood and utilized, so perhaps a word of caution should be offered here before presenting a model of youth ministry.

We need first to understand that any model is an attempt to graphically describe a complex and integrated reality by breaking it down into its various component parts. This has the great advantage and benefit of making the processes and components involved in the totality understandable and discussable; it has the disadvantage of allowing one to lose sight of the whole because of disproportionate or distorted perceptions of the parts involved. Models are very helpful when they are understood for what they are—artificial attempts to analyze and understand complex realities. They can be useless and even bewildering when they are misunderstood or given more value than they deserve.

The model of youth ministry presented here offers both the benefits and problems, the strengths and weaknesses, of all models. It is the most helpful presentation of the many dimensions of youth ministry that I have seen, demonstrating quite logically the processes involved in sharing faith effectively with young people. Its major weakness is that it is *so* helpful and *so* integrated that there may be a tendency to canonize it, to make it *the* model of youth ministry. If the model is recognized for what it is—*one* creative attempt to understand what youth ministry is all about and *one* step toward developing new and better models for the future—it will more than do its job.

It should also be noted here that what we are presenting is not a model of a *present* reality. Catholic youth ministry today is truly in its infancy, and a total and effective youth ministry is certainly more a dream than a reality in the Church today. Rather, the model presented points us toward the future, giving directions to pursue and a sense of cohesion and purpose as we pursue them.

Fr. Don Kimball, a "Christian disc jockey" and leader of youth ministry from the Santa Rosa Diocese of California, has developed what has become known as "the wedge model of youth ministry" because of the shape of its graphic presentation. The model is an attempt to present graphically the dimensions of pre-evangelization, evangelization, catechesis, Christian service, and peer ministry as they can be integrated into a total ministry to, with, by, and for young people.[2] My presentation of the model and my comments on each dimension of it constitute my personal reflections about youth ministry based on past and present experience. Because I have somewhat adapted and modified his original work, Don Kimball deserves any credit that may be offered for the model itself, while I assume any criticisms or disagreements that may be directed at this presentation of it.

The graphic presentation of the wedge model is given on page 44, and a point-by-point commentary on the model begins below. The numbers used in the commentary correspond to those provided above the various dimensions of youth ministry as shown in the model.

1. Relational Ministry

The first stage of youth ministry is what is commonly called *relational ministry,* the building of relationships of trust upon which all further ministry must be based. Many young people, either as a natural phase of their development or because of negative past experiences, go through a period of apathy, negativity, or even antagonism regarding the Church and the faith it preserves, celebrates, and passes on. The causes of these attitudes vary from the "negative discovery of self" common to adolescents that affects all areas of their lives — parent and peer relationships, for example — to difficult home environments and conflicts with individual teachers, pastors, or other representatives of the Church. Regardless of the causes of the negativity, if it is to be overcome the adult members of our parishes should try to make every effort to reach out to individual young people, to demonstrate the sincere care the Church has for them, and to invite them into the life of the community. Michael Warren refers to this as "the ministry of welcome." Until young people feel welcomed by and into the parish community of faith, there is no reason why they should be open to the message of faith it proclaims. The term most commonly used in recent Church documents for this dimension of youth ministry is *pre-evangelization,* in a sense the "tilling of the soil" that is required before the seed of faith can take root and flourish.[3]

Wedge Model

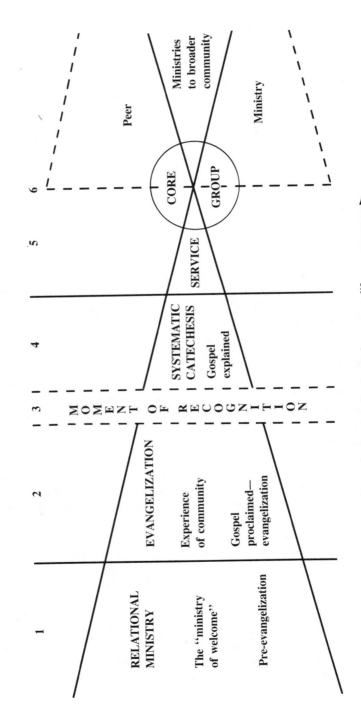

| 1 | 2 | 3 | 4 | 5 | 6 |

RELATIONAL MINISTRY

The "ministry of welcome"

Pre-evangelization

EVANGELIZATION

Experience of community

Gospel proclaimed— evangelization

MOMENT OF RECOGNITION

SYSTEMATIC CATECHESIS

Gospel explained

SERVICE

CORE

GROUP

Peer

Ministries to broader community

Ministry

→ Continually deepening prayer life

Relational ministry is perhaps the most recognized and discussed of all
the dimensions of youth ministry,[4] so much so that many people, unfortunately, feel that this *is* youth ministry in its entirety. The stress upon this "ministry
of friendship" or "contact model" of youth ministry is based on the rather
recent recognition that this very basic, foundational level of the ministry has
been sorely neglected in the past. Many of our young people do not feel
welcomed by the Church; their alienation from the Church has been increasingly evident. Youth ministry must begin there if it is to successfully begin
anywhere. But it cannot and does not stop there.

2. Evangelization

Once young people, as individuals, have been made to feel worthwhile and
welcomed by the community of faith, they will automatically want to share
and celebrate that experience with others. They will want to gather—perhaps
initially for recreational and social activities, later in youth groups involved
in service, study, prayer, and so on. It is in the context of this experience
of community that the Gospel can be effectively "proclaimed."

The *proclamation* of the Gospel can be understood as distinct from its
explanation, that is, from the formal explication and discussion of the symbols, traditions, history, and teachings of the Church. In the early Church
there was no attempt at heady theologizing, no need or desire to analyze
the intricacies of the message shared by and lived out by Jesus. Rather, the
early Christians were driven to shout that very basic message, the "kerygma,"
almost literally from the rooftops. In effect they said, "This is the way it
is. Jesus, whom you have seen crucified, has been raised from the dead and
now lives as Lord of the universe. Turn from your sinfulness, recognize Jesus
as Lord, and be saved. Take it or leave it!"

That rather striking pronouncement, if spoken by individual persons with
no credibility, would have been rejected as laughable, if not the talk of in-
sane people. What gave the message its credibility was the fact that it was
proclaimed by people in communities, communities of love. Those persons
forced to evaluate the early proclamation of the Gospel, and to decide either
to accept or reject it, did so in light of the way the message was affecting
the lives of individuals. They were impressed not only by the internal sense
and vitality of the message, but even more so by the witness of those who
had accepted it: "See how those Christians love one another." The need for
that kind of proclamation of the faith backed up by communal and individual
witness is as desperately needed today as in the past. It is precisely the realization of this reality, and the recognition of the common lack of such witness,
that has led the Church so strongly to emphasize the need for evangelization
in our modern world.[5]

In youth ministry, perhaps the most effective means for evangelization is the youth retreat. Search, COR, and Teens Encounter Christ (TEC) weekends are all examples of intensive community-based experiences for youth in which the basic elements of the Gospel—again the kerygma—can be proclaimed and, on a rudimentary basis, experienced and celebrated. Literally tens of thousands of young people have been deeply touched by such experiences in the last ten years, and perhaps no other single development has better served to keep alive the hope that young people can in fact be deeply affected by and committed to the faith.[6] But there has been an ongoing concern that such experiences, though helpful and even profoundly significant for many, often lack depth and the kind of continual follow-up that is critical to faith development. Some even accuse such retreat experiences of being overly emotional and manipulative. That kind of accusation may be justified if youth ministry is seen to stop at this point, at the simple proclamation of the Gospel. Total youth ministry, on the other hand, recognizes the retreat as just one dimension of a much more involved process.

3. The "Moment of Recognition"

Central to all current understanding of faith development, and therefore central to youth ministry as well, is the realization that one must arrive at the point of personal decision—conversion, metanoia, encounter with Christ—if the faith is to have full significance in one's life. The faith cannot simply be inherited from one's ancestors; it must be personally owned, freely accepted as real and vital in one's life. This moment of personal decision-making regarding faith constitutes the next and very significant stage of faith development and of youth ministry.

I have chosen to call this critical stage of faith development the "moment of recognition." I do this for two reasons primarily. First, I want to avoid the notion implied by words like *conversion* or *encounter* that a person is in some way to be thunderstruck by the faith, in some emotional sense overwhelmed by the presence of God. Though that may in fact be a very real and valid experience for some, my own sense of faith development is that it is neither the most common nor necessarily the most healthful way to move toward maturity of faith. Most of us creep toward maturity of faith in much the same way that we gradually achieve all other levels of human maturity—one step, even one stumble, at a time. There seem to me to be many dangers inherent in the belief that faith development requires a dramatic and sudden turnabout in one's life, not the least of which is the tendency of some persons to try to force that kind of experience upon others.

My second reason for preferring the term "moment of recognition" is that the term at root expresses well what occurs here. The word *recognition* means "re-cognition"—that is, "knowing again." You can only recognize at any one moment that which has been known to some degree previously—perhaps not fully, perhaps not in depth, but known to some degree nevertheless. This is what happens at that moment of recognition in our faith development. All that has been known by us before—our experiences of the symbols and rituals of our faith, the witness of Christian parents, prior religious education, and so on—are at some point in time understood as integrated and personally meaningful realities. Kimball refers to this—and I would agree with him—as the "aha! moment," the sense of discovering, perhaps with great surprise, the fact that our faith makes sense of both our world and our personal lives. Until this happens, all future faith development will be slowed, if not totally stopped, because the faith will remain an external and often unintelligible amalgam of doctrines and religious practices.

An absolutely critical point must be made regarding the moment of recognition. It must be a totally free response of the individual to the unconditional love of God. Though the community of faith can provide an environment in which the individual might find the faith attractive and worthy of consideration, it cannot force the individual to accept the faith or to live out meaningfully the religious practices and doctrinal beliefs that flow from it. It should also be noted that the moment of recognition will occur at different times for different people, with some experiencing a free and true opening to faith in their late teens and others not truly owning their faith as a personally chosen value until the age of forty or beyond. The Church's obligation is to witness to the faith with integrity and conviction and to invite all others to do so as well; whether persons choose to respond to that invitation is totally their prerogative.[7]

One of the very necessary tasks of adolescents is to try out different lifestyles, to weigh alternatives, to play with all kinds of possibilities in life. It is not the time normally for lifelong decisions, for thoroughly considered life choices. As adults we often shudder at the thought of young people sixteen or seventeen years old choosing marriage. And yet we are strangely less skeptical of faith "commitments" made at this age; in fact, we often *expect* such maturity of faith. Youth ministry, when properly understood and implemented, recognizes that adulthood is normally the age for such faith conviction, and that the goal of youth ministry is to make the possibility of such a future decision attractive to young people, not to pressure or in some way manipulate them to move toward that moment too quickly.

It is true, however, that many young people seem to experience the moment of recognition, the "aha! moment." This is often the result of healthy and well-developed youth retreats or contact with particularly gifted teachers or other witnesses of the faith. There is, following that experience, a sincere desire to seek a deeper understanding of the faith. And that desire, that openness to a deeper search of the meanings of our Christian faith, leads to the next dimension, or stage, of youth ministry.

4. Systematic Catechesis

Catechesis, both as a term and as a process or activity, has a very involved and profound history in the Church. It is a complex reality with many layers of meaning. My treatment of this topic here must be necessarily simplistic and centered upon the specific implications of catechesis for youth ministry.[8]

In the sense that it is being used here, catechesis refers to the systematic process of exploring the depths of meaning in the Christian story, studying its many implications for one's personal life, seeking a richer understanding of the faith through the study of the Scriptures and through sharing with other members of the community. One facet of this process can be formal religious education, but catechesis also takes place in less formal ways in the experience of liturgy, in private or shared reflection upon one's personal life experiences, and so on. In light of our previous comments, it could be said that systematic catechesis is the process of *explaining* the Gospel that has been *proclaimed* through the process of evangelization.

As young people experience what John Westerhoff has called "searching faith," the personal struggle to make sense of and to move toward personally owning the faith, they need solid direction and properly developed catechetical opportunities. In the past, the Church tried to provide just this kind of direction through formal religious education programs, either in our schools or through parish CCD programs. The problem with many of these attempts, and the reason for their apparently common failure to interest and fulfill the needs of young people, is twofold: (1) Our religious education often falsely presupposed the moment of recognition, the openness to faith, on the part of young people who had not truly experienced that stage of faith development. Our attempts to explain the Gospel were therefore aimed at many young people who were simply not ready for it and who therefore logically rejected it or reacted to it with apathy. (2) Many of our catechetical efforts, even when directed toward those who were, in fact, open to and ready for them, were simply poorly conceived and ineffectively presented.

If the systematic catechesis of young people (as distinctive from *informal* catechesis) is to be effective, it must be creative, interesting, and enjoyable. Michael Warren has said that our past catechetical efforts have been continual and terminal, meaning we have presented virtually constant formal religious education to our young people from about age seven till Confirmation, at which point it seems to cease permanently. Warren believes that instead we should pursue a youth catechesis that is occasional and lifelong, based on the dictates of human development, perhaps offered seasonally rather than weekly, and then recognized as a process that must be continued into and throughout adulthood. There is no question, whether one agrees with Warren or not, that our catechesis needs to be much more creative than it has been in the past if it is ever to serve the needs of young people. Unique scheduling approaches have to be tested; we have to experiment with a wide variety of teaching techniques, and so on.[9] Certainly our systematic catechesis must be firmly based on the kind of relational and communal ministry discussed earlier, in which individual young persons may freely join with others to pursue their understanding of the faith in supportive and celebratory community environments. I will return with more reflections on youth catechesis later in this article.

5. Christian Service

The next major dimension of youth ministry identified by our model is service. Christian service, in its fullest and richest sense, is the almost automatic response to the dictates of the Gospel when it has been properly proclaimed and explained. The individual Christian who achieves any degree of maturity of faith is going to seek opportunities for sharing his or her personal talents with the community of faith, as well as with the broader community. This not only is the natural desire of Christians but also is one of the most attractive characteristics of many of our young people. The research of George Gallup, Jr., and David Poling, as described in their book *The Search for America's Faith* (Nashville: Abingdon, 1980), states:

> We have heard that young people today are an inward, self-centered generation, who say 'do your own thing' and who have disdainfully removed themselves from the strain and severity of modern life. Our studies reveal the opposite: many are vitally interested in the helping professions and one out of every four people fourteen years of age or older volunteers time to some nonprofit organization." (Pp. 23–24)

For many people, adolescence is a time of great idealism, a time of growing awareness of the problems of the world, but also an almost indomitable — some would suggest, naive — optimism about their ability to affect, if not conquer, those problems. Such young people need to test their limits, to find ways to reach out to others. Well-conceived and properly directed service opportunities can provide very fruitful means for accomplishing these tasks, to the benefit of both the young people and those they serve. The provision of such opportunities is a vital and necessary component of total youth ministry.

Closely related to this discussion of Christian service is the area of consciousness-raising, education, and action for peace and justice — an area that the bishops in their 1971 synod called a "constitutive dimension of the preaching of the Gospel." The major issues of poverty, nuclear armaments, sexism, the draft, and so on, should be of major concern to the growing Christian. The danger in dealing with some of these issues too deeply or too early in adolescence is the possibility of overwhelming the young people with a sense of foreboding, raising their level of awareness far beyond their sense of power to act, and thereby frustrating, if not depressing, them. This is a very delicate question in my mind, one that deserves far more deliberation and study than I can provide here.[10] However, it is my conviction that the in-depth study and discussion of global social issues will not be truly profitable until the latter years of high school, at the earliest, and that organized attempts at concrete action regarding social justice issues may not be truly effective until later in adolescence (eighteen to twenty-five), when many of these issues take on a personal significance that may not be present at earlier ages.

I'll be returning later to the discussion of the service dimension of total youth ministry. We can state here, however, that the *minimum* requirement regarding Christian service, if our ministry to young people is to be complete, is this: those young people who *are* ready to share their talents and gifts with others should be offered the opportunities and guidance they need to do so effectively, and those who are directing such service involvement should do so with a sensitivity to each young person's level of maturity and ability.

6. Leadership Development and Peer Ministry

We come now to an explanation for the conic, or wedge-shaped, graphic presentation used in Kimball's model. The relational dimension of youth ministry involves the hospitable offer of friendship extended to *all* young people, the invitation by the parish community for all young people to join in its faith-life. We have a moral obligation as Church to see that each of our young people senses and tangibly experiences that kind of openness on the part of the adult Church. When that invitation is extended, *some* of them will respond and seek ways to share and celebrate with others in community, a community in and through which the Gospel can be proclaimed. Fewer still of that number will experience the moment of recognition, the "aha! moment," the experience of free and personal openness to faith. Of those who do, some will need and seek out a deepening understanding of their faith through systematic catechesis, and eventually some of that number—by now a real minority group within the context of the total youth community—will want to reach out to others in service.

The point or implication of the wedge, then, is that the natural result of the faith-development process—not the goal, but the seemingly unavoidable result—will be a continually decreasing number of participants as the process continues. This process of gradually decreasing numbers ultimately will lead, in Kimball's perception of youth ministry, to the formation of a "core group," a small community within the whole that will consist of those young people who are deeply committed to the faith and to growth in it, and who because of that faith seek to reach out in service to others. This development is not peculiar to youth ministry. It is just as true among adults: almost any parish includes a small nucleus of particularly committed adults about whom the whole parish seems to revolve and upon whom it seems to depend. The common tendency of such groups is to spend an inordinate amount of time complaining about all the people who are not involved, who do not share their concern. It would seem to be far more productive—and a lot more enjoyable—for that small group to celebrate and thank God for what it shares; the group will then be far more attractive to "outsiders" than it could possibly be when caught up with negativism and despondency. The same will hold true for small youth core groups and those who lead them. Rather than being distressed by the increasingly poor response in numbers to the opportunities provided, we should not only expect it but also celebrate the faith that is shared by those who *do* choose to be so involved.

A final point should be made about this core group, a factor concerning it that is represented by the broken lines on the diagram of this model. The members of this group, because of the process of faith development that each has experienced, will be in a position to reach out to others—young and older people alike—in a spirit of Christian service and commitment. They will become active members of the faith community, thereby continuing the process of sharing the faith with others through the ministries of welcome, evangelization, and so on. They will often function as "peer ministers," young Christians who will enjoy a particular kind of credibility as they reach out with the message of Christ to other young people. In this sense, then, the integrated approach to youth ministry implied and advocated by this model provides for the continual development of its own leaders, thereby assuring that the process will not simply die with the burnout or moving on of its initial leaders.

The Wedge Model in Theory and Practice

It is important to note that the approach to youth ministry represented by Kimball's wedge model is neither entirely new nor contrary to other developments in the Church. Many recent official documents have pointed to the multidimensional scope of Christian education, for instance, and a tremendous surge has taken place in our research in and consequent understanding of the developmental nature of faith.[11] In fact, the basic process for sharing faith delineated by this model is as old yet as fresh as the personal ministry of Jesus himself.[12] Jesus reached out and made contact with people as they were, he invited them to "come and see," he spent time with them and helped them see the profound significance of his teachings, and then he commissioned them to "go and do likewise." What youth ministry as a philosophy seems to be offering is a vocabulary, a theory, and some practical strategies as to how this can best be accomplished among today's young people, and that is a contribution to the Church at large of which all in youth ministry can be justly proud.

I mentioned earlier that one of the dangers, if you will, of this model is that it is *so* helpful and *so* reasonable that we might tend to canonize it as *the* model of youth ministry. My experience in sharing the model with others in workshop situations is that it rings true with most people and, in fact, resonates so clearly with their own experience that the presentation of the model often becomes itself a kind of "aha! moment" for those to whom it is presented. It does not take long, however, before the questions and the problems begin to surface, and the real limitations of models become immediately clear. What happens to all those who do not go through the entire process, for example? Are they ignored or in some way ostracized from the parish? How can a parish respond to all the needs and responsibilities implied by this model? How do we as individual youth ministers respond to the wide variety of needs and levels of development exhibited in any one group of young people? What do you do if half of your group needs heavily relational ministry and the other half wants and needs systematic catechesis? Assuming you can get a youth group to progress in its own development, how can you provide ongoing opportunities for inviting new members into the group who will most likely be at a different level of need and development? How can a parish possibly provide the personnel and resources that seem to be required in pursuing this kind of total ministry to, with, by, and for youth? It is clear that this article is not the forum for responding to all of these practical questions nor, quite honestly, are there necessarily valid and valuable answers available for all of them. We simply have a great deal to learn. Some of my later reflections on the various components of youth ministry may shed light on these kinds of questions and some possible answers to them. For now I would like to offer just two insights that I think can put all of this into proper perspective.

1. A Cyclic, Not a Linear, Process

It is important to note that one does not "go through the process" as it is outlined in the wedge model once and for all, as if there were a linear progression from relational to service dimensions of faith growth that occurs but once in a person's life. Rather, the process, if it can be validly termed that, is more cyclic and recurs throughout one's life, presumably, we would hope, always progressing to greater levels of depth. For example, in my own faith development I have experienced some good catechetical background and have tried to share my talents with the broader community. But I still desperately need people who reach out to me and support me. I have an ongoing need to be evangelized by people of faith. I struggle daily with the need for a deeper commitment of the faith and have had many "aha! moments" along the way. I have a constant thirst for more knowledge about my faith, and Lord knows, I have a long way to go in my willingness to serve others. At different times in my life I struggle with different problems and arrive at different solutions, and yet in the midst of all that apparent confusion and stumbling about, I recognize a pattern, a rhythm of sorts, in my own growth in faith. I find that pattern and rhythm to be well reflected in the wedge model, and I feel as well that the model helps to sensitize me to the pattern and rhythm of faith development in others.

2. A Tool for Evaluating and Directing *Us,* Not *Them*

It should be quickly added, however, that the value of the wedge model is *not* that it helps us to identify the level or stages of faith growth in individual young people. It would be presumptuous, if not downright unchristian, to attempt a personal evaluation of the faith-life of each person we encounter. The wedge model is not to be used as a tool for evaluating others, but rather as a guideline and, to a lesser degree, a tool for evaluating the broader community's ministry to young people. Is my parish one in which young people feel welcomed, and how can we make it even more so? Are the catechetical opportunities we provide successful or attractive to our young people? If not, are there clues provided by this model of youth ministry that can lead us to improve the situation? Are we providing youth retreats, and if so, are these effective and nonmanipulative means of evangelization? Are reasonable and well-conceived opportunities for Christian service offered to our young people? And so on.

The point is that a parish is called to provide opportunities, programs, and services that respond to these multiple dimensions of youth ministry in an ongoing way, and then the young persons *themselves* choose those levels of involvement or those opportunities that best respond to or reflect their personal needs. I will readily grant that this is far easier said than done, but I feel a direction is provided here that makes a great deal of sense.

A Definition of the Youth Minister

Given the model of youth ministry presented here, what can we say about the person called to carry on this ministry, that is, the youth minister? My concern here is simply to attempt a definition of *youth minister*, not to deal with the important issues of job descriptions, qualifications, characteristics of the youth minister, and so on.

A number of current practices that make defining *youth minister* difficult:

1. The term or title *youth minister* is often used so broadly that it seems to encompass everyone who comes into contact with young people: parents, teachers, coaches, parish secretaries, janitors, and so on. The problem here is that the title becomes so common that it effectively defines or describes no one.

2. A second difficulty arises when parishes and others look at a model of youth ministry like the one provided here and simply say, "That's what a youth minister is—someone who does all that." So the youth minister ends up with a job description that includes relational ministry, community-building, sacramental preparation and celebration, religious education, and service programs . . . a job description that a canonized saint could not fulfill. As a result many youth ministers are quickly frustrated or exhausted, the turnover in the field is high, and many end up disenchanted with the whole endeavor.

3. There is also a problem in youth ministry centering around the issue of professionalism versus volunteerism. Too often the title of youth minister is given only to those who are hired and paid to do the work, while those who freely share their talents and gifts with the Church are automatically viewed as less than professionals. It is hoped the weaknesses of this attitude are evident.

A Proposed Definition and Its Implications

So just who is a youth minister? In my mind, **a youth minister is one who is publicly commissioned by and accountable to the Church and who represents the faith community in ministering to, with, or for the young people of the community.** Note the important factors implied by this definition:

1. *All* ministry must be grounded in, arise out of, and be supported by the broader community. Anything less than this will be either ineffective or counterproductive. Many youth ministers are inclined to view themselves as identified with the young people—outside the community, as it were—or to feel in some way in opposition to the community because they serve as advocates of young people. This is a very problematic position to take, almost guaranteeing failure. The ministers to young people must see themselves, and be seen by others, as very identifiable members of the community who reach out with care and concern as representatives of that community. In the same sense, youth ministers must be accountable to the broader com-

munity in order to avoid the sense of isolation and independence that often characterizes this ministry.

2. Careful note must be taken of my definition's emphasis on ministry "to, with, *or* for youth," rather than on the common statement from *A Vision of Youth Ministry* (Washington, DC: United States Catholic Conference, 1976) about ministry "to, with, by, and for youth." The intent here is to clearly locate and identify the *particular* concerns of an individual youth minister within the broader spectrum of youth ministry concerns, and to avoid the common misconception that youth ministers must be "all things to all people." Total youth mini*stry* is the entire Church's ministry to, with, by, *and* for the young people, but an individual youth mini*ster* may only have the talent and desire to minister to, with, *or* for the young people. Some, such as teachers or coaches, will minister *to* youth. Others will minister *with* youth, as in the case of those who coordinate service activities or peer ministry. These people will be fully accepted as youth ministers, even though they do not carry the burden of working on *all* levels of that ministry. A given parish will hire the person with the qualities and abilities suited to its unique needs. And, incidentally, the qualifications of a youth minister—given this definition—will vary according to the responsibilities assigned to each one. The DRE may require a master's degree in religious education, while the counselor will require a far different academic and practical background.

Therefore, in light of our model, a parish will assess its own particular needs and those of its young people and, perhaps ideally, hire a "director of youth ministry" (or, perhaps even more clearly, a "director of youth ministr*ies*") whose responsibility would be to oversee and coordinate the many dimensions of youth ministry and also to recruit and train individuals who would handle the various dimensions of the total ministry to its young people. Notice: such a director is called to oversee, coordinate, recruit, and train, *not* personally to direct all these efforts. In addition to this director or coordinator, then, there may well be many other "youth ministers"—volunteers or professionals—involved in various dimensions of the parish's total ministry to, with, by, and for its young people.

Reflections on the Various Components of Youth Ministry

The Total Community Is Responsible

Youth ministry must be recognized as the responsibility of the entire faith community, not as a specific task that can be delegated to an individual youth minister. It is foolhardy to think that an individual youth minister could effectively develop strong personal relationships with all the young people of the parish, create a sense of community among them, counsel them through their decisions about faith, provide catechesis for those who seek it, and then provide opportunities and directions for Christian service. The mere statement of such responsibilities makes such a job description appear ludicrous, and yet many youth ministers live with just these kinds of responsibilities and expectations. The only rational approach to youth ministry is to recognize that the youth minister's primary responsibility is to help the adult community, as a whole, minister to its young people by identifying, developing, and then sharing the talents of many people in the community.

The Role of Parents in Youth Ministry

In view of the role of the faith community in ministering to youth, a primary concern of the youth minister must be communication with and the involvement of the parents of the young people. In looking back at our model for a moment, parents must be recognized as the key "relational ministers," those who more than anyone else can create the sense of trust, love, and concern that is so foundational to all future openness to faith. Those in youth ministry must help parents to fulfill this vital role, by offering programs in adolescent development, for instance, and by helping parents develop the necessary communication skills with which to build healthy relationships with their adolescent children. Parents must be seen as the 'primary evangelizers" of their children. It has been repeatedly demonstrated that no other single factor more influences the faith development of persons than does the witness and faith-life of parents. This particular point is so important that it deserves further comment.

In my mind we have failed to explain clearly our meaning when we have called parents the "primary religious educators of their children." Properly understood this is certainly true; the problem is, it seems to me, that this has seldom been properly understood, and many of our parents live under the weight of tremendous guilt feelings because of this. Again, I think our model of youth ministry helps to clarify the issue. When we have called parents to be the primary educators of their children, I believe they have taken that to mean that they are to be the "primary catechists" of their children, in the sense that they must be able to deal with, understand, and then effectively present to their children all the profound doctrinal, liturgical, and historical teachings and traditions of the Church. Most parents, even with the training often provided them by their parishes, simply do not feel capable of handling this kind of education, and I personally don't blame them.

My own sense of parental responsibility, again looking to our model for help, is that parents are responsible for opening their children to the wonder and power of the Gospel by loving their children unconditionally and by living their own faith day in and day out with conviction and dedication. *If* they do this, the odds are strong that their children will approach adolescence with a degree of openness and receptivity that will make a true recognition of the meaning of faith possible. At that time, the Church must provide the catechetical opportunities that will be required if that initial openness to faith is to achieve any depth. This will often require professional catechists who have the theological and pedagogical training to provide effective religious education. The parents must surely support and encourage such efforts, but they should not be made to feel in some way solely responsible for their success.

The "Aha! Moment" and Personal Freedom

Regarding the moment of recognition, I have already stated that this must be a free response on the part of the individual to the unconditional love of God. There can be no room for coercion by parents, clergy, or other representatives of the community. And my conviction is that far more young people are ready for this kind of openness to faith than we may be inclined to believe.

As we have seen, the relational dimension of youth ministry is critical to its success. This is where the attempts of youth ministers often begin. On a personal, one-to-one basis we must reach out affectionately to our young people as representatives of a community that cares for them. The need for this kind of ministry—and the depth of the experience it provides for individual youth—will be directly proportional to the young person's past experience with trusting relationships. Some young people will need years of ministry just at this level, because many have been deeply hurt during their lives. Others will need only a smile, a brief comment, and an invitation to "come and see." My experience has been that the need for this kind of outreach is not always as deep as we might think, that many are so anxious for what we have to offer that a simple invitation is all they need or want.

If the invitation is extended to young people and if the Gospel is then effectively proclaimed to them, many will be ready to respond freely and openly. The development of youth groups, well-conceived retreat programs, and so on, can be marvelously effective means of evangelizing young people. In that supportive environment many will readily experience the "aha! moment," the great experience of recognizing the personal significance of a faith relationship with an infinitely loving God.

A Word on Youth Catechesis—With More to Come

The next section of this paper deals with the very important issue of the catechetical dimension of youth ministry. What is the relationship between youth ministry and religious education programs? Are they in conflict with one another? Assuming the need for some kind of formal catechesis for our youth, what approaches can we use that will not completely turn them off to the further development of their faith? These are, in my mind, the most critical questions confronting youth ministry today. More on that later.

Christian Service and the Problem of Mandatory Service Projects

The placement of the service dimension of youth ministry in our model has some extremely important implications. As we have seen, Christian service *in its fullest and richest sense* in this model is recognized as the ultimate response of the individual to the experience of faith in its fullness, that is, as an outgrowth of the faith-development process that has included pre-evangelization, evangelization, and catechesis. My conviction is that when the Gospel is effectively proclaimed, when it is responded to in faith, and when that faith is then deepened by the understanding brought about by catechesis, the Christian will be virtually driven to share his or her talents with the faith community and beyond.

The logical question then is, What about service projects that are *required* of young people *prior to* that kind of faith development? Recognizing full well that there are exceptions to every rule, and acknowledging that many young people have probably had positive experiences in faith growth because of service involvement they did not freely seek, I still must strongly state that I am opposed to such attempts at mandatory service as contrary to the spirit of the Gospel and often counterproductive for healthful faith development. Such required service projects are becoming increasingly popular as a major criterion for acceptance for Confirmation, a sacrament most popularly celebrated in early adolescence in our country. I question whether these requirements truly reflect the maturity of faith they are intended to gauge, and I fear they often teach lessons that we would hope our students never learn. Consider the following two examples:

1. It is not uncommon to require candidates for Confirmation to complete fifty hours of service to the parish or to the broader community. What does this teach? In most cases, I feel, the service requirement is viewed by many young people as somewhat akin to being stretched on the rack. If they just suffer through those fifty hours, if they just endure the agony of completing that project, they will prove that they are sincere enough about their faith to be accepted for Confirmation. And then, thank God, they'll never have to do *that* again! Christian service is therefore seen to be largely distasteful activities with recognizable time limits. The whole sense of freely reaching out to others in consistent ways with love and concern is lost. The sharing of one's personal talents with the community is often reduced to fulfilling specific expectations set by an authority outside oneself.

2. I am also concerned about the "benefactees" of such service projects. This approach to mandatory service often reduces people to projects. This year's eighth-grade students visit the neighborhood "old folks' home" for a few weeks, until their "limit" is reached. They then stop, and next year's class picks up on the project. What happens to the people who are to be served by this? How do they feel? Are they being used as educational tools and techniques, much like films and group exercises? And what are we teaching our young people through all of this?

I realize these are rather strong statements, and they may be slightly exaggerated to make a point. But the concern that motivates them is real.

I am not saying that *all* Christian service must be delayed until a mature faith commitment is reached. Rather, I feel this is a question of approach, a question of perspective. I often used an exercise with freshman students on retreats that will clarify this point. At the end of our retreats, I would ask the freshmen to spend about five minutes in silence reflecting on their lives and the talents that God had given them. I then asked that they first choose the one talent they thought was their best and then go out to find a symbol that would in some way represent that talent. They were to bring the symbol to our closing Eucharist, where it would be presented at the offertory as a sign of their desire to share their talents with the community. A fairly simple exercise, one would think. The fact is that 50 percent of the students came to me after ten minutes or so saying they couldn't think of a single talent they had . . . not one! Few developmental psychologists would be surprised by this. The difficulties with self-image and self-acceptance during adolescence are well documented. My question is, how can these young people have any sense of Christian service if they have such a low opinion of themselves? Do they not need first to be made aware of their own gifts and talents before they can be expected to comfortably reach out to others? I think so.

My approach to Christian service at early adolescent levels would provide opportunities for such involvement *only* for those who freely want it. My concentration would be on the areas of self-image and self-acceptance. I would try to help the young people recognize and then begin to develop the talents and abilities they have been given, without putting them in the often embarrassing position of trying to reach out to others when they have not yet embraced themselves. And I would never require the completion of assigned service projects as a condition of acceptance for the sacrament of Confirmation. I feel such practices serve neither the faith development of the young people nor those to whom their service is presumably directed.

To clarify further: I have been discussing Christian service in, as I have characterized it, "its fullest and richest sense." My point is this: Involvement in service opportunities prior to conversion may be better understood as experiences of evangelization than as expressions of true Christian charity. Through such involvement young people have a chance to get to know themselves better, to test out their skills, to work closely with others, and so on—all laudable tasks in themselves. But Christian service as presented in the wedge model implies a level of altruism and self-giving that may only be expected of mature, faith-filled adults.

As alluded to earlier, I would see mid-adolescence (sixteen to twenty) as a time for providing a catechetical base for Christian social justice, raising a consciousness of the issues of peace and justice, and exploring some of the implications for the mature Christian in terms of lifestyles, career choices, and so on. Issues of real pertinence to young people of this age could be explored in greater depth—e.g., consumerism or the responsibilities implied by the right to vote. Finally, I would generally save direct involvement in social action for late adolescence (twenty to twenty-five) when the young person's psychological maturity would permit a more solidly based involvement and one that would likely have more permanent impact on his or her life than would the more sporadic service-project approach.

The Catechetical Dimension of Youth Ministry

Probably no single issue is more central to present discussions on youth ministry, and in my mind no issue will have greater influence on its future, than its relationship to youth catechesis. The most difficult problems confronting youth ministry today deal with the question of the catechetical dimension of that ministry—who is responsible for it, how do we develop effective catechetical programs, how does youth ministry relate to CCD in the parish, what impact does campus ministry have on the religion department in Catholic high schools, how do youth ministers relate to directors of religious education, and so on. The issue is the subject of discussions—and occasional confrontations—on the national, diocesan, and local parish levels. The clarification of these issues must be a prime concern of all those involved in youth ministry and youth catechesis.

Why the Tension?—A Personal Reflection

Many reasons exist for the tensions caused by the question of youth catechetics and how it relates to broader youth ministry. Perhaps a reflection on my own experience will help. About six years ago, when the term *youth ministry* was just beginning to surface in Catholic circles, I was a director of high school religious education for five parishes in Appleton, Wisconsin. I was beginning to have success with a new approach to our programming—new scheduling approaches, an integrated curriculum, the addition of retreat experiences at each grade level, and so on. Attendance was growing steadily and enthusiasm was high. Then I started to hear about youth ministry—the "new" approach to adolescent faith development. I was told that the new approach was needed because the "old way" had failed. Youth ministry was highly relational rather than "just academic." What was needed, I was told, was the dissolution of all the CCD and religious education programs and the initiation of a broader kind of ministry to young people that would reach them "where they're at"—a ministry that would go into the home, the streets, and the schools, rather than expecting the young people to come to our stale and ineffective programs. Youth ministry was in, CCD and religious education were on their way out.

Please understand that this was *my* perception of the situation, and an obviously biased one at that. But that is precisely my point—that all of us naturally operate out of our own experiences, our own biases, and our own commitments. My reaction to youth ministry was anything but positive initially. I felt, first of all, affronted by it. I felt that my successful programs were being criticized by people who failed in their own educational programs and who were seeking easy alternatives. I became defensive. I found myself looking for the weak links in the youth ministry position, rather than affirming its strong points. In so doing, I think I failed to support a philosophy that would have helped my own students a great deal. In short, I was wrong.

I discovered I was wrong in my initial reactions to youth ministry as soon as I stopped being defensive and started to listen—and to think. To my surprise I realized that objectively I agreed with the advocates of youth ministry on virtually every issue. I realized, again with surprise, that the reason why my own educational programs were successful was that they incorporated the tenets of youth ministry without ever identifying them as such. I realized that youth ministry, as a broad and total ministry to our young people, did not threaten formal religious education efforts but, in fact, enhanced them and supported them. And, as I assume has become clear in this article, I now firmly support and encourage the development of total ministry to, with, by, and for our young people.

My reason for recounting my own brief history with youth ministry—from the perspective of a religious educator—is that I am perhaps arrogant enough to think that my experience is fairly representative of the majority of those in formal religious education programs. I think that many religious educators on the diocesan and local parish levels feel either threatened by youth ministry or overwhelmed by it ("Don't tell me they're going to give me *another* job to do!"). An obvious question of economics is also involved in all of this; the thought of competing even more for an already scarce dollar can be disquieting to say the least. The entire question is loaded with semantic and theoretical confusion, illustrated by those religious educators who feel that catechesis *properly understood* automatically incorporates youth ministry and therefore precludes the need for additional efforts.

The Issues Must Be Faced

The need for serious and open discussion on the issue of youth ministry and its relationship to youth catechesis is evident, and yet I fear that precisely the opposite response is common. It seems to me that the current posture of both youth ministry advocates and religious educators is often one of resigned silence. Having perhaps experienced initial confrontations similar to my own, many now choose to "stay out of each other's way," with neither side wanting to offend the other. The motive here—maintaining peace— may be admirable, but it hardly resolves the issues involved. The issues have to be resolved, or we will all suffer the loss.

- If the questions involved are not openly discussed and resolved, youth ministry will suffer the consequences because North American Catholicism is so highly committed to education that, if forced to choose, the Church would choose formal religious education over broader youth ministry.
- If youth ministry as a vision and as a practical approach to young people does not flourish, our educational mission as a Church will be retarded in its growth—a growth that demands the insights that youth ministry can offer it.

Four Steps Toward Constructive Dialogue

If constructive dialogue is to take place on the issue of youth ministry and adolescent religious education, advocates of both positions are going to have to recognize the validity and potential contributions of each position and strive to achieve not only peaceful coexistence but also harmony and *shared* responsibility for the faith development of our young people. I would recommend the following four steps to the advocates of the two positions:

1. Those involved in and supportive of total youth ministry must avoid the temptation to claim that total youth ministry is needed because educational programs have failed. Many presentations, articles, and workshops on youth ministry begin with a statement of the poor reputation of parish CCD programs or a repetition of the familiar statistics on the "unchurched" millions who are not reached by formal religious education efforts. Even if such statements could be justified logically, they automatically begin the discussion of the issue with a negative tone, with an apparent attempt to find blame. Many religious educators naturally find this offensive and therefore become defensive. Youth ministry can justify its existence with numerous positive arguments—with the valuable insights of developmental psychology, recent studies on faith development, the results of sociological investigation, and so on.

2. Youth ministry must more clearly articulate its commitment to religious education as a major component of total youth ministry. Thoughtful advocates of youth ministry have never denied the need for educational programs, despite the common perception of many to the contrary. It is that common perception that must be acknowledged and corrected. Spokespersons for youth ministry must clearly state that if the Christian faith is to be shared with our young people, it must be studied, investigated, reflected upon in prayer; that is, it must become intelligible, not simply attractive, to them. We must help our young people to understand and to articulate our Catholic Christian symbols, traditions, history, and beliefs. Proponents of youth ministry must continually affirm that our young people need a consistent, ongoing, and gradually deepening understanding of the faith, and the ability and language with which to express and share and celebrate that understanding. This is, of course, the primary concern of religious education and catechesis.

3. Religious educators, on their part, must admit that perhaps the majority of our past educational efforts have been too academically oriented, stressing the teaching of facts more than the development of total persons. They must acknowledge the need for a balanced and integrated ministry to and with our young people that encompasses the many dimensions of their world—such as parent and peer relationships and the impact of our culture and its often confusing, if not outright unchristian, values. Religious educators must acknowledge that they provide for just one dimension—though a vital one—in the Church's ministry to its young people. And, in so doing, religious educators must recognize and support the efforts of total youth ministry.

4. Youth ministers and religious educators—on the national, diocesan, and local parish levels—must join together to develop integrated ministries to those they are called to serve. Every effort must be made to identify and eliminate the causes of confusion and disagreement. All the areas of pre-evangelization, evangelization, catechesis, and service must be recognized as vital dimensions of faith development, and care must be taken to see that opportunities for involvement on all these levels are made available to youth according to their needs. Job descriptions, budgets, and the number of personnel must be evaluated and ultimately based upon the recognition of the need for total ministry to, with, by, and for young people.

Suggestions on the Effective Catechesis of Youth

Catechesis is a vital and necessary component of total youth ministry, but it is equally evident that there are significant problems in actually providing effective catechesis for our young people. How do we catechize; how do we provide an adequate understanding of our faith without turning them off? I have both general and specific recommendations to make on this point, all of which will have to be concisely stated given the limitations of space:[13]

General Recommendations

1. First, we have to become continually more creative in developing effective catechetical approaches to our young people. We have to find alternatives to the often static and mostly ineffective one-hour, once-a-week models of religious education that have been the norm for most parish educational programs. Many such alternatives are now being developed and actually implemented throughout the country.

2. Second, we have to take full advantage of our understanding of human development, recognizing the varying capacities and abilities at each age level and providing catechetical approaches appropriate to those ages.

3. Very importantly, we have to recognize continually that youth catechesis has its own specific and vital goals, and at the same time we cannot allow ourselves to be trapped by the thought that the faith-development process ends with graduation from our educational programs. The sense that we have to "get everything in" by the end of the high school years is a primary cause of the "over-teaching" that so often alienates young people. Youth catechesis must be recognized as preliminary to the kind of continuing adult faith formation that is required if the Gospel is to be fully understood and lived.

Specific Recommendations

The following recommendations regarding the development of effective systematic youth catechesis concern both the persons involved in that catechesis and the programs they are called to develop. The program recommendations are based on somewhat stereotypical understandings of the young people, their needs, and their cultural and social situations. These will necessarily have to be adjusted appropriately to suit local conditions.

1. Awareness of the catechesis of children. First, I think that those involved in youth catechesis must become very conscious and aware of what is going on in grade school religious education today and must make every effort to understand and to build upon it, studying available materials, meeting with grade school teachers and coordinators, and so on. This may seem at first to be an odd recommendation. But I am convinced that the negativity of many youth ministers and others toward formal, or systematic, catechesis is based on their own grade school experience of a catechetical system that may simply no longer exist. Our young people are generally far more receptive to direct input and discussion of the faith than they were just ten years ago, and that is largely due to the tremendous improvement of grade school catechesis and the growth of family-centered religious education. Youth ministers and youth catechists must be fully familiar with these developments, or they may fail to understand the young people who come to them.

   2. Catechesis in early adolescence. Second, in early adolescence, which I would define basically as the junior high school years, we must stress the relational dimensions of our ministry and concentrate on the areas of human development that are foundational to healthful faith development. I think the following concerns should dominate our ministry during this stage:
a. There should be an emphasis on the personal growth and development of the individual, helping young people to understand and deal with their experience of rapid growth and change—helping them to accept their bodies, for example, and to understand their developing emotions and increasingly questioning minds.
b. The relationship with parents should be discussed, and young people must be helped to deal with that changing relationship with minimal trauma and guilt.
c. The area of sexuality should be discussed at this time, not simply from the biological perspective but also from the perspectives of self-image, personal relationships, communication, moral decision-making, and so on.
d. In early adolescence, there should be a heavy emphasis on building a sense of group solidarity and belonging in the context of events and opportunities sponsored by the Church—for instance, field trips, campouts, and social gatherings.
   I know there are those who will object that I am suggesting many relational programs under the guise, or umbrella, of catechesis. There is an adage that during the junior high school years, it is more fruitful to talk to God about boys and girls than it is to talk to boys and girls about God. I don't necessarily agree with that sentiment, but I think it has some validity. This is a stage of development when it is important to provide young people with the opportunity to experience a certain sense of the sacred, to experience the presence of God within the context of these kinds of relational activities. It is a time for establishing the relevance of faith and religion to lived experience, rather than for pursuing a philosophical or theological

understanding of the faith. An intimate prayer service around a campfire will teach the junior high student far more than a six-week course on prayer; adults who can speak personally and affectionately about their God will teach more than an academic course on Jesus. My point is that the junior high years are the peak time for the kind of outreach and relational ministry that we have said is so necessary in the development of faith. If relationships of trust are established at this time, a richer and more direct catechesis will be possible later; if it does not happen at this age, those ministering to older adolescents—say, juniors or seniors in high school—will be left to deal with the common consequences of negativity, closed-mindedness, and boredom.

   3. Mid-adolescent catechesis. In mid-adolescence, then, which I would roughly define as ages sixteen to twenty, I think we should make the following kinds of opportunities available to those who, because of the proper ministry in early adolescence, will be open and responsive to them:
a. This is the time for a full proclamation of the Gospel shared in the context of the faith community. This is, in my mind, the primary function of good youth retreats, which are normally less effective and even counterproductive when offered to younger students.
b. Mid-adolescence is the appropriate time for an integrated presentation of the meaning of our faith, a presentation that basically answers the question, What does a Catholic Christian believe and why? If this has not been force-fed them before, they will be hungry for such input now. Again, it must be remembered that this does not have to be offered in traditional classroom environments and formats. All kinds of alternative approaches are available—the weekend model, extended campouts, youth groups like Young Catholic Students (YCS), daylong programs, summer sessions.
c. Mid-adolescence is a time of tremendous searching, often leading to a sense of confusion, hopelessness, and for some, depression. A strong attempt should be made to share a sense of the meaning of life, particularly the specific sense of meaning provided by Jesus and his message.
d. Mid-adolescence is a prime time for providing the first conscious or systematic understanding of prayer and the opportunities for development of both a personal and communal prayer life.
In other words, I believe that mid-adolescence is the appropriate time for a full-blown catechetical program in its richest sense. Not all young people will be ready for it, and the commitment to total youth ministry will provide alternatives for those who are not. My conviction, however, is that far more will be ready for this than we might initially believe, and that the opportunity for such involvement must be provided for those who seek it.

4. Catechesis in late adolescence. Finally, in late adolescence — from about age twenty to twenty-five — the concentration should shift again to include

   a. the opportunity for personal spiritual direction leading to the development of rich personal prayer life;
   b. opportunities for working out career and lifestyle decisions;
   c. opportunities for personal involvement in service to others, particularly in efforts to evangelize younger people through involvement in youth retreats, and so on, as well as for involvement in social justice issues; and
   d. the development of small, intimate, and self-directed support groups centered on scriptural study, prayer, worship, sharing, and celebration.

A Hope-filled Future

In conclusion, then, I believe that our ultimate goal as youth ministers and religious educators must be to provide our young people with the opportunities to own their faith, to possess it personally, to learn to experience and express it as an integral part of their lives. We are to lead them to personal and spiritual freedom, not to continued dependence upon us. That will only be possible if their lives are founded on the truth shared by Jesus — the truth that *is* Jesus and his message. That is a marvelous challenge. We who are involved in youth ministry should be grateful it has been given us and perhaps awed by the sense of great responsibility that has been entrusted to us. With a continued commitment to work together as youth ministers and religious educators and with a strong desire to support all those who minister to young people — particularly their parents — I am convinced we will succeed.

Notes

1. In my attempt to deal with youth ministry "in as broad a way as possible" in this article, I am choosing to discuss it in terms of the total Church's ministry to young people and, perhaps a bit more specifically, the relationship of young people to their parishes as their most broad-based contact with the broader faith community. In this article, therefore, I do not deal directly with the *particular* and important concerns of Catholic high schools or parish religious education programs. Space simply does not permit the detailed treatment of these specific areas, nor is such discussion the central purpose of this effort. My hope is that all who minister to or with young people — pastors, parents, teachers, volunteers, liturgists,

and so on—will attempt to analyze and apply the implications of what I offer here to their own particular area of concern and interest.

2. The familiar expression of youth ministry as one "to, with, by, and for youth" is taken from the important paper *A Vision of Youth Ministry,* published by the United States Catholic Conference in 1976. People involved in youth ministry at any level should be fully familiar with this statement about the dimensions, goals, principles, and components of youth ministry. It is available from the Department of Education, USCC, 1312 Massachusetts Avenue NW, Washington, DC 20005.

3. Don Kimball, along with many others, dislikes the term *pre-evangelization* and does not use it in his model, because he thinks that all relational ministry carried on by Christians is by definition evangelization proper and should be recognized as such. My feeling is that, particularly in youth ministry, less clearly evangelical ministries such as street ministry, drug and alcohol counseling, education in sexuality, and numerous outreach efforts need to be clearly identified and recognized as offering a vital dimension to our ministry to young people. The intentional separation of the concepts of pre-evangelization and evangelization, in my view, strengthens this reality rather than detracts from it.

4. Jeff Johnson, currently the consultant for youth catechesis in the Archdiocese of Saint Paul-Minneapolis, has contributed a great deal toward our understanding of the relational and outreach dimensions of youth ministry. See his article on the Young Life ministry in this collection (essay 14, pp. 180–191).

5. Don Kimball's own work in radio and music ministry is a fine example of a creative way to evangelize young people today. He and his staff of young people "proclaim the Good News" by using young people's love of music as a kind of bridge between them and the Gospel. For more information on their work contact Cornerstone Media, P.O. Box 6236, Santa Rosa, CA 95406; phone 707-542-8273.

6. The success of the retreat model has been so widespread that Michael Warren has proposed that it become *the* foundational model of youth catechesis. See his article "Youth Catechesis in the '80s" in *Origins,* 10 April 1980.

7. A cynical evaluation of the process of sharing faith implied by the wedge model could lead some to identify this as the approach used by many of the cults: make contact with lonely young people, give them a false sense of security and group solidarity, and then brainwash them. Only the continual and unswerving affirmation of the freedom of the individual can protect our approach to youth ministry from such accusations.

8. I feel that one of our major difficulties today on all levels of discussion in the Church—youth ministry, theology, religious education, whatever—is the lack of a reasonably universal vocabulary with which to discuss major issues. For example, I hesitate to use the word *catechesis* in this ar-

ticle because, as indicated, my use of it here is admittedly simplistic and narrow. Berard Marthaler, for one, sees catechesis as a kind of Christian socialization that might well incorporate all the dimensions of youth ministry offered in our model. John Westerhoff offers a similar, though perhaps even more expansive, definition of the concept. And yet I find the word too valuable and too important to ignore or avoid, so I condition my use of it here with the term *systematic* to indicate the more intentional and perhaps formal dimension of catechesis that would often be called *religious education.* A helpful discussion of this problem can be found in Thomas Groome's *Christian Religious Education* (New York: Harper and Row, 1980), pp. 20–29, which, not so incidentally, is probably the most significant statement on religious education to be published in years. See also footnote 13.

9. My own attempt at such an innovative catechetical approach is represented by my four-year parish program, *Sharing the Christian Message I–IV,* revised edition, and also by my texts and teaching manuals for use with students in Catholic high schools, *Understanding Your Faith* and *Jesus of History, Christ of Faith.* All are published by Saint Mary's Press.

10. An excellent article on the teaching of social justice at the high school level can be found in an article by Charles Shelton entitled "The Adolescent, Social Justice, and the Catholic School: A Psychological Perspective," *The Living Light,* Fall 1980. The article was then included in Shelton's book, *Adolescent Spirituality* (Chicago: Loyola University Press, 1983), pp. 294–319. One cogent quote:

> Both the questioning and formulating of a value system that incorporates social justice principles and the working for social justice might prove difficult in the secondary school years without a deeper sense of one's own identity which includes personally thoughtout values and social attitudes. It might only be in young adulthood (the college years) that the adolescent develops a true attitudinal and value system indicative of identity solidification that is consonant with social justice principles.

11. The National Conference of Catholic Bishops' 1972 pastoral letter on education, *To Teach As Jesus Did,* states that "the educational mission of the Church is an integrated ministry embracing three interlocking dimensions: the message revealed by God (*didache*) which the Church proclaims; fellowship in the life of the Holy Spirit (*koinonia*); service to the Christian community and the entire human community (*diakonia*)" (no. 14). The *General Catechetical Directory,* approved by Pope Paul VI in 1971, and *Sharing the Light of Faith: National Catechetical Directory for Catholics of the United States (NCD),* presented by the U.S. bishops in 1979, both affirm that the purpose of catechesis is to make a "person's faith become *living, conscious,* and *active* through the light of instruction" (*NCD* no. 32, [emphasis added]). The *NCD* also discusses the threefold mission of the Church: "proclaiming and teaching God's word, celebrating the sacred

mysteries, and serving the people of the world" (*NCD* no. 30). .The work
of James W. Fowler is most often mentioned in regard to our understanding of faith development. For a helpful summary of his major theses, see
Thomas Groome's *Christian Religious Education,* pp. 66–73.

12. The beautiful Emmaus story from Luke 24:13–35 is a favorite
biblical model for effective youth ministry. See Groome, pp. 135–136, for
some insights from an educator's point of view.

13. I have done considerable work in the areas of adolescent religious
education and catechesis since this article was originally published in 1981.
Though I have attempted some minor but important editing of this section
on youth catechesis, any substantial elaboration of my current understanding of these areas was precluded due to the limitations of space. Though
I would not characterize any of the information in this article as erroneous,
I do feel that it is incomplete and, therefore, potentially misleading. For
a more complete discussion of my current understanding of adolescent
religious education, see *Sharing: A Manual for Program Directors* (Winona,
MN: Saint Mary's Press, 1985), particularly the essay "Youth Catechesis
in Context," pp. 44–59.

Essay 5

Agenda for Youth Ministry: Problems, Questions, and Strategies

Craig Dykstra

*A few years ago, I was invited to participate in a consultation on youth ministry held at Louisville Presbyterian Seminary. The consultation, conducted over the period of a semester, involved much practical work with young people, intensive study of key writings about youth, and dialogues with youth ministry theorists. I was pleased to have been invited, especially since the consultation was designed by Craig Dykstra, with the help of David Bos, a minister working with young people in the Louisville suburb of Saint Matthews. Dykstra's work had always shown a concern with the communal base of religious education in the Church, and he brought the best scholarship to bear on that concern. Another reason for my pleasure was that, at the time of the consultation, the president of Louisville Presbyterian was C. Ellis Nelson, who had written what for me was a key work on the relationship of education to church life—*Where Faith Begins *(Richmond, VA: John Knox Press, 1967).*

When the report on the consultation appeared, I was impressed by its broad focus and by the way it raised key questions about the quality of the Church's commitment to youth found in church policies and programs. I was anxious to see the report in print and widely circulated, but the pressure of time prevented the kind of rewriting of the report that Dykstra judged necessary before its wide dissemination. For Readings and Resources in Youth Ministry, *however, Dykstra found the time to do the revision that we have in the following essay. His contribution enriches the book and pleases me greatly. Readers from various denominations will find here valuable insights and guidance for their ministry to and with youth.*

Several years ago, I worked with a group of seminary students to gather information about and frame certain issues concerning youth in relationship with the church. We read a good deal of literature in the areas of theology, adolescent development, youth culture, and education. We studied some of the history of youth ministry, particularly in the mainline Protestant churches. We interviewed a number of young people, both those involved and those not involved in local churches. We talked with some parents, pastors, and lay youth leaders in churches. And we consulted with a group of fifteen denominational staff members from churches in the United States and Canada that had primary responsibility for youth ministry programs in their denominations. Finally, we recalled our own experiences as young people in relationship with the church, and we attempted to learn from what those experiences mean to us now. We did whatever we could to gain insights and information that might be helpful to us and to others in positions of responsibility with respect to youth ministry.[1]

The result of our explorations was a set of working papers, each of which addressed a particular theme that we found significant. The present essay draws from, and in certain respects updates, those working papers, in an effort to pull them together into one coherent piece. It attempts to call the attention of parents, youth leaders, teachers, pastors, and church members—as well as young people themselves—to some realities that youth face in our contemporary situation. The essay focuses our concerns on problems and questions that need to be faced together as the church.

The first four of our themes have to do with the dynamics of youth ministry, issues that all leaders would want to keep in mind. These are (1) the struggles of young people in their everyday lives and the need in youth ministry to be aware of and directly responsive to those struggles, (2) the importance of language, particularly the significance of using the language of the Christian faith in our ministry with youth, (3) the need to involve young people directly in the ministry and mission of the church and the necessarily experimental nature of their commitments, and (4) the crucial role that adult mentors or friends can have in the lives of youth. The latter two themes prompt two additional ones: (5) the problem of providing trained leadership and (6) the variety of youth ministry programs that need to be maintained.

1. The Struggles of Young People

Adolescence involves struggle, sometimes quite serious struggle. Effective youth ministry necessarily involves continual awareness and understanding of these struggles. This ministry calls for direct aid to young people at every appropriate point in their struggles—even though those struggles and responses to them may, at times, be threatening to the church as a whole or to those adults most directly involved with youth.

The statement that adolescence involves serious struggles may seem overly dramatic; it may seem to disregard the fact that adolescence is not always experienced this way. Furthermore, the same generalization could probably be made about many other periods in people's lives. Nevertheless, struggles during adolescence have a potential for bringing persons closer to the psychological edge of human limits than the struggles of any other period. Erik Erikson says, "In no other stage of the life cycle . . . are the promise of finding oneself and the threat of losing oneself so closely allied."[2] In many cases, this is true quite literally. Suicide is the second highest cause of death among adolescents, and accidents (many of which may be indirect suicides) are the first.

On the other hand, the struggles of adolescence are particularly open to creative resolution if they are carried out in the context of relationships with caring individuals and in a caring society. But contemporary adolescents are in a dangerous situation in this respect. They live in a society that is often experienced as "care-less." There is major instability in the social and political world, and this generates great insecurity and anxiety in young people. Upheaval, enormous pressures, and conflicting values in schools often do the same. So, of course, do uproar and unresolved conflict in the family. Furthermore, people in typical congregations and families often fail to see the effects of those forces on their young people. They fail to look beneath the surface and see the young people's most troubling concerns. Sometimes, out of good intentions or out of fear, they even encourage the adolescents to likewise avoid looking beneath the surface, thus pushing the concerns to still deeper and less conscious levels.

Responding with Direct Aid

In the context of a careless, fearful society and of church ministry programs that are not focused, adolescents who are in psychological or social trouble often need direct aid. The phrase *direct aid* is intended to emphasize the part of ministry to youth that responds with helps that are not always regarded as church ministry. Included here are suicide prevention centers, child abuse centers, drug and alcohol rehabilitation facilities, juvenile justice ministries, and so forth.

Organizing a real response to such needs can be threatening, of course, to any community that thinks of itself as an ideal place for children, to churches that justify their existence solely on the basis of their delivery of "religious" services, and to individuals whose faith cannot admit that doubt and struggle are inevitably involved in adolescent crises. Nevertheless, the church has a responsibility to provide direct aid of whatever kind to youth who need it. Furthermore, these kinds of needs must be responded to if the message of the church is ever to be heard and if healthy participation in the life of the Christian community is ever to be an option for these young people. This kind of ministry is, for some young people, the most important way they will ever come to know and feel the love of God—that is, through people who love them and care for them just at the point when they themselves feel least worthy and lovable.

The church can choose to play either of two roles in response to the struggles of adolescents: It can moralistically reinforce and compound their sense of personal failure, or it can provide a ground for trust in the future and a forum for new life. Merton Strommen, who has summarized a number of the central struggles of adolescence in his book *Five Cries of Youth,* made the following comments about a needed transformation in adolescent religious understanding:

> Characteristic of adolescence is a moralistic stance. They understand religion as a moral standard to be lived. The view brings a strong sense of guilt with it—of "should," of "ought." Religious transformation for an adolescent means that he or she moves from that natural yet immature understanding that religion is something *humankind* does toward viewing religion as something *God* does, so he or she moves from a moralistic standpoint to one of grace.[3]

Youth ministry is ineffective when it does not reach young people at the level of these struggles. Youth must be aided at these times by a presence that supports and cares for them no matter how threatening those struggles may be. It must enter the "troubled waters" and provide a context of hope and a promise of a future with which young people can align themselves.

Approaches for Local Churches

Engagement with youth in a way that attends to them in their struggles, strives to understand, and seeks to provide direct aid requires a very significant investment of energy and a good deal of creativity. The strategies listed below are by no means exhaustive. These steps, which some local churches have taken to help adolescents in their struggles, can serve as guidelines for others that wish to do likewise:

1. Design curriculums that deal directly with important adolescent struggles. Provide opportunities for discussing such subjects and include material that might speak to feelings of despair and personal fragmentation.

2. Participate in the development of crisis intervention services for youth. In such contexts, the articulation of a faith perspective, appropriately presented and demonstrated, may make a significant difference in helping young people to resolve their crises.

3. Consider individual needs in involving youth in the local church. Provide occasions for one-to-one expressions of concern and caring between young people and adults and between young persons themselves.

4. Encourage adult leaders to become trained in crisis intervention in order to acquire more sensitivity and skill in dealing with typical adolescent struggles.

2. Youth, Language, and the Interpretation of Life

The struggles of many young people are not usually the kind that get them into trouble. But even so, there is another, quieter struggle that goes on. Most young people invest significant energies in trying to understand and interpret themselves and their world in coherent, meaningful, workable, and personally satisfying ways. They search for a sense of personal identity and a way of life.

Erik Erikson describes the process of identity formation in the following terms:

> Identity formation employs a process of simultaneous reflection and observation, a process taking place on all levels of mental functioning, by which the individual judges himself in the light of what he perceives to be the way in which others judge him in comparison to themselves and to a typology significant to them; while he judges their way of judging him in the light of how he perceives himself in comparison to them and to types that have become relevant to him.[4]

In simpler terms, one tries to see how one is seen by others and attempts to shape one's self in response. A person develops a sense of identity when the way one is seen by others *fits* coherently with the way one sees oneself (and when the way one sees others fits with the way they see themselves). This "fit" enables one to use his or her powers and gifts effectively in this world and establishes a meaningful, workable, and personally satisfying identity.

The Struggle of Interpretation

This process of identity formation is a "hermeneutical" process, a process of interpretation. We do not know directly how others see us. We *interpret* their responses to us to be "respect," "disdain," "love," "fear," "friendship," "manipulation," "enjoyment," and so on. Our responses are responses to interpreted actions. This process of interpretation, of course, is not unique to adolescence. All human interaction that is not just mechanical reaction is a complicated interchange of interpretation and response. What is unique during adolescence is the development of personal responsibility for interpretation. During adolescence a person, for the first time, begins to decide how to interpret and respond. One now has to *struggle* to interpret and respond appropriately.

There are many reasons that interpretation becomes a struggle at adolescence. A basic reason is that, developmentally, at this age we gain the cognitive capacities to see that other people's interpretations of things are different from our own. As children, we assume that other people see things the way we do. But this changes by the age of about eleven or twelve.

We also develop the ability to imagine different futures and to know that how we act in the present will shape to some extent the future that is to come into being.

Another reason that interpretation becomes a struggle in this period is that people's expectations of us change. We are not only given more choices than we previously had, but we are also expected to make the kind of choices that our society considers viable for the future. In childhood, our world and the patterns of interpretation that shape it are more or less given to us: alternative patterns are hidden from us; we live in a relatively closed and formed world. But in adolescence we discover that there are other possible patterns of interpretation. We must choose. In choosing, we begin to take responsibility for shaping our world. As we do so, we shape our own selves.

This process of interpretation takes place in the context of communities of interpretation. The school, the peer group, the family, the church, the nation, and so on, are all communities of interpretation. Our interpretations are not isolated and individual. They are interpretations prompted by a larger and broader pattern of interpretation that a community holds in common. As H. Richard Niebuhr puts it, "We interpret the things that force themselves upon us as parts of wholes, as related and as symbolic of larger meanings."[5] Communities of interpretation are held together partly because the various interpretations and responses that go on there are part of a larger whole.

This larger whole is what Erikson refers to above as a typology. Elsewhere he discusses this same phenomenon in terms of ideology. An ideology, or typology, is a broad, widely accepted pattern of interpretation of the world and of the significance and meaning of the events, the circumstances, and the interactions that take place in that world. Erikson argues that adolescents hunger for ideology or a meaningful pattern of interpretation because ideology is the only way in which they can come to interpret the world coherently, find a place for themselves in it, and establish a sense of self in that world.

Patterns of interpretation are carried symbolically. We come to have a world and find a place for ourselves in it by learning the language, the symbols, the stories, the metaphors, and the images of the pattern of interpretation that gives us that world.[6] If we do not know the language of a community, we can neither see the world as that community sees it nor become a part of that community ourselves. When a community's language becomes the language we use, we become members of that community and see the world through the lens of that language. It gives order to our experience, provides the grounds for our interpretations, and enables us to respond in coherent, that is, identity-shaping, ways.

Adolescence is a time of crisis for most people in our culture because there are so many diverse patterns of interpretation available. We live in an intensely pluralistic world. There are many competing subcultures, each with its own language, symbols, images, metaphors, and stories. Ironically, however, it is simultaneously a world in which the great variety tends to limit rather than extend the breadth of our language and the communities of interpretation that carry them. This places contemporary youth in a difficult, even dangerous, situation. In one of his essays, Michael Warren quotes the complaint of Scott Hope, a college teacher of writing, who says,

> Students who enter universities increasingly have available to them only those languages which allow them to communicate with themselves, with their families and with their peers. They seem to feel that they *do not need* [emphasis in the original] a language beyond peer language. . . . Our society is dominated by peer languages, the in-languages used by educators, by sociologists, by EST-graduates . . . by technicians of all stripes, by politicians, by the Pentagon, and so on.[7]

The problem here, as both Hope and Warren point out, is that young people are left with far too limited and much too fragmented a world. As Warren expresses it,

> They are isolated on an island of speech that restricts them literally . . . to the insular world of self, family, and peers. On this island existence is alienated, cut off from the important areas of the human world-mediated-by-meaning. It is also cut off from the past and shows little concern for the future.[8]

In sum, the fragmentation and isolation of communities and "languages" provides no adequate basis for identity formation with a larger scope and contributes to a crisis of interpretation.

The Christian Language

We Christians believe that we have been given a language that does in fact help us to make sense of the world, of a large, broad, comprehensive world with its fundamental issues of good and evil, of promise and limitation, of living and dying, of suffering and joy, of destruction and creation.

We believe that the language of the faith — that is, the stories of the people of Israel; the life, death, and resurrection of Jesus; the church and the saints through history; the images of Christ on the cross and his washing of the feet of his disciples; the metaphors of the Kingdom of God and the pearl of great price; the rituals of being washed in Baptism and eating bread and drinking wine at the Lord's Table — provides for us a pattern of interpretation that gives sense to our experience and draws us into daily experience in ways that really give us identity. Because we believe this, we want others, including young people, to see the world through this lens and partake in the patterns of interpretation and relationship that the Christian language enables. We believe that if people hear and learn and use this language, they will find their most fundamental needs met.

If youth ministry has anything to do with helping young people to establish a sense of identity that is coherent, meaningful, workable, and satisfying, then we must help them to learn this language and see how it affects the life experiences they really do have. Unless we use this language with them, teach it to them, and help them to make it their own, there is no way that they can participate fully in this community of interpretation and response and no way that they can establish a deep sense of identity.

But there are problems with this approach, and they are serious. The most serious problem is whether or not we people in the mainline churches have enough awareness of the Christian pattern of interpretation for it to make sense of our experience. There is considerable evidence that in practice we do not. Repeatedly we have been accused of biblical illiteracy and theological amnesia. Our everyday speech patterns include very little in the way of theological or biblical language (i.e., we simply do not use the words *sin, salvation, redemption, justification, grace,* etc., in everyday speech), and references to key biblical figures and stories are virtually nonexistent. We can hardly bring ourselves even to mention the name of Jesus Christ outside of very specialized, "churchy" contexts.

Most of us completely miss biblical and theological allusions when they appear in literature and art, and preachers cannot depend upon the congregation to bring any biblical or theological knowledge to their hearing of a sermon. Indeed, much of the preaching and teaching itself has abandoned the biblical-theological pattern of interpretation for other patterns thought to be more illuminating for our experience. Psychological patterns of interpretation are perhaps the most prevalent. We are, for example, much more likely to use the concepts of psychological development and group dynamics in our work with youth than we are to use the language of prayer and discipleship.

There are many reasons for this phenomenon. Among the most important are probably (1) the almost total assimilation of the mainline churches into the values and the interpretation patterns of the contemporary culture, (2) the effects of historical-critical approaches to the Bible and history that seem to relativize all truth, and (3) a fear of fundamentalist and authoritarian forms and tendencies.

The three reasons are interconnected. Historical criticism is a major feature of contemporary Western culture. We recognize that all ways of knowing are historically conditioned and relative to that conditioning. Therefore, we know that no one has a handle on all truth. Because we know this, we are committed to mutual tolerance and individual freedom. What we fear most are groups that are intolerant and that deny individual freedom.

But this is exactly what we see fundamentalist groups doing. They have no problem using religious language. They use it to describe a total world in which good and evil are sharply defined — and sharply separated. In fundamental forms of belief, a "we-they" mentality develops, in which one's own position is protected and those in alternative positions are made enemies. This has happened so often that one of the fears we in the mainline churches have of using religious language is that it will quickly deteriorate into fundamentalism. So we tend to abandon religious language altogether.

One important result of this abandonment of religious language to fundamentalist groups is the creation of a religious vacuum in our society. The option, religiously, that most people see is a fundamentalist religious pattern of interpretation or no religious pattern of interpretation at all. The mainline churches have been unable to put forward a constructively critical religious pattern of interpretation. Our pattern of interpretation has become increasingly negative. There is little in it that enables people to make positive commitments, to use it to articulate a social and personal vision by which to live and to which to bear allegiance.

This lack of a positive pattern of interpretation has precipitated an identity crisis in the mainline churches, which only complicates the identity crisis of adolescents. Adolescents need a positive, constructive pattern of interpretation to which they can turn. The fundamentalist churches and cults have one to offer, and (though it is seriously defective) many adolescents do turn to it. The mainline churches do not have such a pattern to offer. Therefore it is difficult for these churches to reach young people in meaningful ways. The pattern of interpretation we do have to offer is so similar to that of the prevailing culture that young people have no reason to turn to the mainline churches for one that will help them to build a sense of personal identity. They can get, and have already gotten, what we have to offer from their schools and their peers.

These reflections lead us to a painful conclusion: Insofar as mainline denominations provide no unique, constructive religious pattern of interpretation that helps young people understand their experience, they have no vital youth ministry to offer. But we can state this conclusion positively as well: We can build an effective and vital youth ministry by developing a pattern of interpretation that (1) is grounded in religious language and history, (2) provides a constructive vision of the world and personal and social life, (3) calls forth the allegiance of young people because it helps them to understand their own experiences and live more fruitful lives, and (4) does not take on authoritarian and fundamentalist characteristics.

A Crucial Task for Youth Ministry

This may well be the most important task for youth ministry in the mainline churches in the next decade or more—the development of a constructive, biblically and theologically grounded pattern of interpretation. We simply must learn how to use religious language in a nonfundamentalist way in our everyday speech. This is, of course, not simply a task for youth ministers and youth leaders. It is a task for the whole church. But youth ministers and leaders are in a position to work on this problem. The way will not be found by academic theologians. It will be found by theologians-in-practice who develop ways of using religious language with people for whom this language is foreign, but for whom an understanding of this language enlightens experience.

This is a very difficult task. It involves two things: first, the development (or renewal) of a pattern of language that is concrete enough to be comprehended by young people, yet critical enough to open young people to the world as a whole; second, the development of a ministry of interpretation.

Fundamentalist groups and cults have a tremendous advantage over us here. They are able to use religious language concretely because they are satisfied with literalistic and univocal religious understandings. Literal and univocal approaches to reality are always the easiest to understand, and they feed our desires for protection and identity over against others. The task of the mainline churches is to learn to use religious language in a way that is at once concrete and understandable *and yet* not literal. Like the language of poets and artists, this language must use the concrete to open up dimensions of transcendence, depth, and mystery. The Bible is full of stories, parables, images, and metaphors that function in just this way. We must draw on these resources.

A youth ministry of interpretation will have to involve teaching young people biblical and theological words, concepts, stories, images, metaphors, and even doctrines. But just introducing people to new words and concepts does not accomplish the task of helping them to make this language their own. David Burrell points out that "language brings with it a structure of consequences" and that "those entailments must reach into the organization of one's life before he can be said to understand in a way that gives him facility with a new language."[9] New concepts and vocabulary need to be *lived* in such a way that the new language increasingly introduces one to a new lifestyle, a new way of living. This new way of living leads to a deepened understanding of the language, which in turn leads to a deepening of lifestyle. Language and action cannot be separated. Thus in youth ministry an exploration of religious language must take place in the context of an exploration of our experience and in the context of a venturing out into new forms of experience. Neither experience without language nor language without experience is sufficient.

This exploration is a struggle that takes time and effort. One cannot be a dilettante. If new concepts are to be introduced, they cannot be introduced at random or too quickly. They must be thought about, talked about, acted on, perhaps written about thoroughly. And they must be dealt with in terms of a variety of personal experiences, especially those kinds of experiences that one strives, in a disciplined way, to have at the impetus of the new language.

For example, if one were working with a group of young people on prayer, one would help the group look at their own experiences in prayer (or lack of such experiences), at biblical and theological understandings of prayer, and at the experiences other Christians have had with prayer. This is important as introduction. But none of this would amount to much unless the youth were encouraged and guided in new experiments with prayer and in a more disciplined prayer life.

Finally, learning religious language will have no effect on the way young people interpret their lives, understand the world, or develop their identities unless this language is used in relationships with other people who also use that language in describing and extending their day-to-day experience. Young people will not learn to use religious language as their own unless the church as a whole uses religious language as its own natural pattern of interpretation and response.

The task of youth ministry is not one of getting young people involved in an interpretation process. All young people already are investing significant energies in this process in order to establish for themselves a sense of personal identity. Our task is to develop a religious pattern of interpretation that is both biblical and illuminating of contemporary human experience. Furthermore, our task is to help young people experiment with this pattern of interpretation, understand it, and increasingly adopt it as their own in the context of a community of interpretation that does the same with them.[10]

3. Experimental Commitments

Adolescence is a time for exploring and making commitments. Young people both need and want to align themselves with persons and communities and with the values, beliefs, and ideals those persons and communities hold. It is imperative that the church in its ministry with youth (1) be a community worthy of fidelity, (2) explicitly call forth the allegiances of young people, and (3) provide concrete ways by which the experimental commitments of youth may be tried.

Exploring for possible commitment and experimenting with actually making commitments are other important means by which young people develop a sense of identity and move into a way of life. The range of exploration and experimentation in making commitments may have some predetermined limits in adolescence, and it is hard to predict what temporary and long-term alignments young people may make over the course of several years or what effect these will have. However tentative and experimental these alignments are, nevertheless they are a preparation for that aspect of adulthood that involves choosing, at various levels of intensity, the communities and life projects with which one will be identified and to which one will give oneself.

Just as the church believes that its language has the power to give life and meaning, so too it sees that, as a body of people with its purpose and mission, it is worthy of commitment. Therefore, it seeks to call young people to align their own commitments with those of the church and to draw youth into committed participation in its life and work.

Attracting Young People's Attention

The first step in calling young people into commitment, of course, is simply to have them take the church into consideration. It must, therefore, find ways to attract young people's attention. We often assume that we have the attention of young people who have been "raised in the church"—and perhaps in many cases we do. But we should not take this for granted. Adolescents have a great deal more freedom in terms of where they spend their time than do children. In addition, increasingly they are developing interests of their own—interests that are really theirs and not the interests that others have for them. In order to be committed to something, one must first at least be somewhat interested in it.

Many congregations work very hard at doing something that will attract the attention and interest of youth. Some of the attempts range from the faddish to the bizarre. Many of them go no further than attempting to replicate or compete with what already has grasped the young people's interest elsewhere. In the long run, those approaches are self-defeating. For if the appealing interests are not consistent with the kinds of commitments the congregation wishes to invite, that church community is involved in a contradiction right from the start. David Ng, in his book *Youth in the Community of Disciples,* points to the dilemma:

> In most churches youth ministry is a struggle. Attendance is sporadic. The interests of young people are elsewhere. The activities are irrelevant. . . . In some churches the youth program is highly successful in terms of numbers, activities, and fun. These churches run high-powered programs which are planned and conducted by professional youth workers who can provide good food, good singing, ski trips in the winter and river trips in the summer, et cetera, et cetera, et cetera. Yet, after three or four years of either type of youth program, small and struggling or big and eventful, a young person may not have heard the good news that God loves her, that she has an identity and purpose in life, that her sins are forgiven, that she is called into community, that she has support for her individuality and a place for corporate action and witness.[11]

In the one case, there is no interest and hence no commitment. In the other case, there is interest, but not in the things to which the church calls young people to be committed. Commitment in the church does not arise out of simply enjoying being there. It arises out of finding the church to be what it is called to be. It arises when young people sense and experience the church as being itself and carrying out its ministry and mission with integrity.

Integrity and Clarity of the Church

If commitment in the church arises out of finding the church to be what it is called to be, then a crucial question for youth ministry concerns not so much young people and their interests but the church and its integrity. Will the church be perceived as worthy of commitment? Or will it be one among many sources of disillusionment? Will commitment in and to the church bring experiences and understandings that are empowering and life-giving to youth? Or will commitment in the church be for young people an experiment that does not—and in all likelihood will not—bear fruit? In order for a church community to be attractive to youth, it must be perceived by them as worthy of fidelity. It must have integrity in theory and in practice, a quality for which the young often have a very keen eye.

Regarding the commitment of youth and the integrity of the church, one point is crucial: The church will never be perceived as, nor will it actually be, worthy of commitment unless the local church itself is vitally committed to youth in a clear and concrete way. If a church cannot make available good, caring individuals for its young people, why should they become committed to that church? If a church makes no provision for youth in its budget or no space available in its facilities, should it come as any surprise that the young people are hesitant to commit themselves in that church? We all become committed to someone or something when we sense that we are also the "recipients" of commitment. The interest of others in us is often the most important factor in our becoming interested in them. Certainly we cannot sustain interest or commitment in another person or group who ignores us, expresses little or no interest in us, and shows no sign of commitment to us. This is no less true for young people. A church, to be worthy of the commitments of youth, must first express its commitment to them.

A second aspect of commitment in the church has to do with its values and beliefs. The church—as the body of Jesus Christ with a mission in the world—cannot be the church if its only commitment is to itself. The commitments that the local church is to call forth from young people are not primarily to the congregation but to the community's reason for being, to its purpose and end, to its Lord. Thus we call the young person first of all to the commitments *of the church* rather than simply to a commitment *to the church*. But what if the commitments of the local church are confusing or unclear? Unless we are able to articulate what we are committed to as a church (and what we are not), young people will have little grounds on which to choose for or against us. When it is difficult for young people to tell where we stand, it is difficult for them to choose to stand with us or against us. So they just ignore us.

Harvey Seifert, in his article "Unrecognized Internal Threats to Liberal Churches," asserts that these denominations are threatened by a failure to clarify their mission, their basic theological and social convictions, and their constituencies. Seifert defines *liberal denominations* as those

> whose theological positions are comparatively receptive to the conclusions of the physical and human sciences, and whose social witness is relatively thoroughgoing and comprehensive and includes some basic criticism of major social systems. . . . At the same time liberal churches are appreciative of major elements in the tradition as still valid, and they stress the importance of emotionally vital, personal religious experience. They aim to join the warm heart to the clear head and busy hands.[12]

But, Seifert argues, such churches have great difficulty projecting an unambiguous and highly visible image of what they in fact are. Perhaps they do not really believe in what they believe. Perhaps they lack confidence in who they are. Seifert suggests that because these denominations fear they might alienate conservative members, they compromise and obscure their message to the extent that they blunt their own distinctive emphases.[13] Perhaps this blurring is one of the major reasons that the mainline churches seem to have difficulty in calling forth the commitments of youth. They seem to young people to stand for nothing clear and distinctive in the larger life of the culture.

Genuine Responsibility in the Congregation

Commitment, then, will need to be called forth to something genuine and something at least relatively clear to young people. But such a commitment within a congregation will come only through actual involvement in the practices and engagements by which that church exercises and carries out its commitments. Thus the church that does not provide youth with genuine responsibility in the total life and mission of the congregation does not provide adequate means by which the young people can express and test their commitments.

Unfortunately, much of youth ministry simply does not give young people things to do that are really worth doing. It is not so much that what we do with youth is boring—which it often is—but that even when an activity is not boring, rarely does it lead to anything significant or accomplish something worthwhile. By not taking anything seriously, the activity thereby implicitly suggests that the young people themselves are not taken seriously. We are often astonished at how much youth can accomplish—in athletics, in the arts, in science, in craftsmanship, in service to others, in so many arenas of life— when they are given the challenge, the guidance, and the encouragement to do so. But how seldom it is that young people accomplish significant things in the church.

The Christian life and mission is, when you get into the thick of it, an adventure of high proportions that taxes the best in us and often involves risk and even danger. If this is not the Christian life for us, we have failed as Christians. And if the challenge and risk of the Christian life do not somehow become apparent to our youth, we have failed them as well. Youth ministry that calls forth commitment will be a ministry in which adolescents' resources are taxed and tested, in which their present capacities and skills are stretched to the limits, and in which the excitement and daring of being a Christian is experienced personally.

A central means by which a congregation may call forth the commitments of youth is, first of all, to identify the gifts that the young people have (even in cases where they themselves are not aware of their gifts) and, secondly, to put these gifts to use in the church's life and mission. The gifts of the young must be put to use if the young are to want to give their gifts to the church. Then, as these talents are used in the church, they are developed, enhanced, strengthened, and made firm. When the church becomes a place where youth see that their gifts are recognized and used and that their own capacities to give their gifts can grow, young people will find the church a place they wish to be. They will find its people a group with whom they want to spend time. This becomes all the more true when the gifts and the giving of them by the young people are publicly recognized and celebrated by the church.

Adolescent commitments, as we pointed out earlier, are often experimental in nature. This means that the intensity and the duration of these commitments may vary a good deal over time. Young people may follow through on some things and give up quickly on others. Some things may generate a good deal of enthusiasm at one time but hardly any interest later on. This variability, however, does not mean that these experimental commitments are not vital and formative. Adolescence is a time of testing and searching, and the testing often includes failure and drawing back as much as it does achievement and engagement. Youth need to be given the freedom to make *or* relinquish, to alter *or* retain commitments. They need opportunities to carry their commitments as far as they are able to take them. They also need the freedom to get out of these commitments at times without engendering others' hostility and recrimination. They need to be allowed to commit themselves again, even if the commitments and promises they once made were broken. This is, of course, true for all of us. But it is something to be particularly aware of and careful about with adolescents, since experimenting with commitment is especially crucial to this period of life.

Specific Challenges and Expectations

An important implication for strategy arises from these reflections: Regardless of the experimental nature of adolescent commitments, young people ought to be confronted with specific challenges and expectations so that they may have a true opportunity for testing out and exploring what commitment in the church might ultimately involve. With this in mind, consider the following suggestions:

1. Young people are more likely to gain a sense of identity in the community to the extent that they are regarded as full-fledged (rather than junior) members of that community. Give them opportunities to serve as leaders, not only of youth organizations (although that role should not be downgraded or eliminated), but also at the level of the official board and committees of the congregation. Do not condescend to young people in matters of giving time and money, but rather expect them to pledge financial support and time and to be faithful to their pledges. Also expect them to perform tasks for the church outside of the typical youth service.

2. Include young people both in the planning and in the execution of these service projects of the congregation. The service projects of youth groups ought to include the involvement of adults. Such service projects also need to be linked explicitly and in various ways to the theology and purpose of the church, in order to demonstrate for youth the integrity of theory and practice in these projects.

3. Plan for the participation of young people in all congregational events, including worship, suppers, and business meetings. Assign an individual or a group to make sure that this kind of planning for their participation takes place.

4. Educate youth in the beliefs and convictions of the church. This should include straightforward considerations of the church's public stands on social and political issues and of its methods of biblical interpretation. Contemporary theologians should be read and studied, and their differences with literalistic and fundamentalist understandings emphasized and discussed.

4. Adult Mentors

As our research team analyzed the interviews we had with young people, as well as our own pilgrimages through adolescence, we found again and again that, for many adolescents, *one particular adult* had made a profound impact. So often it was the case that a particular significant adult had helped the young person to deal with struggles and make the Christian faith come alive and had invited and supported commitment. We arrived at the conclusion that the presence of a significant adult in itself was an important theme. We came to see that the adolescent needs to be in relationship with an adult friend or mentor, a person with whom the young person can communicate and in whom he or she can see what it means to be Christian. We also became aware that we must insure that our programs in youth ministry facilitate and nurture, rather than impede, such relationships.

Characteristics of a Mentor Relationship

It is important to note that when such relationships develop between young people and their adult friends, it is usually because the relationship is characterized by some combination of the following five characteristics:

1. The adult takes a personal interest in the particular young person. From the adult side, this interest seems to be marked by a sense that this young person, more than others, has characteristics and qualities that are uniquely attractive to that adult. The young person shows a kind of promise that makes the adult want to invest something of himself or herself in the young person. From the young person's side, this interest is noticed and appreciated. The adolescent comes to feel a sense of personal worthiness just from seeing his or her particular and unique worth reflected in the eyes of an adult who is not a parent. As a result, the young person becomes particularly interested in and attracted to this adult.

2. The adult tends to become a model for the young person. The adolescent sees in the adult the beliefs, the attitudes, the values, the patterns of behavior, the accomplishments, and the style of life that, to a significant degree, the adolescent desires to emulate and adopt as his or her own. The adult's response is to become teacher, guide, counselor, sponsor, and host to the young person. As teacher, guide, and counselor, the adult articulates the beliefs, the convictions, the values, and the attitudes that are central to him or her as a person and explains their significance and meaning. As sponsor and host, the adult often includes the young person to some degree in his or her own life world. He or she provides opportunities for the young person to meet and be with some of the people the adult lives and works with, to share some of the adult's important experiences, and even at times to carry out some of the tasks and responsibilities that are part of the adult's everyday life.

3. The adult acts as a guarantor for the adolescent. George I. Bustard, Jr., says, "A guarantor is one who swims across the lake and waves encouragement from the other side. 'If I can make it, you can.' "[14] As guarantor, the

adult does more than provide a model of the future for the adolescent. He or she also reaches back to the place where the adolescent is. He or she lets the young person know that in experiences of struggle, doubt, and confusion or during feelings of inadequacy about the journey ahead, the young person is not alone. Others have been there before, have found resources within themselves that they did not know were there, and made it.

4. The adult provides an open ear to the adolescent. He or she is ready and able to listen to the concerns, the hopes, the dreams, the ideas, and the feelings of the young person. The adult responds in a variety of ways: with agreement, criticism, humor, advice, or whatever else may be appropriate from the adult's own point of view. But whatever the response, it is grounded in a basic attitude of acceptance of and care for the young person. The young person responds to this attitude by opening up himself or herself, by sharing what he or she does not share with parents and friends, and by taking the adult's responses into careful consideration.

5. The adult sometimes takes on the role of advocate. As an advocate, the adult will stand up for the adolescent when the young person comes up against destructive opposition. In such situations, the need is for

> someone to stand with youths in their strength and vision, someone to speak for them and plead their case, someone to take their needs seriously and cut through their loneliness, someone to show them how to . . . use their influence successfully, or how to learn from their failures.[15]

In short, the adult empowers the young person when the adolescent's own power is not enough.

The above five characteristics describe what we call a *mentor relationship*. Although leaders of youth groups are sometimes mentors for certain young people, and although elements of the mentor relationship are important in relationships between young people and their youth group leaders, the significant feature of the mentor relationship is its individuality. People are not mentors for groups; they are mentors for individuals. They may be mentors for several individuals, but they focus on them as individuals rather than as group members.

People who are mentors are mature people. They know why they are and are not threatened by the differences between them and their young people. Often they are people in their forties and fifties (or even older) who have made peace with themselves and with life. They are "anchored" and therefore can be anchors for young people. They may not be able to lead a group or keep up with an adolescent's physical pace. But they can do the things that mentors do.

The term *mentor* is borrowed from research in the field of adult developmental psychology. Daniel Levinson's *The Seasons of a Man's Life* is the main source.[16] But the term is used in a different context there. In Levinson's work, the mentor relationship (1) is a relationship between a young adult, usually between the ages of twenty and thirty, and another adult approximately ten to twenty years older; and (2) focuses on the issue of career. The mentor in that case is one who carries out the functions we have described, but for a young person who is striving to enter the world of work and to live out the lifestyle that he or she envisions in relation to that work.

In spite of this difference in context, we have found the characteristics of a mentor described in Levinson's work to be applicable to the relationship between a particular adult and a particular adolescent. Adolescents need and have found mentors, just as young adults do. Mentors in both cases play analogous roles. But in adolescence, the emphasis is on vocation as a way to be a self (particularly in the context of the Christian community) rather than on vocation as an occupation. The question is not so much, How can I be a lawyer, an artist, or a union leader? as it is, How can I be a person? — and perhaps implicitly, How can I be a Christian person? The mentor provides a living promise that there are answers to that question and a living bridge to those answers.

Mentor relationships do not last forever. They arise when adolescents are getting some new distance from their parents and are in need of alternative adult models and confidants. These relationships may last less than a year or may go on as long as three or four years. Often the breakup of a mentor relationship is painful and filled with conflict and disappointment. The younger person may have to break from the mentor's influence in order to stand by himself or herself, just as he or she had to break from parents. Or the relationship may dissolve as the young person grows older and becomes the mentor's colleague and equal. Mentor relationships are not meant to last. But their impact is powerful. They provide a path through adolescence and a door into adulthood. They are never forgotten.

Fostering Mentor Relationships in the Congregation

As things now stand in most churches, mentor relationships are impeded rather than facilitated. Adolescents are frequently sequestered in youth groups and institutions where they relate largely to their peers and a few adults. Most young people simply do not have many opportunities to get to know adults (especially those who are over forty years old), and most adults in churches know few, if any, adolescents with any degree of intimacy. Our congregations are highly age-segregated. Even where they are not, church life is often so compartmentalized from everyday living that young people have no entree into the full life of any adults other than their own parents.

To the extent that age segregation and compartmentalization can be broken down, mentor relationships are more likely to grow. These relationships are rather natural. Both young people and adults find value and pleasure in them. But in our society, intentional efforts have to be made to produce the soil that will grow these relationships. Here are several strategies that pastors, youth leaders, and others responsible for youth ministry in a congregation can use:

- Act as "matchmakers" between young people and adults who have similar interests. For example, if a particular adult is interested in repairing cars, suggest to that person that he or she invite a particular young person who is also interested in this to help him or her on a project (likewise for people interested in music, theater, sports, etc.).
- Provide programs in vocational counseling that emphasize one-on-one relationships between persons in particular occupations and young people interested in considering those occupations. Daylong or week-long visits on the job are especially helpful, as are internships, if they can be arranged.
- Develop educational programs that make use of one-on-one teaching relationships between adults and youth. Albert C. Winn's *Where Do I Go from Here?*[17] provides a particularly fine model.
- Involve adolescents in intergenerational and family cluster models of educational and service programs.
- Plan occasional youth group programs to which adults from the congregation are invited and in which opportunities for dialogue between youth and adults are provided.
- When young people are placed on church committees and boards, support them in their responsibilities by assigning adult members to be their special colleagues.
- Develop adult education programs that help adults understand young people and their needs and interests.
- Facilitate "adopt-a-grandparent" programs and other such opportunities for intergenerational friendship.
- Hold an "exchange-a-teen" weekend in which young people trade parents and families by living in another teen's home for a weekend.
- Keep an eye out for adults who have high potential to be mentors. Invite them to come along on a retreat or attend some other youth function where opportunities for informal conversation are likely.

These few strategies may suggest many other possibilities to readers. The principle behind them all, however, is to intentionally bring adults and young people together in settings where they can befriend each other, share something personal, and perhaps plant the seeds for deeper and more extended relationships. Adults in the congregation are potential mentors for youth. Mentor relationships can be among the most formative in a young person's life. They can provide concrete images of the Christian life and help that is needed along the way.

5. The Need for Trained Leadership

Our discussion of mentor relationships touches on and leads us more fully into the issue of the need for adult leadership in youth ministry. The investigations our research team undertook brought us to the conclusion that the lack of such leadership is a major problem in the mainline churches. It is often the case that adult youth leaders are hard to find and that, even when such volunteers can be found, they often are not well prepared, not adequately interested and committed, or not creative. This is not the fault of those who step forward. The fault, in these cases, lies in the lack of an adequate strategy for developing leadership. A particularly significant failure appears in the lack of adequate training programs and leadership opportunities for young people who have recently graduated from high school and for "early" young adults.

Well-conceived and well-run youth ministry programs depend upon well-trained leadership. There are two aspects to this leadership. First, young people themselves must be given opportunities for leadership and leadership training within their own groups, in the congregation, and in other church settings (including, for some, regional and national positions). Second, adult leaders are needed who enjoy young people and can communicate with them, who understand their needs and circumstances, and who are able to provide needed care, support, and guidance. These adults need to know the Gospel and how to communicate it, in deed and in word, as it relates to the young people's own experience. Adult leaders should be able to plan well *for* and *with* youth. They should be persons of faith and integrity in whose lives young people can see examples of the Christian life.

The two aspects — youth leadership and adult leadership — are related: Good adult leadership tends to foster leadership opportunities and training for youth. Young people who have learned to be leaders in their congregations have an important foundation for becoming adult youth leaders later on. This is why it is important that the development of leadership in youth ministry be based on a process of ongoing, cumulative training. Training for leadership in youth ministry must begin during adolescence, continue in the years after high school, and be reinforced and deepened during adulthood. Our perception of leadership development for youth ministry in the mainline churches is that this kind of ongoing, cumulative training does not occur very often.

Seminary Training

In the mainline Protestant churches, the major strategy for developing adult leaders for youth ministry is included in seminary education. This is the only strategy we have that is in any sense ongoing. Young people who show promise as leaders in the church during adolescence are often encouraged to consider the ordained ministry as a profession. If they decide they are interested in exploring this option, they are given some further encouragement but usually little practical help. Ordinarily, they go off to college where, in most cases, they are on their own.

During the college years, these young people may or may not become involved in youth leadership on campus or in a congregation near the college campus. But their involvement is seldom coordinated, or even known, by the home congregation. In Presbyterian churches, some of these young people register as candidates for the ministry with their presbyteries. Similar processes are available in other denominations. But guidance toward youth ministry per se is minimal, and training in youth ministry is virtually nonexistent. Any formal training in youth ministry does not begin until these persons enter seminary.

Seminary students do receive training that is valuable for youth ministry, and they sometimes receive training in Christian education and youth ministry per se. Upon graduation, these students often are expected to take major roles in the adult leadership of youth ministry, as assistant or associate ministers in multistaff situations or as sole pastors of smaller congregations. But there are several problems with using seminary training as the major strategy for developing leadership in youth ministry.

The first problem is that a gap still remains in the development process. During the years of college between high school and seminary, the young persons going through this process may have little or no involvement in youth ministry or church life. What involvement he or she does have is unsystematic, sporadic, and dependent almost entirely on the initiative of the individual. This means that during a period when important leadership skills are being developed and tested and when a significant contribution to the church and to youth could be made, these people are separated from the church's youth ministry. The loss of the vital contributions that these people could be making to youth ministry and the lost opportunities for developing their knowledge and skills in this area should be of great concern.

Second, the training that is available to these persons once they come to seminary is woefully inadequate and, in some cases, counterproductive. A good deal of a seminary student's experience and training in youth ministry comes through field education. A majority of seminary students who do field education in a congregational context take on the responsibility for youth ministry in those contexts. How this works out in practice is often unfortunate. In the first place, many students who are given the responsibility for youth ministry in their fieldwork do not want it and resent it when they get it. They are just not interested. But they are forced to do youth ministry because fieldwork helps pay the bills and because congregations think "doing the youth group" is what seminary students can and ought to do. Furthermore, youth ministry done as a field assignment is conditioned by that reality of its being nonvoluntary. It often provides a poor experience of youth ministry even for those seminary students who are motivated to do it.

Most often, this fieldwork is done solely on weekends in places far from the seminary campus. Seminary students have little opportunity to get to know the young people at any significant level of depth. They can neither be involved in their day-to-day lives nor minister to them or with them in situations and contexts that come up during the week. The field assignment usually lasts no more than nine months, so that continuity in the youth ministry program, both for the congregation and for the seminary student, is impossible. Most significant youth ministry takes place only after the young people and their adult leaders have come to know one another, trust one another, and plan together. The second, third, and fourth years of work with youth are generally much more likely to be fruitful than the first.

In addition, the fieldwork model of youth ministry usually works against the involvement of lay adult leadership. In most circumstances, congregations think that giving the responsibility for youth ministry to seminary students means that lay responsibility is no longer required. Even when church members are involved, because the students are in the congregation for a limited time each week, it is very difficult for the lay leaders and the seminary students to communicate adequately in order to coordinate their work.

Also students who do youth ministry as their fieldwork find little support and supervision in this work from their supervising pastors. It is not unusual for a pastor to hire a seminary student in order to get youth ministry off his or her own back. When this happens, the pastor often stays as far away from youth ministry as possible. It is no wonder that many seminary students find youth ministry to be a frustrating, discouraging, and unrewarding experience. Once they have "done their time," they wish never to do youth ministry again. Like their supervising pastors, they avoid it at all costs in the future.

The field education issue is not the only problem for youth ministry in seminary training, however. The classroom work in Christian education in general and youth ministry in particular is insufficient in breadth and depth. Students do not come to seminary to learn youth ministry. They come to learn to be ordained ministers. Although training for the ordained ministry in general has dimensions to it that are essential for youth ministry, only a very small portion, if any, of a seminary student's classroom work is devoted to youth ministry in particular. But ministry with young people demands knowledge and skills that are peculiar to it—particularly adolescent development, adolescent culture, and educational strategies that fit the needs and capacities of youth. Most seminaries do not have these classes in their curriculums. Moreover, classroom work in youth ministry, when it does take place, is rarely coordinated with the experiences that students are having with youth ministry in the field.

Finally, seminary classroom work and fieldwork are usually done in isolation from any professional associations or support groups that exist among youth ministry leaders in the church. Clergy who are involved in youth ministry to any significant degree know that within and among denominations there are people who support one another personally, share common concerns, and carry out cooperative ventures in youth ministry. Students who are being trained in youth ministry in the seminaries ordinarily do not even know that these networks and associations exist. Their training and experience is gained apart from these supports, and they are isolated from any denominational or interdenominational efforts that are currently under way.

Even when seminaries do manage to deal with these problems and offer adequate classroom and field training, there are many students who do not take advantage of it. This would not be a problem if these persons were not given responsibility for youth ministry upon graduation. But they are. The first position for many seminary graduates is either a staff position that involves major responsibilities for youth ministry and Christian education or a pastorate in a small congregation. In either case, most seminary graduates are given responsibility for youth ministry and Christian education. They often resent these responsibilities because they do not want them, or they fulfill them inadequately because they are not trained to undertake them. In either case, youth ministry is deprived of trained, committed clergy leadership.

The image of seminary training in youth ministry we have depicted is, perhaps, a "worst case" scenario. Obviously the situation is not this bleak in all these respects for all students. Some students do learn a great deal in the area of youth ministry in seminary, have positive and rewarding experiences in field situations, are introduced to the support networks that exist, and leave seminary with competence in and commitment to youth ministry. But most of the evidence suggests that the "worst case" scenario is the most typical and is one that has a profoundly disabling effect on the youth ministry of the mainline denominations.

Even if the problems with the seminary training model were to be significantly improved and more clergy were well trained in youth ministry leadership, the model would still have some problems. First, a heavy dependence upon clergy leadership tends to overprofessionalize youth ministry, segregate it from general congregational responsibility, and obscure the need for ongoing, cumulative, *lay* training. A vital youth ministry depends upon the significant involvement of laypeople in it, just as Christian education as a whole does.

The Sunday School Movement, for example, was a lay movement from its inception. For more than a century, this movement drew its power partly from the fact that it was organized, carried out, and eagerly supported by committed laypersons who invested significant time and money in developing Sunday schools, teaching in them, and gathering regularly for training.

A strong case can be made that the professionalization of the Sunday school through the Religious Education Movement during the early twentieth century sapped a good deal of the life out of it. Ellis Nelson has occasionally commented that it was the professors of religious education who killed the Sunday school.

It seems worth considering, then, whether the current vitality of such groups as Young Life and Youth for Christ might not be due partly to the fact that these are largely lay-organized, lay-supported, and lay-implemented organizations. It is also worth noting that these organizations do not depend upon a seminary training model exclusively, but they carry out training programs for laypeople that are ongoing from youth through adulthood, and they include large training schools or camps and annual rallies.

One of the positive effects of a lay-based process of leadership development is its effect on young people. When the adult leadership of youth ministry consists predominantly of clergy or seminary students, the young people are not given an adequate model of Christian leadership. They see no clear example of what it would mean for them to be Christian lay leaders. The implicit choice given to many young people is this: Become a minister or forget about leadership in the church. Young people who cannot or do not wish to become ordained ministers need to have models of Christian leadership who are informed, articulate, committed, caring—and not ordained. They especially need such models who are not too many years older than themselves. They need young adults between the ages of twenty and thirty who can provide for them images of the Christian life that can guide them during the next several years of their lives.

A Strategy for Developing Leaders

What all this suggests is that the mainline churches need to work on a strategy of leadership development that (1) is ongoing and cumulative from adolescence through adulthood, (2) involves post-high school adolescents and young adults, as well as others, in leadership in youth ministry, and (3) places more emphasis on the training of laypeople than is currently given.

Among the possible results of such a strategy might be more of a balance between laypersons and clergy in youth ministry leadership, as well as enhanced cooperation between them. Also, this strategy can increase the ability of congregations to take responsibility for youth ministry, provide visible models of lay Christian leadership for youth, and ensure better-trained lay and clerical youth ministers.

It is easier to say what is wrong with the present strategy of leadership development than it is to actually improve it—especially when heavy financial and personnel constraints exist in the budgets for youth ministry of all the denominations. Nonetheless, it seems that significant improvements are already being made. The interdenominational youth ministry training conferences that have been held under the auspices of Joint Educational Development, a cooperative effort of twelve Protestant denominations, have been an attempt to expand the support network among youth ministers and to involve both clergy and laypersons in further training.

Several denominations, too, hold summer youth conferences at which youth, lay leaders, and ministers gather for fellowship, Christian education, and leadership training. Regional judicatories (dioceses, conferences, synods, presbyteries, etc.) seem, in many locations, to be giving more attention to developing structures and holding events that facilitate relationships among young people in different congregations and that enhance the training opportunities for youth and lay adult leadership.

An important experiment is being carried out in the Presbyterian Church (U.S.A.) with its "Tithe of Life" program. This program attempts to deal with ongoing, cumulative, lay leadership training in youth ministry during the post-high school years by enlisting young adults into two years of voluntary work in youth ministry. This experience in ministry provides support, pre-service and in-service training, and a network of colleagues for those taking part in it. All of these efforts may be expected to bear fruit, and they need to be continued and expanded.

However, other approaches are worth considering. The seminary training model should not be abandoned. But it needs to be supplemented by a greater emphasis on lay training, and it must be significantly improved in itself. Lay training and involvement in youth ministry during the crucial college years will provide a background of experience for those young people who do decide to enter the ordained ministry. This can make their seminary training much more effective. Strategies to involve these people in local congregations, in regional and national youth conferences and camps, and in conferences designed especially for them might be tested.

Seminaries also must develop ways to better integrate classroom learning and field experience, and they need to enlarge the offerings in Christian education and youth ministry. Above all, the conditions under which seminary field education in youth ministry is carried out must be greatly improved. Students need better supervision and support. Internships in youth ministry should be expanded, while the weekend task of "doing the youth group" should be reduced or somehow transformed, if not eliminated.

Also worth considering is the possibility of a national training school in youth ministry for lay adult leaders and young people. Whether this could or should be done within denominations or interdenominationally would be an important matter to consider. If such a national school did seem to be a reasonable venture, college students, seminarians, and young adults ought to have important leadership roles for planning it and carrying it out.

Finally, the development at local, regional, and national levels of more models of youth ministry that are not based solely on the fellowship group might be considered. Some possibilities for such models include denominational or interdenominational vocational counseling programs in connection with church-related colleges; an interdenominational network of crisis counseling centers; regional and national centers for training in peer ministry; regional and national church drama groups, orchestras, and choirs consisting of young people; and regional and national theological institutes for church youth and post-high school young adults.

None of these efforts individually would have a great impact on the problem of leadership in youth ministry. But their total effect would be significant. The problem of leadership in youth ministry is not one that can be handled entirely at the congregational level. It is a problem to be solved by the youth ministry enterprise as a whole, and its solution will depend upon efforts at all levels—regional, denominational, and interdenominational.

6. A Variety of Responses

The conclusion of our section on leadership pointed us toward the need for variety in the organization of youth ministry. This need warrants further scrutiny, both in order to help us see what the range of options might be and to make a case for fostering such variety within the total "ecology" of youth ministry in any one community.

A Typology

Our discussion of this issue begins with the following claim: In the total ecology of organizations that minister to youth, a variety of types with various functions and theological stances try to meet the differing and changing needs of adolescents. But it is difficult for one organization or group to be all types—that is, to carry out all functions that are needed or to be faithful to all theological stances at the same time.

This claim involves a rather obvious plea for pluralism in youth ministry. It is also a plea for cooperation rather than competition among youth ministry agencies. No one group can be "all things to all people" at all times—but "all things" are needed. This, no doubt, seems obvious. But in practice the reality can become difficult to live with. This is especially true when the aims and procedures of some groups are seen as antithetical to what others believe is most important, healthy, and productive in youth ministry and when these groups consequently compete with one another. For example, we have seen the unhappy and antagonistic relations that often develop between local church youth leaders and leaders of Young Life or similar organizations—or between leaders of large church youth groups and leaders of small ones.

Types by Function

In our research, we have been able to identify some types of youth groups according to the function that each plays for its members. The list of types is not exhaustive but suggestive. The types, too, are not mutually exclusive. A group may be considered of one type because of how it functions for its members, but it may also be seen as of another type because of a different one of its functions. However, we have arranged the list in terms of poles of emphasis, according to functions that are quite opposite. A group that is strong in one function will find it difficult to also be strong in a function that is its polar opposite (e.g., a group that can be classified under "1*a*" probably will not be able to be classified under "1*b*" as well). These are the types we have identified, according to how they function for their members:

1*a*. Groups in which *emotional experiences* of religious commitment are emphasized
1*b*. Groups in which *critical reflection* on religious and personal issues are fostered
2*a*. Groups that have *firm boundaries* and explicit initiation procedures
2*b*. Groups that have *flexible* and porous *boundaries* and no discernible rite of initiation
3*a*. Groups that are highly *task oriented* and organized for productivity
3*b*. Groups that are highly *relationship oriented* and lack formal organization
4*a*. Groups that encourage and provide opportunities and assistance for increased *involvement in wider church structures*
4*b*. Groups that provide a context for *rebellion against* or a moratorium on the values, beliefs, and institutional roles of *wider church structures*
5*a*. Groups in which *intimate interpersonal relationships* are normative
5*b*. Groups that provide opportunities for *relative anonymity* and protection from intimacy

Types by Theological Stance

Groups may also be differentiated theologically. One way of making this differentiation is to analyze the degree to which religious language is used in the speech patterns of the group and the way in which religious language is understood. We have identified the following types by theological stance:

1. Groups whose theological stance is *precritical orthodoxy*. Such groups are generally characterized by literalistic approaches to biblical interpretation and a stress on right belief and right practice (both of which are clearly defined). Religious language is used extensively.

2. Groups whose theological stance is *critical confessionalism.* Like orthodox groups, these groups have a strong sense of confessional identity. But the pluralistic nature of the world is affirmed and appreciated. Beliefs and values are open to critical examination in the light of experience, and practices may change as a result. Religious language is used extensively.
3. Groups characterized by *nonconfessional cultural Christianity.* Such groups have no strong sense of religious identity. Religious language is used sparsely. The group uncritically adopts the practices, the language, and the beliefs of the surrounding culture. The point of reference for the group is its place of meeting.

Our research on these types of groups according to function and theological stance has not yet led us much beyond the commonsensical. It would be most valuable to employ tools presently being used in the fields of social psychology and organizational behavior to analyze in a more sophisticated way the dimensions of organizational structure and function that do indeed differentiate youth organizations from one another. It would be especially helpful to know to what degree any of these separate factors correlate in a factor analysis of the data. But such research has not yet been done.

Even without a more adequate means of discrimination, however, a typology such as this one can be helpful. It suggests, at least, that when youth ministry is considered as a whole in light of the needs of adolescents, the desirability of having a variety of different types of groups available becomes evident. Such variety is desirable because all of the needs that these various types of groups meet are found among the adolescent population. In addition, using this typology helps us to be more clear about what forms best address the different needs.

Groups to Fit Many Needs

Young people are not all alike. Some are searching for religious experiences that engage their emotions. Others are trying to think through religious and personal issues in a cognitive and critical mode. Some need a group that tells them in clear ways whether they are in or out. Some need a group that they can move into without great commitment in order to try it out for a while. Some are in search of intimate personal relationships. Some need a place to be with others without having to share too much of what is inside them. Some are interested in doing and accomplishing. Others just want to be together with people they like. Some find theological orthodoxy the only way to begin to make any sense at all of what is happening to them and their world. Only there do they find an identity that is concrete enough to save them from confusion and chaos. Others find such orthodoxy stifling and confining. We believe that all of these needs are legitimate and that we must foster a variety of groups to meet those needs.

It is also true that individual adolescents change over time. What was a need for a person at one time may no longer be so. New needs develop. Movement to a new group is sometimes necessary in order for the new needs to be met. The following hypothetical scenario illustrates this movement:

> Ann was rather quiet and easily overlooked in a crowd. Her shyness prevented her from making friends easily. This difficulty was augmented when Ann's family moved into a new neighborhood, and she enrolled in a different school. Ann discovered that many of the members of the youth choir at her church attended her new school. Though she had difficulty making friends at school, she joined the choir. There she became a close friend of Jill and of Lea and even began dating some of the young men in the choir. As a result of these experiences, she gained confidence in herself and seemed to be less shy. The number of her friends at school increased, and she became involved in several extracurricular activities there. After a while, she dropped out of the choir.
>
> As a result of Ann's newfound activeness in the world around her, she began to develop interests of her own. Through participation in the school's drama club, Ann discovered that she was a good dramatic storyteller. The next summer, to keep from being bored, she participated in her church's summer recreation program as a Bible storyteller. She enjoyed the experience and was left with a greater desire to learn more about the Bible, to learn more about working with children, and to meet some young adults who enjoyed working with children. She simultaneously began attending her church's senior high Sunday school class and the meetings of Young Life in her high school.
>
> In both Sunday school and Young Life, Ann found she had some real leadership skills. Her adult leaders encouraged her. She felt, however, that the Sunday school class and the Young Life group did not provide a broad enough context in which to test herself. She joined the youth group at her church. It was not long before her leadership abilities were recognized there. She ultimately became the group's president. This position brought opportunities to become involved in her denomination's summer leadership training camp and in its regional and national youth organizations.[18]

Ann is a hypothetical person, but the story illustrates something that happens to many young people. As they grow, they abandon some groups and join others because their needs, interests, and circumstances change. We believe this process ought not to be discouraged.

Through our interviews, we found that this pattern of changing groups is rather widespread. We also found something we had not expected to see: Many adolescents are members of two or more church or parachurch youth groups simultaneously. We noted with interest that many of these young people were members of groups that had opposite functions. For example, some felt a need to be in one group that was highly task oriented and a need to be simultaneously in a different group that was highly relationship oriented. Neither group satisfied both needs, but both needs were there. It took two groups to handle them. Although we have not tested this hypothesis scientifically, it does seem that often the persons who are most involved in youth groups are persons who are involved in more than one group. That is, involvement in one group does not necessarily detract from involvement in another. It often enhances it.

Because adolescents have a variety of needs (not all of which can necessarily or easily be met by any one group or type of group), it is important for youth ministry leaders to attempt to foster a variety of types of groups in a community. In order to do this, a systematic typology of youth ministry organizations could first be developed, by means of which the ecology of youth ministry in a community could be analyzed. Persons concerned with youth ministry could then determine whether there were major gaps in that ecology and attempt to fill them. Such a perspective would also aid the process of mutual support that needs to exist among leaders and organizations that carry out distinctive (and in some cases, competing) forms of youth ministry.

Furthermore, it is useful to see part of the task of youth ministry as a kind of "brokering" of the movement between groups. Youth leaders should know the local ecology and attempt to help particular adolescents find the groups that best meet their needs at a given time. The other side of the coin, of course, involves *allowing* youth to make movements from group to group. We must resist putting strong social pressure on young people who choose to go elsewhere than our own group and inducing guilt in them. A young person's leaving of a group we happen to lead is not necessarily a sign of unfaithfulness.

Finally, each group or program needs to have a clear sense of what its purposes and functions are. It must then try to carry those out as effectively as possible, without trying to be all things to all people at all times.

Conclusion

These six issues are, we think, of key importance for those of you who plan, sponsor, carry out, and engage in youth ministry. Ponder over them, think them through, and keep them in mind. They are, quite obviously, not the only key issues. Nor are these reflections on them the end of the discussion. Indeed, our intention has been primarily to generate discussion, as well as action. Our hope has been to place six items—some rather perennial, some perhaps new—on the agenda for youth ministry in the coming years.

Notes

1. The project was undertaken at Louisville Presbyterian Theological Seminary and funded by a research grant from the Lilly Endowment, Inc. I would like to express my appreciation of and thanks to the members of the research team. The student members were Patrick Clark, Robert Edmundson, Forrest Krummel, Sue Davis Krummel, Brett Mouran, John Pehrson, Scott W. Simons, Teresa Snorton, Keith Sundberg, Gerald Stephens, and Herminia E. Trinidad. Many of the ideas that have found their way into their current forms in this essay were first born in papers by these students and in discussions with them. Dr. A. David Bos, the executive director of the Saint Matthews Area Ministries in Louisville, was the project's research associate. Dr. Bos was deeply involved in all aspects of the project, and he coauthored with me several of the working papers on which this essay is based. I am grateful for his constantly stimulating collegiality. Finally, thanks are due to Dr. C. Ellis Nelson, the former president of Louisville Seminary, and Dr. Robert W. Lynn of the Lilly Endowment, for their encouragement and support of this project.

2. Erik Erikson, *Identity: Youth and Crisis* (New York: W. W. Norton, 1968), p. 244.

3. Comments made in a discussion with our research team at Louisville Seminary.

4. Erikson, *Identity,* pp. 22–23.

5. H. Richard Niebuhr, *The Responsible Self* (New York: Harper and Row, 1963), pp. 61–62.

6. *Language* includes here not only the words people use in speech or in writing, but also the music they play and hear, the art they produce, their "body language," and the visual images used in the various mass media (television, movies, magazines, etc.).

7. Quoted in Michael Warren, *Youth and the Future of the Church* (New York: Seabury, 1982), pp. 106–107.

8. Ibid., p. 107.

9. David Burrell, *Exercises in Religious Understanding* (Notre Dame, IN: Univ. of Notre Dame Press, 1974), pp. 22–23.

10. For further discussion of this issue, see my essay "Youth and the Language of Faith," *Religious Education* 81 (Summer 1986): 3.

11. David Ng, *Youth in the Community of Disciples* (Valley Forge, PA: Judson Press, 1984), pp. 49–50.

12. Harvey Seifert, "Unrecognized Internal Threats to Liberal Churches," *Christian Century* 96, no. 35 (31 October 1979): 1057.

13. Ibid.

14. George I. Bustard, Jr., "Times That Are Changing—Phase Two: The Guarantor," *Strategy* 3, no. 4 (June–August 1973): 12.

15. George I. Bustard, Jr., "Times That Are Changing—Phase Three: The Advocate," *Strategy* 4, no. 1 (September–November 1973): 8.

16. Daniel Levinson, *The Season of a Man's Life* (New York: Alfred A. Knopf, 1978).

17. Albert C. Winn, *Where Do I Go from Here?* (Chicago: Science Research Associates, 1972).

18. Adapted from an essay by team member Teresa Snorton written for our research project.

Essay 6

Components of Successful Youth Catechetical Programs

Michael Warren

The following essay was written to summarize my findings during a two-year period of investigating successful parish catechetical programs for youth that were known to be enjoyed both by those initiating them and by the young people participating in them. At the time the study was done, youth catechesis for older teens had virtually come to a standstill in the United States, and it seemed important to search out programs that had a certain catechetical genius. My study showed that in almost every diocese such programs could be found and that they took varied forms in an array of different settings. My hope was that such programs could be studied by others who were unsure of what direction to take in youth catechesis and that this study would thus lead to a kind of revolution in youth catechesis.

Unfortunately this revolution in youth catechesis has hardly begun, and the work of identifying and appreciating creative youth catechesis is just as important today as when I first did my study.

This essay is reprinted from Youth Ministry: A Book of Readings, *ed. Michael Warren (New York: Paulist Press, 1977), pages 84–92.*

During a two-year period, 1973–75, I conducted a national survey of Roman Catholic dioceses on the situation of youth catechesis in out-of-school programs. I met with representatives of almost every diocese in the country to discuss the directions of youth catechesis in their own and neighboring dioceses. However, as a follow-up to this diocesan-level survey, I tried to identify parishes running model successful youth programs. I was curious to find out whether my own three-year experience in parish clusters in New York and Virginia was similar to the experiences of those running catechetical programs in Tucson, Spokane, and Orlando. I also wanted to find out if I could uncover components common to successful catechetical ministry to young people at the parish level.

In order to get this information, I asked each diocese in the United States to identify two of its best parish youth programs, and then I wrote these parishes asking for a detailed description of their youth catechetical programs. The following report is a summary of the data sent in by the relatively small number of twenty-nine parishes that responded to this request for detailed information. It took weeks of poring over the descriptions of these parish programs before the common elements hidden in the various reports could be discerned. After all, the reporting parishes were geographically and demographically diverse. Some programs were based in homes, some in area centers. Some parishes used only professional teachers as catechists; others invited a cross section of adults to engage in this ministry. Thus the first and most obvious feature of successful catechetical programs for youth in various parishes in the United States was the variety of approaches that characterized them.

More study, however, revealed another more unifying common element among these various programs. It was this: in each program there had been careful attention to relationships among all those involved in the program. Another way of expressing this commonality: every program reported was in some respect a community-centered one. Great care was given to the way people came together. Attention was paid to relationships among all in the program — among the adults, among the young people, and between the young people and the adults. Where parishes were successful at the relational level they were also successful catechetically. The following section describes in some detail the community-centered component of these parish programs, and the final section describes other features common to them: variety, planning, and informality.

1. Community-Centered Programs

What do we mean by community-centered programs? To repeat, these are programs that successfully develop relationships among the adults, between the adults and the young people, and among the young people. At this point, I would like to examine each of these relationships in turn.

Relationships Among Adults

These relationships are fostered and encouraged in many different ways.

As a Support Group

In many well-planned parish youth catechetical programs the adult catechists actually form a support group in which individual catechists find help and encouragement. In such parishes, adult catechists meet regularly but in informal settings. Such meetings sometimes occur as debriefing sessions after a program. Intelligent use of debriefing can turn a weekly meeting into an in-service training program for all involved. Here the adults discuss what happened and why—in some places over beer and sandwiches. This is an atmosphere where they can share their successes and failures, knowing that even failures can be a source of learning and future growth. Under a leader who convenes this group these adults can also exchange ideas about what is happening in their program and about future directions they would like to take. Thus they become involved in the evolution of the program. Such adults work not in isolation but in co-relation.

As a Fellowship

In some parish catechetical programs, adults form a fellowship of faith. They pray regularly together. In addition to meeting to plan, they also meet to share their faith with one another. Such faith-sharing sessions take many forms: periods of prayer at the end of other types of meetings, days of recollection, retreats, celebrations of unity in the Eucharist. There is no formula for developing a faith dimension among adults. It is more a matter of attitude, especially in the coordinator or the director of a catechetical program. This attitude recognizes that if adults are to assist the young in growth in faith, they too must be actively engaged in their own development. It may be that when adults find that their catechetical ministry is aiding their own development as persons, they will be most inclined to continue as catechists. At a recent meeting of catechetical leaders in Atlanta, a trainer of catechists shared the following insight based on her work: *Those adults who have developed an ability to pray together and to talk about their own faith tend also to be the most flexible and comfortable in dealing with young people in nonclassroom situations.* These adults are quicker to realize that classrooms are not the only, or even the best, places in which to help young people grow in faith. They tend to be more free in trying out other models. Thus this trainer has built into her program a prayer and faith-sharing dimension. It makes sense. As their own understanding of faith becomes centered in their personal lives and able to be expressed in personal terms instead of solely in doctrinal formulations, these catechists rely less on a highly structured catechesis.

As a Friendship Group

I cannot say what levels of friendship develop among catechists in good youth catechetical programs. Yet from the low-key contact with one another as a support group and as a faith fellowship, one would suspect that, in addition to a good deal of friendliness, various degrees of friendship also emerge.

Relationships Between Adults and Youth

These programs also attend to relationships between adults and young people. Obviously, some of the good relationships that evolve between youth and adults come about naturally. A mature, well-balanced adult who has a sense of humor and a love of young people will easily develop a good relationship with youth. But what I am referring to here is something that happens because it has been planned at the program level. By what means?

By Joint Planning

Young people help plan and run the catechetical program they themselves are in. The adults have provided for a young, authentically participative role in running the program. Representatives of the young people are given a say in program development, implementation, and evaluation. Moreover, the young may serve on a variety of other working groups, dealing with publicity, service programs, and social or athletic events. In short, the input of all is actively sought, recognized, and appreciated. More and more parish programs for youth, and especially for older youth, are relying on the input of the young themselves.

By Creating an Atmosphere of Friendship

Some parishes have paid special attention to the atmosphere or setting for youth catechesis. The program has been organized for informal interaction between the adults and the young. The program is not limited to rectangular spaces called classrooms, within which from ten to thirty young people sit and listen to the words of a single adult. Rather, the program is designed around a variety of activities, all of which encourage the young and the adults to be together in a friendly, mutually enriching way. Retreats, a rap session, field trips, and, as we shall see, a variety of other approaches are used to create a relationship of friendship between the teens and the adults.

In *Five Cries of Youth,* Merton Strommen remarks that the basic or primal ministry to the young is the ministry of friendship. This fact is something skillful catechists have long known. In this connection, the choice of language by some of these parishes was interesting. Many avoided the term *teacher* to refer to their adult catechists, preferring instead to call them simply *adults* or *leaders* or *resource persons.* One report described the role of adults as "catalyst, participant, facilitator, motivator." Such a use of language may highlight a distinctive role for the catechist dealing with youth in out-of-school programs.

What are some of the things individual adults do to foster this bond of friendship with young people? Some, recognizing that telephone conversation has a special intimacy for young people, make a point of phone contact with their young persons. Others attend sports and social functions their youth are involved in. Some bring their wives or husbands to catechetical programs on occasion, so the young people will get to know other dimensions of their lives. Some adults are eager to be on retreat teams, because they recognize the close bond that can develop on a retreat weekend.

At the program level, adults are not put in the position of functioning primarily as disciplinarians. Programs are designed for flexibility, for a very low-key sort of discipline with few sanctions. Lyman Coleman–type group programs are designed to allow for much informal chatter while learning is going on. The only rule, and often an unwritten one, in such programs is that of listening when someone is speaking to be heard. That is simple politeness and ordinarily not a problem for young people. One group of parishes designed a program so that kids could miss a week without causing any difficulty to others. It was a large-group program, based on a different theme each week. The themes were not sequential, though they were announced in advance. The young were encouraged to come to the programs that appealed to them. However, the strategy among the adult leaders was to make certain that each week those who didn't come would regret having missed an exciting, rewarding evening. And so it was. I am told that enrollment grew from week to week until two groups had to be formed. This move toward greater flexibility and a more relaxed atmosphere paid off in a better relationship between the young people and the adults. Such programs are not highly structured, though they are carefully organized. In general, the looser the structure, the more careful the organization and the preparation needed to ensure its success.

Those parishes that give a priority to adult-youth relationships recognize that catechesis is not something a privileged group does for an underprivileged group. It is rather a joint venture in which both groups grow together through their efforts on one another's behalf. Catechesis is not a soup kitchen operation; it is not done in handouts from the haves to the have-nots; it is much more like a family dinner table where parents and children alike are nourished not only by the food but also by one another's presence.

Relationship Among Young People

Successful youth catechetical programs also pay attention to the relationships among the young people themselves. Again, as with interaction among the adults and between the adults and the youth, there is a preoccupation with how people come together. These programs have shifted emphasis from the quantity of sessions and of participants to the quality of relationships among participants. If the priority is the quality of time spent together, the emphasis is not on attendance but rather on the growth of those who do attend. That approach seems to help the attendance problem solve itself. Some of the forms this emphasis on peer relationships takes are as follows: There is a great deal of emphasis on small-group discussion and on other types of *sharing* among the young people. Whereas catechesis for young people was once dominated by input, there seems to be a shift to expressivity, that is, to procedures that will encourage them to make sense out of what they have been told and to express what it means in relation to their own personal lives. Some parishes are doing youth catechesis out of a basic service model. The young people engage in service projects as an effort to express their faith in action. They come together at regular intervals to pray about, talk about, and learn more about the further dimensions of their Christian service. Input is handled exclusively in full-day, retreat-type programs that are planned as they are needed.

Successful catechetical programs also emphasize leadership development. Young people are asked to take leadership roles in running various aspects of their own programs. I have already mentioned something about this important development. Retreats are probably the most concrete example of a valuable type of leadership development. The majority of youth retreat programs now in this country make use of young team members who give carefully prepared talks based on their own personal experience of the Gospel. I have heard many such talks over the past ten years, and they have a unique and very moving power. Such a role in a retreat develops not only leadership but also an authentic ministry among the young themselves. What I am saying is that the best catechetical programs are now developing a catechetical ministry among the young. Their young people are becoming skilled catechists in their own right. That is why one small-town catechetical center could report that 50 percent of its adult catechists had gone through the center's programs themselves when they were younger.

As a result of such indirect leadership training, catechetical programs are helping teens exercise a peer ministry, a ministry to their own age-group. That ministry is at root a ministry of friendship, which provides basic care and concern so needed by the young. Once this dynamic of caring and service to other young people takes root among even a small group of leaders in a catechetical program, the complexion of the entire program changes for the better. The program then generates its own life. It ceases to run at the impetus of adult pressures and cajoling. It is energized by a communal life of its own.

2. Other Features of Successful Parish Programs

Planning

Careful planning has been the underlying motif in the above explanation of the successful parish program. There is not one-time planning, that is, planning in September for the entire year. Planning usually is done in segments. The first sequence of events is planned, run, and then evaluated before the next sequence is run. This type of planning is admittedly time-consuming. Yet it pays off, especially if the planning process involves the young people themselves.

The following planning strategies are also being used by parish programs:
- sending a weekly or biweekly bulletin to the adult leaders, informing them of the precise goals and procedures of a particular week's programs;
- holding a regular weekly debriefing session among all the adult leaders of a particular age-group
- taking time for a special planning session run over several weeks between the fall and spring sessions, during which the weekly program is shut down for "inventory" (one parish schedules three planning workshops each year)
- keeping the young people informed of at least the general directions of the program, in addition to providing them with a written bulletin of events and activities

Variety

One of the results that careful planning makes possible is a deliberate variety of programming. At any rate, most of the parishes reporting in my survey showed a good deal of variety in what they were doing for youth. The most common format in use is a presentation by the catechist followed by a small-group discussion. However, active educational procedures like educational games, role-playing, problem solving, guest lectures, field trips, all-day and weekend retreats, and large-group celebrations are all apt to be utilized at times in the course of a program. One parish reports using "everything from panels to rap sessions, dramatic playlets and the rock opera *Tommy* to expanded liturgies and full-length films."

In addition to a variety of educational procedures, parishes also report a range of other activities serving various needs of young people. Some offer one-to-one counseling for those desiring it. Others have lively social action programs, as well as regularly scheduled social activities, such as recreational trips, dances, and talent shows. Offering social activities to which the young can invite their friends who do not participate in the catechetical program appears to be a useful means of publicity.

These, then, are some of the common elements found in parish catechetical programs that have been identified by diocesan catechetical staff persons as successful. It is important to keep in mind the variety of approaches that characterize these programs. Such variety suggests that a successful catechetical approach to youth cannot be neatly blueprinted from somebody else's design. What might be appropriate to a large urban parish might not be feasible in a rural area. On the other hand, the interaction that characterizes the programs studied suggests that good catechesis emerges from efforts at becoming a common unity, joined in a common faith in Jesus and in a common love and respect for one another. Such a common unity does not just happen. It is an achievement, the result of careful effort by all involved. One might expect the results of such efforts to be their own reward.

Essay 7

Principles and Procedures in Youth Ministry

Richard Costello and Michael Warren

The chief author of the following essay is Richard Costello, who has a special talent for creative planning and attention to practical details. This talent can be seen also in essay 15, which begins on page 192.

Readers should note that although we use the term youth ministry *in the title, our chief concerns in this essay are catechetical. Significantly, in the essay we even name ourselves a "catechetical team," chiefly because so much of our work has been with adult catechesis and so much of our concern has been with the role of catechesis in building credible parishes. However, our catechetical work with youth needs to be put into the context of the broader ministry to young people, and I hope readers can detect the "youth ministry sense" underlying what we have written here.*

This essay is reprinted from Youth Ministry: A Book of Readings, *ed. Michael Warren (New York: Paulist Press, 1977), pages 114–124.*

How do we lead contemporary young people into the circle of the faith community? How do we lead them to share our cherished values of Church, prayer, and the loving God revealed in the person of Jesus? The authors believe there are two important ingredients for carrying on a successful ministry to young people. The first has to do with the competence and the attitude of the minister and the second with the methodology he or she employs. Part 1 of the following reflections will propose some attitudes needed by those ministering to the development of youth, and part 2 will offer some positive suggestions for designing programs for young people.

Part 1

Youth Minister Attitude 1:
Be Ready to Hand Over Your Faith

The most important thing we as adults have to offer to the young is not our expertise at giving multimedia presentations or our skill in using a text effectively. It is our faith. If we do not believe that revelation has taken place in our lives and that we have responded to it through faith, then everything else we do is simply an exercise in technique. Still more, believing that God has touched our lives and transformed us is not enough; we must be willing to try to articulate that experience.

Actually, this is the task that in the earliest days of the Church was done by the mystagogue. The mystagogue had the privileged role not only of instructing people in the secrets of the Christian mystery but also of leading them in a very personal way into the mystery that is in them. Jesus himself is the mystagogue before all others, the exemplar, because he shares with us the holy mystery that he himself experienced and that he now wants to evoke in us. As Donald Gray put it recently,

> Jesus' ministry is a grace in our midst, but it also summons us to a task. Jesus has enacted on our behalf the essential meaning of man's relationship to the holy mystery that is God, but it must be reenacted by us on our own behalf and in our own way for it to become salvation. The mystery of destiny and freedom that I have already pointed toward in Jesus reappears, not surprisingly, in the journey of the self.

We no longer have to be sources of infinite knowledge. We must no longer feel that we have to answer all the questions. (That is not to say, however, that information is not an important segment of religious education and ministry, but rather that it needs to be put in its proper context.) However, if we do believe that revelation has occurred in our lives and that we have tried to respond in faith, then we also know that we have responded to a mystery. We have been touched by the person of Christ and in turn have reached out and touched him, but that reciprocal action has not solved all our problems or answered all our questions. Nevertheless, we know, and must help the young to see, that Christ is at the heart of the Christian mystery. He does not solve problems or answer questions but simply says that it's all right not to understand completely; it's all right not to have all the answers; it's all right to be uncertain about the future and our place in it.

Youth Minister Attitude 2:
Be Ready to Hand Over True Responsibility to the Young People

As persons involved significantly with youth, we must be prepared to give real responsibility to the young people with whom we work. Theologically, all of us would agree that youth are, in every sense of the word, *full members* of the Church. But the reality experienced by the young is often quite different. Parish councils are set up with little or no representation from youth. Folk Masses are organized and often run without the involvement of the young or with their involvement limited to playing the guitar. As one young person put it to one of the authors recently, "I wonder if the Church really takes us seriously; many times I feel that I am only being offered token gestures in an effort to ensure that I continue to go to Mass—or if I stop, that I come back. I'm always looking for the gimmick."

Yet all of us would probably agree that the lessons of life we learned best were the ones that cost us the most, because we felt personally responsible for a particular project. We adults, then, must offer young people opportunities to experience failure or success in something that is important.

Here is an example. A few years ago, when the authors were members of a catechetical team working with the young people of eight parishes in Flushing, New York, the team spent almost four months listening to their views and complaints about the Church. These young people had little or no real concept of what the Church is supposed to be, but they were very expert at zeroing in on the weak points of what it is. The authors decided that the best solution would be to give these young people a chance to learn what the Church is all about through an experience that would involve true responsibility.

So the authors went to the pastors of the eight parishes and asked them if they would be willing to let the young people try to establish a separate, autonomous ninth parish composed of and run by the young people themselves. Much to the authors' delight, the pastors agreed. The authors then chose a core of about forty of the most critical young people to initiate this project.

The project began with a study phase, with the youth reading books and articles on the nature of church and the authors conducting sharing and discussion sessions. The young people were then offered an opportunity to go away for a youth parish weekend, at which they were asked to tackle such questions as the membership of this youth parish, its organization, its services, its finances, who its pastor would be, and where the parish would gather.

The limitations of space do not permit us to explain here the eventual outcome of the project. It did not continue, but mainly because many of the pastors and the parish councils came to be threatened by it. Discouraging as this outcome may sound, the project was a learning experience for the young people involved.

Admittedly, in most parishes youngsters are not taken seriously or given a real say. Merton Strommen's research reported in *A Study of Generations* points to the sense of alienation and powerlessness found among young Lutherans. The same could be said of Catholic young people. Actually they are ready to have a say and to exercise true leadership. Of course they need guidance, but they also need a chance. The need for a chance at leadership is highlighted in the recent report *The Education of Adolescents,* by the National Panel on High School and Adolescent Education. If this need for greater opportunities is needed in secular education, then surely it is also needed if our young are ever to feel themselves truly members of the beloved community.

The authors strongly believe, however, that it is most important that adults always be involved both in catechetical and recreational programs for young people. The question is, how should the adults be involved? Too often we set up our programs first and then try to find the personnel to make them go. But, as anyone knows who has set up a teacher-training program for adults who will work with youth, many of these adults feel very uncertain about their ability to handle such work.

Youth Minister Attitude 3:
Be Ready to Adapt Programs to the Gifts of Your Adult Leaders

Programs must be established in such a manner that the adults concerned will be able to act and relate to the young people as each adult person is. We must be careful, for instance, not to structure programs in such a narrow way as to discourage adults who would like to become involved with young people but are afraid of working in a highly structured classroom situation.

In connection with this topic, it is important to realize that those of us who are in charge of training adults to work with the young need not accept all who apply. The authors know the difficulty of resisting the temptation to accept anyone who volunteers, since it is so difficult to get adults interested in such work. All the same, if we strongly believe that a particular adult will not be effective in dealing with the young, then we have an obligation to that person, as well as to those he or she would be working with, to say no. Three questions suggest themselves as criteria in selecting adult leaders: (1) Do they see Christianity as a way of life or as a set of rules and commands? (2) Do they need young people more than the young people need them? (3) Are they comfortable with themselves?

Youth Minister Attitude 4:
Be Ready to Continue Your Own Way as a Pilgrim

Young people need to realize that we too are struggling and trying to grow in faith. All of us have surely had some young person say to us, "You keep talking about Jesus as an example. You tell us that we should imitate him. But we can't really, can we? After all, he was also God. He didn't sin. He didn't know what it was like to be tempted—I mean *really tempted.*"

We pose at least an analogous problem to young people by the attitude and the stance that many of us take toward them. Are we willing to admit to them that we are not perfectly formed adults and Christians? Do we project the image of having arrived? of having achieved the plateau in life called "Adulthood"? I believe that it is extremely important for us to show young people by word and action and attitude that we too are in process, that we too are trying to become more mature—in faith and in other ways as well. To do otherwise is to place ourselves outside their experience.

Isn't it the experience of each of us who work with young people that they force us, in a sense, to become more consciously pilgrims and to take our own journeys seriously? So in a way, they have ministered to us, through their questions, their doubts, their insights, and their own efforts to grow closer to the Lord. Which of us hasn't grown through their witness?

Part 2

In the light of the above attitudes of persons ministering to youth, the following are offered as suggestions for planning that affect our methodology.

1. Plan Short Rather Than Long

Programs should be designed to last for a limited period of time, and overall goals should be established for the entire program as well as for each session. It is difficult to keep young people interested in a program that lasts for a whole year; as P. T. Barnum said, "Always leave 'em wanting more." Six weeks seems to be a good length, followed by an evaluation. If the group thinks the program has been worthwhile, ask them whether they would like to continue with another six-week program.

About goals, it is important that each program be designed to lead to a particular, specific conclusion. For example, if you conduct a program with a vague goal such as "providing better liturgical experiences in the parish," you may find that what you have actually accomplished by it is to make the young people feel more relaxed with one another and with you.

This might force you to be more realistic and to consider what programs would be necessary prerequisites for a future liturgical program.

2. Plan Simple Rather Than Complex

It is impossible to convey all our theological insights in one sitting. *Programs or presentations should be designed to make only one or two points, with plenty of examples.* Alka Seltzer has made a fortune on people who overindulge in eating and drinking. Whenever we overindulge, we suffer. The same is true in catechetics, except that when we overindulge in programming or in presenting material, it is those with whom we are working who suffer—not us. Consider the pattern of Catholic school education: all doctrine and church history in grades 1–8, all doctrine and church history in grades 9–12, all doctrine and church history in four years of college. And CCD programs try to do the same thing with less time and motivation.

On the other hand, one of the problems plaguing catechesis in formal school settings is this insufferable repetition of curriculum. Offering all doctrine and church history in grades 1–8, again in grades 9–12, and again in four years of college is clearly a mistake. Let not those ministering to youth outside of schools make the same mistake. We have an opportunity to be much more realistic and creative in communicating new understandings to young people.

3. Plan Inclusive Rather Than Exclusive

In conducting any program, involve the participants as far as possible in the planning and the implementation, and always involve them in the evaluation. We would think it extremely odd if someone were to suggest to us that we were hungry, then prepared the food, fed it to us, and afterward told us how much we enjoyed it. Yet this is what we tend to do in religious education. By involving the participants in the whole process, we are telling them that they are the most important part of the program. Especially with regard to the evaluation, by sitting down and talking with them we are admitting that we don't have all the answers and that we can learn from them. We are thereby increasing the grassroots level of support for the next program.

4. Plan for Their Needs, Not Yours

Our starting point in programming must be where we find the young people, and we must challenge them to grow in their faith from this point. One of the biggest mistakes the authors have found themselves making over the past two years is to give answers to questions that the young people haven't even formulated. But when we discover what questions the young really are asking, then we can help them see where they really are and challenge them to grow. At times that challenge must take the form of a personal invitation from the adult: How do you pray? Would you like to go for a hamburger?

5. Plan for Atmosphere and for Further Planning

Atmosphere and careful planning are both extremely important. The idea of creating a coffeehouse type of atmosphere is good, but the place can't be the boiler room of the school. And how many programs that were well conceived have been total flops because of minor difficulties: the bulb burned out on the projector in the middle of the movie, or the record player didn't have a long enough extension cord. The attention of the young is so limited and so tenuous that you need all the breaks you can get to hold their attention. Proper planning and care in choosing the environment will not ensure success, but it will at least give you a fighting chance.

6. Plan to Waste Time on the Young

We need to be *willing to spend time* with the young people with whom we are trying to work. Dealing with youth is a full-time job. If you expect them to be there when you run a program, then they expect you to be there when they have something to talk about.

Young persons need lots of time to feel comfortable with you and with one another. At times it is simply enough to be present to one another. An example of what this means comes to mind. Recently, the uncle of one of the authors, who is deaf, was in the hospital. He had practically given up trying to communicate with people because of his hearing problem. Each day a nine-year-old girl came to this uncle's bed and offered him some candy, gave him a picture she had drawn, or showed him a present she had received. No words were ever said between the two, yet much was spoken. We in religious education must also learn to speak as much by our presence as by our words.

7. Plan to Expect and Then to Accept Failures

Our experience has been that for every "successful" program that we have run there have been at least two or three total flops. Perhaps the greatest failure many of us experience is that no one comes to our programs or that the half who do come the first week don't show the next time around.

All of our programs will be flops if we allow ourselves to get into the numbers syndrome. "We had forty young people at tonight's program. It must have been a great program." Statements like this are spoken all the time, and they are not necessarily true. In fact, many times large numbers militate against effective programming. Each one who comes should feel that he or she has had an opportunity to be heard and a chance to participate and that his or her presence was noticed.

It is instructive for ministers to youth to go through the Christian Testament on occasion and see the patience of Jesus with his disciples. In one sense he seems to have picked a group of complete losers. But then note the patience he shows. He knows that the fruit of his work with his disciples will appear only very slowly and gradually. In so many other aspects of his own life, Jesus shows the attitude we must have—of waiting for the time of fullness to come, of waiting until God's hand will bring good out of our efforts. Remembering "God's own good time" might be a helpful corrective to our passion for measurable objectives.

8. Plan to Learn by Doing

Learn to trust in your own creativity. Often it is so easy to simply show a filmstrip or slavishly follow a text. All of us have a tremendous amount of untapped creativity—creativity that could be employed in program planning. The most effective medium in religious education is the medium of the person. Each of us, young and old, has a wealth of religious experiences that are part of our lives—experiences that, when shared, become a powerful religious education tool. All of us love stories, and the greatest story that we have to tell is the story of our relationship with God.

Another way of using the person as a medium is through the use of skits or dramatization. Skits based upon the Scriptures or upon simple themes such as courage, hope, or faith could well be employed by religious educators. Involving the young people in participatory education gives them the chance to use their own creativity and their own religious experiences as a medium.

Summary

The goal of our effort with our young people is to lead them to adult faith. When people speak of the crisis of faith among youth, we often find ourselves thinking of the more serious crisis of faith among adults. It is questionable whether young people can come to and survive in faith without the aid of adult communities of living faith. This fact is being highlighted again and again in publications such as *Sharing the Light of Faith: National Catechetical Directory for Catholics of the United States* (Washington, DC: United States Catholic Conference, 1979), and John Westerhoff's book, *Will Our Children Have Faith?* (New York: Seabury Press, 1976). More and more it is becoming clear that we need adults who will share the secret of their faith with young people. Programs that avoid that aspect of youth ministry, in my opinion, are doomed to failure. Young people are hungry to experience the holy. Experience of the holy seems to be something that is handed on by people who themselves have experienced it. That's our challenge as adults excited about our treasure called Good News.

Essay 8

Developing Religion Curriculums in Catholic High Schools

Tom Zanzig

In the following essay, Tom Zanzig offers a sort of "examination of conscience" for religion departments in Catholic high schools, but one that could also be adapted to elementary schools. Centered on issues of curriculum, these questions could guide a religion department in coming to a more explicit consensus about their goals, replacing the implicit consensus, which says, "Well, this is how we do things, and I guess it is okay." An important aspect of the process suggested here involves the examination of assumptions about the nature of the study of religion in the Catholic high school.

This essay is reprinted from Ministry Management *6, no. 3 (Winona, MN: Saint Mary's Press, 1986), by permission of the publisher.*

During the past few years, I have spent considerable time reflecting on the kinds of principles that might guide us as we attempt to develop religion curriculums, both in schools and in parishes, that reflect the following characteristics:

- theological integrity
- sensitivity to the developmental patterns of adolescents
- recognition of both the opportunities and the limitations experienced in the parish and the school settings

Yet this essay is not an attempt to simply share the results of my own thinking about the development of religion curriculums. Rather, I want to stimulate *your* reflection or discussion with members of the religion faculty at your school about this important dimension of the total ministry of the Catholic high school. The essay presents two separate but related approaches to this issue:

- a series of six questions for reflection and discussion, each suggesting a principle of design, intended to help us focus on our current religion curriculums; and

- a process that a religion faculty may wish to follow in designing a new — or perhaps simply a revised — religion curriculum that more clearly expresses the school's desired goals, content, and approaches in religious education.

Questions for Reflection and Discussion

1. Does our religion curriculum provide a clear, sequential, and integrated presentation of the essential content of the Christian Story and Vision?

This question is clearly loaded and deserves some elaboration. Implicit in the question are a number of my personal convictions about curriculum development. In and of themselves, these convictions warrant some discussion, if not debate:

a. There is a body of information about our Catholic faith that is not arbitrary, and this information should be included in any curriculum that strives for theological integrity.

b. The curriculum's content should unfold in a logical way, that is, with concepts in one course building in a sequential way upon concepts previously learned by the students.

c. The entire curriculum should have some unifying principle, a clearly identified and recognizable "integrating thread" that weaves and connects the curriculum's courses into a reasonable whole.

   As suggested, all of the above convictions are open to some debate. What they refer to and critique is a far too common situation: A school's religion curriculum has been allowed to simply evolve in a haphazard and, at times, even contradictory way over the years. The resulting "curriculum" is a series of courses with no apparent relationship to one another. Such a result will come about, for example, if courses are randomly incorporated into the curriculum purely on the basis of the experience or the biases of individual teachers. The answer to a question of why a particular course is part of the curriculum in such a school is that "at one time we had a teacher who was 'into' that topic." But the integrity of the curriculum can also be violated through omission rather than commission. That is, at times a central dimension of the Christian message might be avoided or eliminated because "we have no teacher able or willing to teach it." Neither including nor omitting courses purely on the basis of the experience or interests of the teachers is acceptable if one of the characteristics we seek in our religion curriculums is theological integrity.

   A related point should be raised here. There is no one, universal "integrating thread" that should always be present in every religion curriculum.

If such unanimity across schools and religion faculties were possible or even desirable, there would be only one acceptable design for a religion curriculum. Such is clearly not the case. By way of example: For quite some time the integrating principle in many religion curriculums was the theme of *salvation history*. Commitment to this approach led many schools to offer a course on the Jewish Scriptures to freshmen; the rationale for this was that all of salvation history could only be understood in light of the religious history of the Jews. However, more recently, an integrating principle in religion curriculums has been our emerging understanding of the *religious and faith development of adolescents*. Advocates of this approach base their curriculum designs on the evolving capacity of young people to understand and personally appropriate the content and meaning of Christian faith. Both approaches, as well as others, can be supported. The point is that a school should be able to identify what it is that integrates its religion courses into a reasonable curriculum. Can your religion faculty do that?

2. Does our religion curriculum consider and reflect what we know about the religious and faith development of adolescents?

I will readily admit that this question demonstrates my own bias toward sensitivity to student needs and abilities as a major integrating principle for developing a curriculum. My understanding of learning theory leads me to the strong conviction that failure to take into account the developmental characteristics of the potential learners virtually guarantees failure in the attempt to teach anything, religion included. This is not to suggest, in the context of our comments above, that material such as the Jewish Scriptures cannot be taught to freshmen (though I do have my reservations on that point). The thrust of this principle is, however, that whatever we choose to teach at whatever grade level, the needs and the abilities of the students should dictate at least how we teach the material. If a teacher is seeking a text for teaching the Jewish Scriptures, he or she should not look for a text that simply covers the material adequately. The text must also be attuned to the starting point of the students with whom it will be used. Think about each one of your existing courses at each grade level: do the content and the processes incorporated into each course reflect a real sensitivity to the starting point of the students at that level of their development?

3. In our curriculum, does the learning of concepts take precedence over the learning of facts?

It is unfortunate that religion, like history, can be taught by having students simply memorize information, with little concern for whether or not they truly recognize and understand the significance and meaning of the concepts often hidden behind the information. This fact-oriented approach is far less likely to happen in the teaching of mathematics or the sciences; in those cases, the student's failure to understand one concept quickly shows up in the failure to understand a subsequent and dependent concept.

In the teaching of religion, though, we have to guard against the ease with which students can move from one course to another with little comprehension of the material presented. Methods for both the presentation of material and the testing of student understanding should be sensitive to this reality. For example, a lecture method of presentation followed by testing to determine if the students simply listened well—that is, whether they can give back the information as it was presented—tends to provide facts to the students, promotes little real learning. Group processes, personal reflection, open discussion, and approaches to testing that require more reflection than memorization (e.g., essay questions or the keeping of a journal) will lead to more effective learning of the theological content. Do the methods incorporated into your various religion courses foster learning rather than memorizing?

4. Are our students allowed, and even occasionally encouraged, to question, doubt, argue against, and perhaps even temporarily reject what is being taught, without fear of reprisal?

This question clearly deserves more discussion than I can give it here, so much so that I was tempted to avoid including it in this essay. But I believe the question is simply too important to neglect. We have come to realize that the struggle to achieve maturity of faith nearly always demands that individuals experience what John Westerhoff calls "searching faith." The essential task of that search is for individuals to reevaluate their inherited religious beliefs, traditions, and practices in light of their increased maturity. At some point, then, they freely choose whether or not to personally appropriate those culturally imposed religious realities into their own identities. At times this process can be very difficult, leading some individuals to a "crisis of faith"; for others the process can be relatively pain-free. In either case, the process appears to be essential to our growth as Christians. Does your religion curriculum help or hinder students in their journeys through "searching faith"?

5. Does our curriculum unfold in such a way that the students are prepared to assume personal responsibility for their continuing faith development beyond high school?

This question raises a number of related issues, among them the ultimate goals that we seek with our religion curriculum, our methodologies, and the skills we attempt to provide our students. Further questions may help us to more clearly focus on our ultimate goals: What kind of world will our students confront as they leave high school, and does their experience in our school provide them with the tools they will need to deal with that world as maturing Christians? These are tough questions, to be sure, but ones that get right to the heart of our efforts as religious educators of adolescents. Consider some others: Does our curriculum develop within the students a clear sense of their Catholic identity—one that is rooted firmly in an understanding of the Gospel of Jesus as it has come to be known and proclaimed within our Catholic tradition? Are our students learning how to pray? Can they find their way around the Scriptures, and can they interpret those Scriptures (to a reasonable extent), using acceptable approaches to biblical interpretation? Can our students make moral decisions that are grounded not in legalism but in a sound understanding of the values of Jesus? If we can answer such questions in the affirmative, we are on the right track. If not, perhaps we must reevaluate our entire curriculum, as well as the total life of the school— which brings us to our last question.

6. **Is our religion curriculum understood within the context of the total life of the school community, so that it both speaks to and is enhanced by the other dimensions of school life?**

This question relates to the discussion of "campus ministry," that is, the implementation of a vision of total youth ministry within the Catholic school setting. Again, the limitations of space here preclude a lengthy discussion of this very important factor in our discussion of religious education in the Catholic high school. Suffice it to say that the attainment of the results implicit in question 5 above would seem to demand a commitment to a philosophy of campus ministry in the high school. Skills cannot simply be taught in classes; we learn what it means to live as Christians by doing it, not simply talking about it. Opportunities to engage in prayer, liturgical celebrations, retreats, service on behalf of peace and justice, peer ministry, and so on, are all vital to the adolescents' growth as Christians. On its own, a religion curriculum cannot lead students to Christian maturity, regardless of how well planned and implemented the curriculum is. Its primary task is to shed intellectual light on the realities of our faith. But these realities must be experienced in other areas of our lives—in relationships with family and peers, within our own personal experiences of the presence of God in our lives, within the context of communal worship, and more.

A Process for Developing a Religion Curriculum

The process given on pages 126–127 is intended to be only suggestive; the exercise can be adapted in a wide variety of ways. It can be used as a discussion activity or, perhaps, as a yearlong project to be undertaken by the school's religion department.

Catholic High School Religious Education:
A Process for Developing a Curriculum

In the left-hand column are listed twelve basic themes that could be included in a curriculum of religious education for adolescents. To develop a curriculum for your school, or to evaluate the present one, join with your religion department faculty — and perhaps other interested parties — in following this process:

1. In column 1, rank order the curriculum components listed, in terms of their *doctrinal or theological importance,* writing 1 for the most important theme, 2 for the second most important, and so on, up to 12 for the theme that you think is the least important from a theological point of view.
2. In column 2, rank order the themes in terms of your sense of their *importance from the students' perspective.* That is, which themes do you think the students will be most interested in or attracted to?
3. In column 3, put a check mark (ν) across from the themes or topics for which you are sure you can find a *qualified* teacher.
4. In column 4, based on all your responses in the first three columns, and weighting their values according to your own theological and educational convictions, put an *X* across from all those *topics you definitely want* to include in your curriculum.
5. Finally, in column 5, organize your selected topics (from column 4) in terms of their *preferred sequence* in your curriculum. That is, write 1 across from the topic you wish to treat first in sequence, 2 across from the topic you wish to treat second in sequence, and so on, to your last topic, which presumedly would conclude your curriculum in the senior year.

	1	2	3	4	5
Sacraments and liturgy					
Prayer (communal and personal)					
Morality					
Comparative religions					
Survey of basic doctrine					
Death and dying					
Adolescent development and faith					
Christology					
Justice and peace					
Christian lifestyles (e.g., marriage)					
Church and/or church history					
Scripture					

Additional Thoughts on the Process
for Developing a Religion Curriculum

- Each step of the process should be completed first by the individual participants in the activity. After a given step is completed individually, attempt to arrive at group consensus on that point.

- What constitutes "doctrinal or theological importance" in the first step of the process is clearly subject to much debate and discussion. That is precisely the intent of the process—to surface such convictions on the part of the faculty members and to strive for some consensus. If the teachers are not in harmony on this basic point, the entire curriculum is weakened.

- The second step of the process involves assessing the needs and interests of the students regarding curriculum choices. This can be approached in a variety of ways, depending on how far you want to carry the process. In an abbreviated version, for example, the teachers might simply project how they think the students would respond. In a more extended approach, the students might actually be surveyed, using any one of a number of survey techniques.

- Regarding the students' responses, it is not implied here that the school should automatically include those subjects that the students want, or that courses that attract little student interest should be eliminated from consideration. Rather, the intent of assessing the students' perspective is to include that as *one factor* in determining not just *what* but, perhaps more importantly, *how* certain subjects will be taught.

- Regarding the third step of the process, it was stated earlier that the availability of a qualified teacher should not be the sole determinant of whether or not a course is included or excluded. This availability will certainly, however, have an impact on planning. If a course is clearly desired but no teacher is available, that reality will influence future hiring decisions. Or more likely, it will point to the need to provide opportunity for further education or training to current staff members to enable them to handle the desired course material.

Essay 9

Understanding the Weekend Format

Michael Warren

Originally I wrote the following essay to encourage those who looked with misgiving on weekends of Christian living to take another look and consider the very positive aspects of these weekends. By putting these weekends into the broader context of developing trends in catechetical ministry, I hoped that those running such weekends would see that they were not engaged in a fad. Thus the context for the essay was a time in which there was considerable criticism of these weekends by those who feared what they called "emotionalism," and the clear purpose of the essay was encouragement.

I continue to stand by the essay in those two purposes. However, in recent years I have become concerned about the lack of change and evolution in these weekends and even more so about their slight concern for other catechetical matters, particularly social justice issues. I have set forth these questions in the article "Youth Ministry: Further Dimensions of the Weekend Retreat," Origins *14, no. 6 (21 June 1984): 90–96.*

This essay is reprinted from Youth Ministry: A Book of Readings, *ed. Michael Warren (New York: Paulist Press, 1977), pages 141–151.*

Chroniclers of the catechetical scene in the United States during the 1960s and 1970s will have to note the dramatic growth of the weekend retreat as a specially useful format for the development of faith. My own relationship with these team-centered weekends has been a happy one, in spite of difficulties at the beginning. In 1964, when Frs. Douglas Brown and James Tugwood of Brooklyn began the Christian Awakening program for young people, their radical move away from the silent, monastic-type retreats so common in Catholic high schools caused some consternation. Skeptics told them they were engaging in faddism and were developing a program certain to fizzle fast. However, just the opposite has happened. That program and others like it have been growing steadily ever since those early years. Moreover, in my own development, I now see that working on these weekends has, more than any other single factor, shaped my own understanding of the tasks of adolescent catechesis.

My purpose here is threefold: to put these youth retreats, which I prefer to call "Christian experience programs," into the context of the current situation of adolescent catechesis in the United States; to give some reasons for the popularity and success of these programs at the present time; and to reflect on some of the problem areas that have surfaced in this important aspect of youth ministry.

The Situation of Adolescent Catechesis

In the recent past, adolescent catechesis has fallen on hard times. A few years ago the Diocese of Cleveland published ten-year statistics on CCD attendance by young people, figures that many found to be representative of what was happening in dioceses far from Ohio. In 1964, 31 percent of Cleveland adolescents in grades 9–12 were in CCD programs, 33 percent were in Catholic high schools, and 36 percent were involved in no catechetical programs at all. In 1973, those in Catholic high schools had fallen from 33 percent to 21 percent, those in CCD programs had fallen from 31 percent to 16 percent, and those in no catechetical programs of any kind had jumped from 36 percent to a whopping 63 percent.

A survey conducted by the Department of Education at the United States Catholic Conference in 1974 showed that the Cleveland statistics were generally valid for the entire country. Almost all respondents to the survey questionnaire noted that attendance at catechetical programs for young people was down. However, while acknowledging serious problems and even widespread discouragement in their dioceses, more than half the respondents saw signs of hope in two developments. One of these was the gradual emergence of a comprehensive ministry to youth. The other was the growth of the youth retreat movement.

Retreats: Christian Experience Weekends

Without exception, where retreat-type programs were mentioned by respondents to the USCC survey, they were given as examples of successful programs. These programs have a variety of names and formats. The most common ones mentioned were Search and Teens Encounter Christ (TEC). Since young people themselves are members of retreat teams in many dioceses, several respondents saw the retreat movement, at least in part, as a ministry of youth to youth. One might conclude that in some areas retreats are no longer looked on as adjunct elements in catechetical work but as core elements in youth catechesis.

What this USCC questionnaire tells me is that, far from being a fad for 1964, retreat-type programs for youth are more and more answering a need expressed by young people. These programs are growing all over the country. More and more dioceses are getting involved in one or another type of Christian experience weekend.

Information from the written questionnaires was backed up in regional meetings held in 1975 with representatives from more than 150 dioceses. One of the items on the agenda for those meetings was the following question: What kinds of catechetical programs for adolescents have been most successful in your diocese? Overwhelmingly, the programs offering the greatest satisfaction and success in dioceses represented at the meetings were those that had evolved out of a retreat model. These programs currently have a variety of formats, especially of weekend formats. In many cases the basic weekend program has been adapted to two-day, one-day, or shorter time segments more suitable for young teenagers.

That summarizes the current situation of youth catechesis as I have been able to determine it. The summary underlines the important place of Christian experience programs in current work with young people. But why are these weekend programs so successful? Is it possible to account for the growing success of these programs at the very time when other attempts to work with youth are experiencing growing failure? I believe it is possible. As I see it, the success of these programs stems from the solid theological and cultural presuppositions on which they are based. Let us examine these somewhat briefly.

Search, Teens Encounter Christ, Christian Awakening, and COR weekends—all these programs and those similar to them rest on a theological presupposition that Jesus is present in the life of each person. What happens in the process of conversion is that a person recognizes that the Christian message is the answer to one's own deepest hopes and longings. When one discovers that the Christian mystery makes sense of the absurdity of life, then one is ripe either for conversion or for another step in one's response to that mystery. These programs have great confidence in the power of the Gospel to speak even to those who profess to be nonbelievers.

Actually these Christian experience programs affirm something Karl Rahner wrote several years ago:

> Christianity has to grow from its own principle of life. Of course, it also has to be transmitted to men from outside. But it would be a false understanding of what preaching is, whether by the authoritative *magisterium* or the pastor in his official work, to suppose that it can or should transmit Christianity to a man as though he were, at best, an empty hollow space ready and waiting

for it, or a schoolboy learning of Australia for the first time in a geography lesson. The grace of God has always been there ahead of our preaching; a man is always in a true sense a Christian already when we begin to commend Christianity to him. For he is a man, already included in God's general will for salvation, redeemed by Christ, with grace already living and working in his innermost heart at least as the proffered possibility of supernatural action. Hence, our preaching is not really an indoctrination with something alien from outside but the awakening of something within, as yet not understood but nevertheless really present; something that is not, of course, to be misunderstood in the modernist sense as a natural religious need in the human subconscious, but which is a grace of God.

Any approach to a man in words from outside, if it is Christian, is always an appeal to God who is already speaking by grace within him and being in some sense heard; any communication of Christianity is always a communication of what is already there, alive, within a man. And if it often seems to be otherwise, if people get the impression that we are preaching a very extraordinary, remote doctrine, intelligible only to experts, which no normal man could find interesting unless he stopped being an ordinary man, it is not because Christianity is really like this but because we have not rightly understood it. ("The Significance of the Individual Member," *The Christian Commitment* [New York: Sheed and Ward, 1963], pp. 102–103)

What Rahner describes as the process of leading the individual to faith could easily be applied to the group process on our weekends. What happens so often is that the group that begins as a more or less loose gathering grows to become a dynamic community of faith. The Gospel ceases to be a word from outside the group's life and becomes rather a word reflecting the inner life of the group itself. I myself have seen intense excitement generated by the scriptural readings at Mass, when those present recognized that their own group experience authenticated the truth of the Gospel. I like to call communal experiences like these "Emmaus experiences" because, like the disciples in Luke's account, the group members recognize that Jesus has been present in their midst, even though they only vaguely realized it at the time.

As almost a digression, I would like to point out that the kind of doctrinal understandings attained through such experiences of a community of faith tend to be well integrated and profound, and we should not apologize for them. What we are doing is getting back to the practice of the early Church, where it was presumed that the most effective grasp of the Christian message could be gotten from the actual life of the community of believers. We must avoid the mistake of categorizing these weekends as experiences of community, as if they were not at the same time experiences of doctrinal realities of our faith. One diocese I know of has a policy of making the Search weekend available to all its young people as an experience of community. In addition, each young person must attend twenty-five hours of doctrinal instruction. What bothers me about such a policy is that it over-compartmentalizes Search as an experience of community. Community and doctrine are not so neatly separate, especially in a well-run weekend of Christian living. That policy is fine so long as we recognize that the weekend itself is an experience of doctrinal realities, but as a much more direct and possibly vital way of learning them than by merely studying them in the abstract. As I see it, these weekends provide the best contexts for sound doctrinal instruction. But more about this aspect later.

There are cultural reasons why these programs are succeeding at a time of catechetical malaise. First, these programs deal with the problem of the "statuslessness" of youth. Young people are at a point in life where they feel capable of shouldering responsibilities but at the same time find themselves excluded from having any real say in the life of their churches. As a result they drop out. At least such is one of the conclusions reached by Merton Strommen in *A Study of Generations,* his study of Lutheran church members.

Strommen found that for most youth there is a sense of being on the outside of their congregation's interests and life. Over half the youth he surveyed (aged fifteen to twenty-three) felt that older people in the congregation were suspicious of them. They also felt that they had no influence on the decisions being made by the congregation. In other words, the institutional life of the congregation has evolved in such a way that leadership and influence are in the hands of people over thirty. Up to one-half of the youth agree that "hardly anyone in the congregation would miss me if I stopped going." Strommen says, "We found that the strongest predictor of youth's attitude toward his church is how well he fits in with groups in his congregation. The acceptance that he feels is the best indication of how he will evaluate his congregation."

Programs like Search are dealing directly with this problem of the "statuslessness" of young people. Such programs provide them with a communal life within which they have an indispensable role. These programs offer the young an opportunity to develop their own ministry to their peers and beyond their peers. It is no wonder young people who are looking to be taken seriously are solidly committed to these programs that put them into a central role. I suspect that in some parts of the country, Christian experience programs are forcing parish CCD programs to make much greater use of the young people themselves in planning and running weekly CCD sessions. As far as I can determine, where such participation is encouraged, CCD is in pretty good shape.

A second cultural reason why Christian experience programs are succeeding is that they provide the kind of ongoing dialogue needed for the maintenance of the process of conversion. In their book *The Social Construction of Reality* (New York: Doubleday, 1966), sociologists Peter Berger and Thomas Luckmann point out that the crucial part of the conversion process is not the actual moment of conversion but the ongoing process of main-taining the new (or renewed) worldview of the person converted. They hold that conversion involves a new way of approaching reality and the accep-tance of new values. The convert begins to inhabit a different universe of meaning. The maintenance of this new world is achieved through ongoing conversation and dialogue.

Most of the Christian experience programs I know about encourage those who have been on one weekend to come back to others in one or another capacity. There is a whole system of renewal that many of us refer to as follow-up. Reunions, second-level weekends, and training programs are all means by which to assist the young in maintaining and even growing beyond their original Christian experience weekend. Further, these programs foster a network of relationships within which conversation about faith can be main-tained. All of us have to shoulder the burden of what can happen if we fail to make provision for these follow-up programs: the final state of the young people may be worse and more disillusioned than their original state.

Obviously I feel very strongly about the value of these programs, a value that is becoming obvious to more and more people each year. As I see things developing, these programs are going to become even more important in the future than they are today. As a way of helping us face the future and begin to improve our programs, I'd like to suggest the following six aspects of the programs for greater attention and for some improvement:

1. The first aspect needing continued attention is the Christ-centeredness of our programs. Being together for a weekend in an atmosphere of love and caring would most probably produce a keen sense of community among the participants. Such a community would probably also be a community of faith, that is, of faith in oneself and in one another. As leaders of our programs, we want—must have—that kind of root human faith, but I think we must actively pursue a further goal of becoming a community of faith in Christ. To pursue such a goal means that the directors and the team members (including young people on the team) must have a keen sense of the power and the presence of the Lord in their own lives and in their work with youth. To do less is to be inauthentic. It is to mask the Christ-centeredness of our motivation and to settle for a weekend of communication skills or group therapy. My point is that we know there is more. Here I go along with Rahner in his assertion that the greatest of gifts to the human person is that of being consciously Christian.

I realize that to keep our programs Christ-centered demands that in fact our motivation and lives be actually centered on Jesus. Yes, that is the hard part about catechesis. There is no way to pass on the Gospel credibly to others—to pass it on as Good News—except as it has meant something in our own personal lives. Nobody wants a disembodied Gospel; it is ridiculous, unbelievable, incredible, uncredible. The hard part of catechesis for all of us is that whether we like it or not, we ourselves must somehow embody deep faith in Christ. The Gospel becomes most real when it is inscribed in a life and not just in a book. Especially with our young team members we must make our faith in Christ very explicit so they will be encouraged to make their own faith explicit.

2. Second, we have to pay special attention to the freedom-centeredness of our programs. If we are not careful, they can easily become manipulative. I think adult leaders in these programs should be preoccupied with freedom. Some weekends can be so high-powered, especially when the group or communal process gets rolling, that some individuals can be effectively denied a chance to disagree or perceive differently. Not all the kids are at the same place when they come; why should we expect them all to be at the same place when they leave? Not even all the team members can be expected to be at the same place.

In my experience, it is the young team members who must be reminded again and again about the issue of freedom. They have to be taught to reverence the rhythm of growth in individual lives. Older, more experienced team members probably have less trouble with this matter. However, I have met many young team members who are so concerned about the success of the weekend that they find it difficult to tolerate differences or the person who won't go along. The whole area of freedom is a matter we adults must be right on top of during our weekends. If at the start we have in our minds some sort of preset response we expect from each youngster, then we are already off on the wrong foot.

3. Third, I'd like to call attention to the need for good adult input on our weekends. Some may disagree with this idea, especially since some Search programs are exclusively peer-to-peer. However, I myself believe that such weekends are excellent opportunities to make simple and clear presentations of core aspects of the Christian mystery. And I believe that these matters should be presented by well-qualified and well-prepared adults. I am not speaking here of abstract truths. I'm speaking of presentations dominated by witness and filled with the kind of personal examples we have all found so effective in these programs.

Let me restate this point. I do not believe that all the presentations on a Christian experience weekend should be given by team members who are young people themselves. Possibly two-thirds of the formal presentations should be given by young people, with the remaining third given by adults who have worked out, with help from appropriate consultants, clear and personal explanations of central aspects of the Christian message. Our weekends are the right time to give such input, when it can be discussed and then later integrated into worship and other activities. Nor should such presentations be merely pasted onto a weekend experience. They must be integral, pointing to the significance of what all are experiencing on the weekend.

In this connection, it seems crucial that all presentations given by young team members should be reviewed beforehand by members of the team, especially by the adult members. Otherwise we run the danger of having glib, carelessly prepared team members. I know this matter requires time. However, the alternative is a poorly run program.

4. A fourth area for consideration is that of evaluation. Evaluation is becoming more and more an accepted part of modern life. Evaluation, long an accepted practice in industry and education, is becoming more important in the other professions. It is possible that many of us have had firsthand experiences of the usefulness of the regional educational association's evaluation of a school. Such an evaluation forces all in the school to sharpen up their performance and face up to hidden weaknesses. It might be helpful if we made it our business to have outsiders come in once a year to one of our programs and evaluate it according to criteria agreed upon beforehand. It might be ideal if the evaluators were connected with an entirely different kind of program: for example, we might have someone from a TEC program evaluate Search in our diocese. At any rate, we can find Search evaluators from the Search program in a neighboring diocese. In my experience, these programs can be so satisfying or even exhilarating to the adult leaders that we can easily grow complacent and blind to the need for our programs to grow and improve.

5. Fifth, I see a need for some kind of sharing among leaders of the different Christian experience models. The whole youth retreat movement appears to me to be growing rapidly. The leaders should be getting together, sharing organizational problems, and swapping ideas for new developments. Exactly how much sharing ought to take place, I am not certain. I feel certain, however, that such sharing will never take place without (a) the direction of talented leadership and (b) the careful avoidance of rivalry, jealousy, and suspicion. The healthiest sign of the youth retreat movement, in my opinion, is exactly the kind of variety that has grown up in these programs throughout this country. Our motto must be Encourage All Initiatives. There are so many young people needing our services that no one program, be it Search or TEC or COR or Christian Awakening, can take care of them all. Search is not the last word in Christian experience programs. There is no last word. All our programs should be seen as beginnings. In addition, the true sign of the professional is his or her respect for fellow professionals and eagerness to learn from them. So in these kinds of programs you might want to discuss a broader kind of sharing.

6. Finally, let us give more attention to the parents of our young people. I think we should be in touch with them and make ourselves available to them. Obviously we have only limited time and we can't do everything. It is just that this may be the one thing we cannot afford to leave undone. Let the young people plan the program for parents and then run it. We all know stories about what happens when there is a clash in the home over Search. Such clashes are painful for all. I'm not certain they are always necessary. Sometimes the parents need a taste of the very kind of experience

the youth had on one of the weekends. Well, we may want to consider how to provide it for them.

In conclusion, all of us in this ministry have much cause for joy. Our work is making a difference in the lives of many young people. And, yes, we ourselves are making a difference in those lives. We can all imagine how much poorer our lives would have been if we had never had the chance to do this work. That's what we all have to rejoice over—that we have been called to a privileged ministry.

Essay 10

Christian Experience Weekends: The Role of the Director

Michael Warren

A majority of the young adults now seeking full-time ministry positions in various dioceses of this country have come to ministry not through the hothouse training programs of seminaries and novitiates, but rather through years of in-service apprenticeship on youth retreat teams. Through these teams they grew in their own sense of ministry and developed considerable skills for it. Often enough, in the background of this development are the people who direct these weekend programs. They are the ones responsible for nurturing the seeds of ministry within so many young people. Theirs has been the specially privileged role of being "ministers to the ministers."

The following article speaks directly to those responsible for the direction of these weekend programs. Even though some of the material in this article overlaps with that in the previous piece on the weekend format, it is included here because it attempts to summarize some of the principles and caveats that have been shared with the writer over a period of years by dozens of directors of such programs. The true value of these weekend programs for any diocese goes far beyond their value for a particular group of young people participating in a weekend program. That value lies, rather, in the success of such programs in developing the leadership needed for authentic ministry in today's Church.

This essay is reprinted from Youth Ministry: A Book of Readings, *ed. Michael Warren (New York: Paulist Press, 1977), pages 154–161.*

Christian experience programs are continuing to develop in the United States, as is evidenced by the two well-designed faith experience weekends in the high school catechetical program of the Green Bay Plan and by the spread of older programs like Search, Teens Encounter Christ (TEC), and Christian Awakening of the Diocese of Brooklyn. As Christian experience programs continue to expand, a key person continues to be the director of these

weekends. In this article, I want to focus especially on this role while doing the following:
1. outlining the characteristics of these programs, using as one model, the Brooklyn-based Christian Awakening program;
2. showing that these programs are in accord with the thrust of modern catechetical theory; and
3. treating five special problems that should concern a youth director in developing new programs.

What is a Christian experience program? Actually *Christian experience program* is an umbrella expression used to cover a wide variety of programs that have sprung up over the past ten years. They follow naturally from developments in personalist psychology, from communications theory, and from pastoral efforts like the Cursillo. Although these programs can be of a single day's or even of only several hours' duration, most of them resemble retreats. They involve a substantial period of time spent in a group considering matters of personal faith development. Unlike retreats of old, the talks are not given by any one person; instead the program is run by a team, often comprised of both adults and teenagers. Even though these programs make use of formal presentations or talks, the emphasis is rather on activity, on discussion and interaction among those making the program. The topics of these presentations and discussions might include the meaning of our relationship to the Trinity (grace), the role of the sacraments in Christian life, the place of prayer, the functions of Christian leadership, obstacles to God's friendship, and the role of the community in Christian living. Even though all talks tend to be of a high caliber theologically, emphasis is on witness, that is, on the Christian mystery as it is revealed in the living document of a person's life. Emphasis is also on the community or group and on concrete learning rather than on some master or teacher and on vertically imposed abstractions.

In the Christian education of the young, I believe that these programs are the way of the future. The reasons are numerous.

Young people are painfully conscious of the need for relationship, and these programs meet their need.

These programs are well suited to the nature of the Christian message. In the early Church, groups met to talk over "the events of recent days" and in so doing, came to discover the Risen Lord in their midst.

These programs are successful at a time when other catechetical efforts with the young are falling apart at the seams, both on this continent and in Europe.

The programs fit in with recent catechetical theory, especially as it has been developing since 1960.

Four dominant themes in modern catechetical theory are reflected in Christian experience programs. These are (1) the centrality of the group,

(2) the importance of context, (3) the principle of adaptation, and (4) the centrality of Christ.

Centrality of the Group

The *General Catechetical Directory* (*GCD*) states, "For adolescents and young adults, the group must be considered a vital necessity. In a group, the adolescent or the young adult comes to know himself [or herself] and finds support and stimulation" (no. 76). The conclusions of the 1971 International Catechetical Congress held in Rome also emphasize the importance of groups. This is a rather new emphasis. All of us can think back to youth retreats that set the participants in neat rows of pews for talks, before sending them out alone and in silence to reflect on what they heard. At the same time, meals in silence attempted to keep the group physically together while stifling group interaction. Today, however, stress is placed on tapping the dynamic of the group, encouraging it to function in a healthy and open way. We have finally come to trust groups and the healing and educative value of group learning.

In most programs, the basic principle in operation is this: a group influences a group. Thus the team members themselves come together prior to the weekend for meetings totaling six to eight hours so that they can form a group or community of prayer, reflection, and work. Together they attempt to come to agreement on their common goals in serving the people who will be participating in the weekend program for the first time.

During the weekend itself the team attempts to be seen as a community of faith, prayer, and service to others. The participants are broken into several stable subgroups, and two team members are assigned to each of these. Since the group itself is central, these team members do not function as discussion leaders but rather strive to function as fully as possible as peer group members.

This process places the youth director in a new role where authority is more horizontal than vertical, for the director is not the only person in the group knowledgeable about matters of faith. The director should try to practice "leadership of the closed mouth" rather than make pronouncements from "on high." Far from being the star of the weekend, he or she must earn the privilege of entering into the total group or any subgroup. Such a role demands particularly good balance and group sense. I presume that not all diocesan youth directors can function in such a role; thus the weekend director may very well be different from the diocesan director. The diocesan director may see his or her job as identifying personnel who can function with this crucial sort of horizontal leadership.

Importance of Context

In our past catechetical efforts, we have not always recognized the importance of the context in which learning takes place. We have been largely
unaware that all learning takes place in situations. All learning is contextual.
The *GCD* states, "They (catechists) are responsible for choosing and creating
suitable conditions which are necessary for the Christian message to be sought,
accepted, and more profoundly investigated" (no. 71).

In a Christian experience program, much attention is given to atmosphere
and environment. This is because learning does not come from any one person's word but more from the total context of openness, freedom, care, and
service. The youth director and the team foster the climate of openness chiefly
by listening and by attuning themselves to the individuals in subgroups. If
freedom is to be another characteristic of these programs, the youth director
will have to encourage teen team members to resist any tendency to exert
pressure on the participants that might impair the freedom needed for real
growth. Finally, the team needs to show in subtle and astonishing ways the
same sort of delicate caring and service that mark Christ's washing of his
disciples' feet. Eventually, the team creates a climate of openness and receptivity in which participants can relax enough to consider the most important
issues of their lives.

Principle of Adaptation

Central to current catechetical thought is the principle of adaptation: The
Christian mystery is radically a message for human persons, a source of joy
for them, if only it is communicated so as to shed light on their experience.
The possible adaptations of the message are as numerous as are the varied
situations and experiences of persons. Among the most effective catechesis
I have seen has been the carefully worked out presentations made to young
people on these weekends—at times by young persons close to their own age.

This principle of adaptation is especially seen in the use of language.
The message is given in language that young people can understand. But
there is another angle to the question of language, and here the director's
role is a crucial and ticklish one. Because these programs are based on a
principle of dialogue, they attempt to allow faith to find its own language.
When that happens one can expect to hear young people speak excitedly of
the Christian mystery in their own words. What I see going on in these situations is something profoundly significant; it is faith seeking a language. I
believe that most young people have faith, but they do not possess the words
with which to articulate that faith. In these programs young people try to
define a new language for faith.

Centrality of Christ

In general, my measure of the worth of a Christian experience program is this: How Christ-centered is it? Catechesis has launched its renewal precisely on the issue of centering the message in the person of Jesus Christ, and not on dissected creed, code, or cult. "What we preach is Christ and him crucified." Unfortunately we all have that very human tendency to put first things fifth or ninth or to neglect them altogether. We face this same danger in our catechetical programs. We can get caught up in our group dynamics or with our theology and somehow lose focus on Christ. I believe that conscious allegiance to Jesus Christ is one of the great gifts of human existence, and the youth directors must ask themselves if they are comfortable and willing to share their own faith openly with others.

In sharing our faith in Christ, it is not a question of giving participants the impression that we have arrived. We can be honest in admitting that we are in the process of renewing our faith search again and again. And as happens in so many resurrection accounts from the Christian Testament, the Lord appears to those who puzzle over him or search for him. Hopefully one of the outcomes of a Christian experience program will be a deep understanding of the presence of the Risen Lord in the midst of a community of faith.

Even though these Christian experience programs are quite in line with current catechetical thinking, they are not without problems and dangers. Let us look at five of these problems. The first is the lack of a critical sense. It is all too easy in such programs to become self-satisfied with our efforts because they seem to have such an impact on those they serve. Yet, if these programs are to be truly effective, they must be continually evaluated with such questions as these: Was the team careful to respect the freedom of those making the retreat program? Were the talks well prepared? Did the team work well together? Was the weekend Christ-centered? Was the program concerned about the next step for the participants, that is, carrying over some of what they learned into their everyday lives? Was an opportunity offered for individual counseling with a qualified adult?

A second problem in these programs is the lack of follow-up. Sometimes a weekend experience can help youngsters to become more deeply conscious of their own feelings and thoughts, but they scarcely have time to assimilate all they experience. They will need some kind of support if they are to stave off discouragement when they return home. Or sometimes a young person may have confided for the first time thoughts of suicide or homosexual fears. Such a person may need only a few more sessions of counseling, or he or she may need referral to a therapist. Follow-up is so important that it makes necessary this rule of thumb: If there is to be no follow-up, it would be better to have no program.

Tied to follow-up is the problem of preparation and training. As in good baseball, good ballet, good writing, good anything, the secret of success is careful preparation. There is no substitute for it, especially for teenaged team members. Any preparation takes time. That is why any director working with these programs must be ready and able to give the kind of time that is demanded.

A fourth problem is that of unrealistic expectations. The secret to achieving goals is to limit them. A weekend program is one experience in the total life of an individual. It does not have to accomplish everything—because it cannot. I do not want to deny that one of these programs can have a very significant influence on a person's life; I do want to deny that it is likely the influence will be total. We will let ourselves in for many unnecessary disappointments as youth directors if we do not understand realistically the limitations of our efforts.

The final problem is the one I am most concerned about. It is that of not being in touch with the parents of our young people who make these programs. I am not saying that in order to run experience-centered programs you have to take on the entire pastoral ministry of the Church. It is just that today more than ever before, we owe it to parents to keep them informed about what we are doing. For example, I should think that sometimes after a weekend experience, the young people should be invited to come with their parents to meet the directors of the program and hear from them a description of what the program was like. Perhaps the parents could be encouraged to participate in experience-centered programs for adults, such as the Cursillo or Marriage Encounter. I should think that having some adult laypeople, possibly parents, on a youth program would be most desirable. The point is that we are kidding ourselves if we think that the faith crisis today is most acute among the teenaged crowd. Crises of adult proportions are to be found among adults.

Whatever the risks and problems of attempting to run experience-centered programs, they are worth the effort; in fact the field is wide open for new, imaginative efforts along these lines and at many different levels. Experimental formats should be tried with junior high students, as well as with those of college age and with adults. Follow-up weekends of greater depth for those who have already been through one weekend are also needed. Whatever further developments are to come in this area, we can expect they will come from leaders who possess faith, vision, and a deep sense of care.

Essay 11

Effective Ministry to Youth
Merton P. Strommen

One of the leading American researchers of youth's attitudes is Lutheran sociologist Merton P. Strommen. The following section is excerpted from Strommen's book Five Cries of Youth, *a report of research done among more than seven thousand young people, representing a variety of Christian denominations and a sampling of nonchurched youth. The "cries of youth" heard by Strommen in his research are the cry of self-hatred, the cry of psychological orphans, the cry of social protest, the cry of the prejudiced, and the cry of the joyous. Though highly interpretative, Strommen's book is filled with insights valuable to parents and all others active in ministry to young people.*

The section presented here describes the attitude of effective leaders who work with young people and suggests some basic stances local parishes might take toward youth. Strommen's ideas could be the basis of a fruitful discussion among people concerned about youth in any of our Catholic parishes.

This essay is reprinted from Merton Strommen, Five Cries of Youth *(New York: Harper and Row, 1974), pages 118–126, by permission of the publisher.*

How Effective Leaders Approach Youth

How does one reach out in a helping relationship to youth?

The persons best qualified to answer this question are youth leaders who themselves excel in reaching out. In order to hear what they say, we first had to locate the cream of the crop.

Through a study conducted in 1970, we developed criteria for effective youth leaders. Once the criteria were ranked, we asked the heads of national youth organizations to nominate leaders of high-school youth who exemplify some of the highest ranked criteria.

Ninety-one youth leaders were named by the following groups: American and Southern Baptist (10); Roman Catholic (6); Christian Church (9); Church of God (9); Evangelical Covenant (7); Episcopal (4); American and Missouri Synod Lutheran (21); United Methodist (6); Greek Orthodox (2); United Presbyterian (1); and Young Life (16). The ninety-one workers then told, through questionnaires, why they intervene in the lives of youth, how they approach them, and what accounts for their effectiveness.

Motives

The first of three questions put to the workers was: Why do you intervene in the lives of young people—that is, what contribution do you feel that you can make to their lives?

As might be expected, over half the respondents cited religious motives: "I want to share my faith," "I can guide them to a full Christian commitment," and the like.

Virtually all, in some part of their free responses, used a desire to influence youth in directions consonant with the Christian way of life as their predominant motive. And this motive clearly arose out of love, concern, and profound respect for youth.

Many responses showed that the leaders were keenly sensitive to the autonomy of youth and committed to techniques which would not violate it. Thus, they did not speak of evangelizing youth, controlling their environment, supervising their behavior, preaching the gospel to them, or other tactics that might be interpreted as applying pressure. Instead they made statements like "I can listen," "I can communicate," "I can be a friend," "I can be a significant adult in their lives," and "I can share my happiness."

A number of insightful youth leaders also recognized that their motivation includes self-realization. "They contribute to my goals." "They keep me young." "I can learn from them." But there was no evidence of self-aggrandizement at the expense of youth, only self-fulfillment as a consequence of helping others develop their potential.

Methods

Three questions were directed to the skills exercised by successful church youth workers. The first question was: What ways of approaching youth have you found helpful? How do you get next to them? Responses revealed six groups of skills:

1. Building Relationships
- Knowing them—home life, school, friends
- Exhibiting deep, sensitive, personal concern for them
- Showing them courtesy
- Participating with them as an equal
- Showing appreciation for a job well done

- Helping them if they ask
- Sharing mutual experiences
- Sharing my own feelings about life

2. Being Genuine
- Being adult
- Speaking in my own vocabulary
- Being honest and open
- Stating my convictions while leaving freedom for theirs
- Boldly speaking out in radical situations
- Admitting I don't know all the answers
- Dealing with my own hang-ups first

3. Being Available
- Going to their events when adults are welcome
- Spending time with them and their friends
- Working and playing with them in various activities
- Taking kids to "away" games
- Picking up hitchhikers
- Inviting them to my home for dinner
- Initiating interviews

4. Showing Interest
- Remembering their names
- Learning about their world
- Being åble to speak their language
- Listening to their music
- Adopting their symbols—beads, long hair, beard
- Finding areas where I can be of help
- Making phone calls and letters re their accomplishments, interests

5. Communicating
- Talking to them every opportunity I get
- Slow, quiet listening; waiting for the chance to say some things
- Listening with the third ear for emotions
- One-to-one counseling

6. Leading
- Discovering and using their talents and interests
- Involving them in planning, decision-making, and executing activities
- Letting them find their own thing and do it
- Accepting their decisions
- Face them with the issues
- Holding unpopular positions which I think are best for them
- Giving them provocative, challenging books

- Offering them a host of options
- Presenting a better alternative by the way I live and act
- Getting them interested in trips, studies to benefit them
- Creating celebrations and experiences for free expressions
- Getting them to camps, retreats

The second question of this group, What are you doing to accomplish [your] purposes [with youth]? revealed three new groups of skills:

7. Teaching
- Training others to reach out on a one-to-one basis
- Training leaders to program "exposure events"
- Reeducating adults to helping roles with youth
- Teaching the Scriptures, presenting verbally and non-verbally the message of the love of Christ
- Teaching a class relating Bible, youth, and culture
- Personally confronting each youth with the claims of Christ
- Relating youth's ideas to Christian faith

8. Creating a Community
- Helping them to get to know each other
- Encouraging group awareness and sensitivity in everyday life
- Finding Christ in each other, in everyone we encounter, in everything we do
- Through involvement, make them aware of loneliness, deprivation, friendliness
- Helping forgiveness and acceptance to happen
- Developing teamwork among youth in their activities
- Trying to build a staff community

9. Encouraging Involvement
- Involving kids where they can grow, experience, relate, share— volunteer work, seminars, schools, inner city, community
- To Mexico yearly for service projects
- Getting young people into the establishment
- Creating opportunities for kids to think about, talk, act out their concerns
- Discussing issues and trying to do something about them

The final question was, If you were to describe the secret of your effectiveness, what are some of the ways of working with people that you have found effective? It elicited no skills beyond those already revealed, but some new illustrations emerged for number 8, Creating a Community: "developing groups who share at the deepest possible level" and "keeping the group open to friends of church youth."

Helping Youth into a Life of Faith

Research on Religious Development, a review of research literature on the religion of youth (1900–1969), established that adolescents who have direct personal experience of the presence of God differ from those who do not. Our study shows in what ways they differ: outlook on life, relations with people, motivation, and sense of moral responsibility. It demonstrates that relationships with God, man, and self are inextricably linked. This is why a personal faith is deemed important by those who have it; it is why a parent will ask, How do you help a son or daughter know a personal, caring God?

A fitting answer is given by leaders in Young Life, international youth organization, who underscore the necessity of first taking the time to establish a relationship of love and trust. Once an open and cordial relationship is established, then questions of ultimate significance begin to surface.

"I don't know what I would do if God didn't exist. But does he?"

"Why doesn't he make it easier for us to believe?"

The Searching Questions

It is natural for the adolescent to feel that his faith depends upon himself, that he has to "make it" with God. And so he asks, Am I good enough?

Assuming the negative answer, he concludes that "God is not interested in me." Added to this concern is youth's fear of losing the respect of admired adults. Some are embarrassed to admit to parent or pastor that they struggle with doubts and question some things they have been taught.

Mingled with these feelings is the wistful, unvoiced question, "How do I 'get' faith?"

When the Bible is quoted, its words become enmeshed in the quicksand of further doubt. "The Bible was written for people centuries ago. By what stretch of imagination can I assume that it speaks to me? How do I know that interpretations I make (or you make) are correct ones?"

How can the words of Scripture ever be windows through which one sees an invisible God?

Finally, because youth respond as total persons, illness, depression, fatigue, or the pressure of circumstances tend to increase their feelings of religious uncertainty.

Times of Reflection and Decision

Youth retreats, informal discussions in a home, and personal conversations provide choice occasions for helping young people think into their relationship with God and voice both their lonesomeness for God and their desire to flee him.

At times like these, young people, preoccupied with standards of right and wrong, come to recognize an issue deeper than the matter of sins, per se. It is the question of authority: Do I remain the captain of my ship, or do I acknowledge the love and authority of God who created me?

During times of reflection and decision, youth need the freedom to discuss the mystery of their rebellion and their proneness to go it alone. One can only encourage them to remain open to God's voice, allow times for listening, and take advantage of moments when he can be heard.

These are not times for a hard sell or for "thought-terminating cliches" which can force an artificial conversion that is mere acquiescence to a religious culture, without knowledge of the love and grace of God.

Youth need to understand that Christianity is a relationship with Christ, in which doubt is admissible because one relates to a person and not to a set of doctrines. Accepting a personal, caring God comes first; in coming to know him, one learns what is embodied in propositional truths.

When youth hear what God has done in the past and can do again for them, conversations about God become hope-inspiring occasions. Youth's attention shifts from themselves and their problems to the promises and possibilities of the Christian faith. The emptiness of a lonely life and the drawing power of love implicit in God's promise motivate them to enter God's possibilities as a child returns to his father's arms. In receiving a Savior, youth come to a personal transcendental experience with Jesus Christ.

A Supportive Congregation

A personal faith needs the sustaining power of a group. But what can give youth a sense of welcome and identification with his congregation?

Of the thirty-five possibilities tested, two were highly associated with positive, warm feelings toward one's congregation: the first, to feel that one fits in well with some group in the congregation; and the second, to feel inspired at worship services.

It is hard to overemphasize the identification youth feel with their congregation when they are secure in a small group. If the youth interact first even in discussion groups of twelve to fifteen people, they later find the freedom to share themselves in the larger group.

An enigma for youth is why gatherings to celebrate their faith, such as Sunday morning worship, are often dull. Many find inspiration totally lacking in this function of their church family.

Percentage Inspired by Local Worship Services
Ecumenical Sample
(N = 7,050)

	Percentage Saying Yes
A. Never inspired, only bored	11
B. No longer inspired, but I once was	11
C. Very often inspired	13
D. Quite often inspired	17
E. Sometimes inspired	32
F. Seldom inspired	15

Unlike adults, youth today are conscious not only of God's transcendence but also of his immanence. They look for more than a service that stresses his holiness, transcendence, and awesome greatness. They want more than the solemn beauty of a service where architecture, music, and liturgy create the sense of God's presence. Youth also want to worship the God who sits next to them in the fellowship of believers.

Youth want to worship a Christ, not only divine but also human, who is a part of rhythm, melody, and ordinary speech. They want a service that inspires, encourages, and helps them to feel what they are unable to make themselves feel.

One group of youth, after several weeks on the issue, agreed on three things they want in a morning worship service. First, it should be a time of singing, of expressing happiness over what God has done and is doing. If a service does not lift one's spirits, why speak of Good News?

Second, they want to learn something new and be stimulated intellectually by fresh insights into Christian truth.

Third, they want to participate and meet God in the presence of others. They want the service to impart a sense of warmth, love, and community.

A Stance Toward Youth

Though this book is written for parents and youth leaders, it should not be assumed that adults have outgrown youth issues. On the contrary, the preceding analyses show how much adults are linked to youth needs.

Low self-esteem is probably passed on from parents.

Family disunity centers in parental conflict.

Social concern is characterized by youth's sharp criticism of congregational adults' lack of manifest caring.

Prejudice is found more readily among adults than among youth.

Loss of faith is an issue that is no respecter of age.

A ministry to youth is best seen as a collaborative effort—mutual seeking, helping, and working—in which adults freely admit their need to be helped in ways similar to youth. To believe that "no one has arrived" enables everyone, regardless of age or experience, to express the need for rebirth or renewal, for judgment and forgiveness.

The stance of common need reduces the age prejudice that characterizes most adults and mitigates the generational chauvinism of youth who feel superior to adults in such personal values as openness, honesty, and feeling for people.

It does not require that young people be seen as little adults. One can still view adolescents as possessors of special qualities—liveliness, enthusiasm, honesty, idealism, and potential—and rightfully say, "I enjoy them," "They keep me young."

The preceding reflections draw attention to at least two imperatives in a youth ministry—*mutuality* and *mission*. Youth of all subcultures want the warmth of an accepting group which is *mutuality*. They need activities which give them a sense of purpose; that is *mission*. Within these two polarities, there is powerful need for *educational experiences* for youth and adults that open minds, develop skills, clarify values, and encourage commitment.

Essay 12

Adolescent Girls: A Two-Year Study

Gisela Konopka

Persons active in youth ministry often express the need for good research on the attitudes and needs of young people. Many are already aware of the value of Merton Strommen's recent research on the attitudes of youth. Less well publicized but equally valuable is the research of Gisela Konopka, director of the Center for Youth Development and Research at the University of Minnesota. Dr. Konopka's work has the special value of having focused exclusively on adolescent girls. My own growing conviction, supported here by Konopka's research, is that those wishing to pay special attention to the exploitation of young people should look first and most closely to the situation of adolescent girls because they are most "at risk" in a sexist, patriarchal society.

Supported by a grant from the Lilly Endowment, Dr. Konopka and a staff of specially trained researchers in twelve different states undertook to identify the wide variety of needs, aspirations, and concerns of girls twelve to eighteen years old. The 920 girls, interviewed in both rural and urban settings, represented every racial, religious, and ethnic group and a range of socioeconomic backgrounds. One-third of the young women were adjudicated delinquent, one-third were active in youth organizations, and one-third fell into neither category. An informally structured but open-ended sixty- to ninety-minute interview with each girl was taped. Subsequently, these sessions were analyzed according to the girl's views, beliefs, and feelings on education, careers, marriage, children, the women's movement, adults, friends, drugs and alcohol, sexuality, social and political concerns, relationships with adults, and experiences with and recommendations for youth organizations.

Dr. Konopka's book containing her findings and recommendations based on them is titled Young Girls: A Portrait of Adolescence *(Englewood Cliffs, New Jersey: Prentice-Hall, 1976). Poems by the girls quoted in the following presentation are taken from this book. Readers who find the following excerpt and interview to be of special value may want to be familiar with Gisela Konopka's classic essay "Requirements for Healthy Development of Adolescent Youth,"* Adolescence *31 (1973): 291–316.*

This essay is reprinted from Center Quarterly Focus *(Saint Paul: University of Minnesota's Center for Youth Development and Research, Fall 1975), pages 1–8, by permission of the author.*

I have always maintained that when we set out to talk about people we should first let *them* talk about themselves. I cannot bring 920 girls here to speak to you in person, but I can let a few speak through their poetry. They write beautiful poetry. This poem was written by a 15-year-old girl in a delinquency institution. She talks about herself and her generation:

> I am a bottle
> sealed with feeling
> too deep for anyone else.
> I am a bottle
> floating in an eternal ocean of people
> trying to help.
> I am a bottle
> keeping my fragile content inside it,
> always afraid of breaking and exposing me.
> I am a bottle
> frail and afraid of the rock and afraid of the storm,
> for if the storm or rocks burst or crack me
> I sink and become part of the ocean.
> I am a person, I am a person
> in the people of the world.

Though I have to generalize about what we found in our study, it is important to remember that *every person is somewhat different from any other.* I also want to say at the outset that I am talking about reality—what we actually heard, not necessarily what we wished to hear. This poem by a 16-year-old speaks to individuality:

> I used to be a grape in a bunch
> and all the other grapes were the same,
> But now I am an apple, crisp and fresh
> and everyone is different.
> My, how life has changed.

These 12- to 18-year-olds were born into national and international strife with the beginning of inflation and depression. The general environment of their parent generation was characterized by prosperity, though it does not follow that all of them participated in prosperity. Their grandparents lived through the depression of the 30's. Each generation grows up in a different kind of context. The girls we interviewed hold high hopes of better justice for all. Their generation comes after the fighting generation, and they are experiencing the harsh reaction against the preceding rebellion. They are very self-conscious adolescents, even more so because they are female. Though we rarely heard the girls talk abstractly about their self concepts, everything they said was permeated by their concept of self.

I shall try to report what they said according to what I thought was significant to them: (1) their present drives, their dreams for the future; (2) their family, important as a supporting and limiting power; (3) their friends, important as mirrors of themselves; (4) the organizations they joined; (5) the school, again important as a supporting and limiting power; and (6) the political and social scene.

1. Life Goals

Marriage

This generation of young women wants both marriage and a career. They have thought it through in rather a calm way. In general they do not expect to marry early. "I want to get married when the time comes and the time is right. I don't want to rush it because I want to make sure. It's like if there was a problem you have to pay so much money to get a divorce and I don't think it's right. If two people love each other they should be able to stay together without those laws between them." I'm not saying there will be no teenage marriages, but on the average they think after 22 is a good time to get married. One thing stands out: marriage means a great deal to them but they do not want to be married to a domineering male. Again there are exceptions, but this is feared with great realism, particularly in the poverty area. "I would rather be more like friends with my husband. That comes first." "I just want to marry someone who shares a lot of the same interests I do and we can get along with each other."

Children

Many girls want children, but they know they have a choice as to when and how many. Most of them wanted three; many wanted fewer; very few wanted more. They thought of raising children mostly in terms of very young children. This business of really raising a human being had not sunk in very deeply.

Divorce

We found an extraordinary fear of divorce. When they talked freely this terrible fear came through. Typical statements: "What is the use of getting married if you just get divorced?" "The children will be hurt."

Careers

The choice of careers is influenced by life experiences — by what we might call adult models. Organizations and schools have given them very little conscious exposure to such models. Counselors in schools seemed to be especially ineffective. "Talking to them is like talking to a brick wall." White collar jobs are preferred. The most tradition-bound group were the adjudicated girls.

2. Sex

Sex is talked about very calmly by most of the girls. They accept themselves as sexual beings. This is not to say they all wanted to have premarital sex, but practically all of them were very tolerant of others who do. Even if they said, "That's not for me," they were tolerant. "I want to wait until I get married, but I don't look down on a friend."

There was enormous fear, however, of being used sexually. They believed a boyfriend should be an equal, a friend, "gentle, nice, someone who listens." *Listens* was written large. Practically none of the girls would want to just go from one love affair to another.

Sexual Abuse and Incest

We found that first sex experiences which had been disastrous and harmful usually happened to girls in their own homes. I'm not talking exclusively of incest. Sometimes it was the father, of course, but often it was a brother, another relative, or the mother's boyfriend. The tragedy is that these girls, when they run away from an intolerable situation, are treated as offenders, not as victims. We do exactly the most harmful thing in such a situation: we put them into institutions where they are separated completely from men and cannot learn any healthy relationship to the other sex. Furthermore, they are labeled. As one of the girls said, "Well, if they put me there, I am bad." This increases their sense of inferiority. They become outcasts.

Pregnancy Before Marriage

The attitude of most of the girls toward pregnancy before marriage again is one of tolerance. This is not a militant generation. Many would want to keep the child, but tend to think of the child only as a baby. Some talk about adoption. They discuss abortion openly. About half of the group were strongly for abortion, half were strongly against it.

Sex information was incredibly poor—an absolute disgrace in 1975. To be sure, there were exceptions. One girl said, "When I first found out I was pregnant I didn't even know what pregnant meant and I went to the nurse and she told me 'that means you're going to have a little baby,' and I said 'What?' And then I told my parents and then I thought I had really been bad." Many did not even know about menstruation.

To summarize, I don't think we found a sex revolution, but there is greater tolerance for premarital sex. There is still an enormous need to help people understand sex. The institutionalized girl was the worst off. She had gone through horrible experiences and most of the time was a victim. She was treated as the offender and made to feel an outcast.

3. Relationship to Adults

Generation Gap

I would like to discuss the relationship of the girls to adults in terms of three myths that we must destroy. One is the much publicized generation gap. Naturally there is always a generation difference, but I would not say it is a great gap. The values the girls hold are often quite similar to those of the adult world. What they expect of people is what we expect of people, too. Negative qualities of adults they mentioned were "phony, nosey, grouchy, greedy, self-conscious; they stereotype us, they don't like us." Positives named included "fun to be with, understanding, respect us, will listen, care, trust us and deserve trust, are patient, fair and just."

Relationship to Parents

The second myth is that the family is totally falling apart, that young people want to get out of the family. We found they want a family very badly, yearn for a family if they don't have it. A girl who was thrown out by her family said in a poem: "Loneliness is missing your family, it's not knowing what to say."

Really surprising to us was that the most significant adult named by a majority of the girls was the mother. They want to be related to mother and often have very good relationships with their mother. "She is just fantastic. She can yell at us, but we really respect her. She is always there to help. She understands, she works, and she knows who she is." That last sentence was rather typical. The nonsense about the working mother being the worst is not true. I think young people are quite realistic about parents.

Next in rank among significant adults was father. Yet he showed up as more authoritarian, often less communicative, and tending to lose contact when the girls reached adolescence. Fathers, it was reported, don't want daughters to grow up; they want them to remain their little girl. "Oh, he's quite tolerant about a lot of things, but, oh boy, if I go out, oh my little girl, that shouldn't happen."

Another finding, not startling but exciting, was the warm relationship with the grandparent generation. These are real people whom the girls love. This is also true of uncles and aunts. "I can talk with them. My grandmother tells me she wasn't always good, but my mother would never say that."

Permissiveness

The third myth I want to hit hard is that this is a permissive society. We found incredibly authoritarian families, the vast majority in fact. We found the battered adolescent. "When I do something wrong he beats the shit out of me. If I wouldn't clean the table right, or especially if I talked back, or if I started to cry or showed any feeling, my stepfather would beat me up." Or, "She wouldn't let me go nowhere. She beat me with braided ropes, extension cords, yardsticks, boards, whatever she could find when she was mad." A girl described being brought in by police for something she had done. The parents turned to the policeman and said, "What would you do?" He said, "Well, if she were my girl I'd give her a good beating with a police belt." "All right," the father said, "give me your belt" (it has a big buckle) and in front of everybody the girl is beaten with the belt. She gets hysterical, falls on the floor, starts laughing and laughing. The more she laughs the more they beat her. Then she walks upstairs and vomits all day. Again, as with sex offenses, these girls are not treated as victims, always as offenders. With some exceptions, the treatment in delinquency institutions is abominable. Too much still is done to degrade the girls. One girl said, "My mother always told me, 'Whenever you see anyone crying, just try to talk to them.' But up here you can't do it because they will start yelling at you, 'You shut your mouth or you will get three days strict you know.' Being locked up, that's the worst. You can't get out, you can't say what you want, you can't do what you want. They bust teenagers for just anything. There is nothing you can do. They're just over you." The hate such conditions create is illustrated by one girl's solution: "Blow everybody up and get people to know what they are doing." Some institutions do try to provide help, especially those that are smaller. Quoting another interviewee: "Our counselor here will try to help you. If you don't want to go to her you can talk to one of the girls."

4. Peers

Another important subject we explored was how adolescent girls feel about their peers. What about the loneliness that showed up so strongly in my previous study, *The Adolescent Girl in Conflict* (Prentice-Hall, 1966)? It is still there. Friends of their own age are very important, but adults are just as important. The girls stressed that friends must be trustworthy and you must be able to talk to them. That goes for both boys and girls, not just girls. What they do when they are with friends is pretty much the same, whether the group includes boys or not. Some have sex relations, but they want the boy also as a *friend*. The delinquent girls talked a great deal about how their boyfriends support them, give them some sense of value. This prop is taken away the moment they are placed in an institution. These girls also suffer from distrust by the community. One interviewee who had become pregnant before marriage was not allowed to go to the same school she had attended, a youth organization of which she was a member immediately excluded her, the parents of her friends did not allow their daughters to communicate with her, and she became a total isolate. This kind of thing we heard frequently.

We found few gang activities. Where they existed, girls were part of the gang, not just the auxiliary. Though there was violence in the gangs and they retaliated with violence, most girls disliked the violence.

Suicide attempts were frequent in our survey population. The reasons are the same as those found in any other population. Enormous loneliness, which we find again among the aged, is one. I was interested in a couplet quoted to us by girls across the country:

> Loneliness is a silent jail
> Without cellmates, parole or bail.

Other reasons for suicide attempts were severe conflicts, either with the boyfriend or with the parents. Occasionally they were related to depressive drugs, especially alcohol. I am often asked if we found much homosexuality or lesbianism. The answer is we didn't. We certainly found it in the delinquency institutions, but all of us know it flourishes there because of the total segregation from boys. Oddly enough, in terms of attitude, homosexuality was the most disliked quality. Tolerance about sex did not seem to extend to homosexuality or lesbianism.

5. Drugs and Alcohol

Not surprisingly, we found an increase in alcohol use, partially because there is less conflict with society about it and partially because it is often fostered by parents. The girls themselves stressed the negative effects of hard drugs. They see them as a danger, but as for marijuana—most of them hardly consider it a drug. They want it to be legalized. Half of the girls said they do not use drugs but they all knew of them. That applies just as much to rural areas as to urban areas. A question we asked was: "Why do you think girls take drugs? Is it different from why boys take drugs?" They said no, it was kind of the same: curiosity, peer pressure, finding drugs agreeable. But they thought boys also take drugs to prove their masculinity. Whether they evaluated the boys correctly I don't know.

We thought drug information often increased curiosity, but on the other hand it showed quite well the different effects drug use can have. We felt that strong motivation is required to stop taking drugs. "My boyfriend doesn't want me to take drugs and I want to please him." Or "I want to have healthy children, so that's why I stopped." They feel they cannot talk to adults about drugs. Most of them thought their parents did not know it when they took drugs. Among girls who belonged to youth organizations (one-third of our sample) most knew about or had taken drugs, but they said, "Oh my goodness, we would never mention it there!"

6. Social and Political Involvement

My first impression when I looked at this part of the material was: this is really catastrophic! They are terribly self-concerned, they don't know how to participate in the political scene, they are disenchanted about things political, they don't feel responsible as citizens. After more careful reading of the material and discussion with my researchers, I recognized that first of all we must think of adolescence as a period of basic self-concern anyhow. Second, many adults do not participate in the political scene either. We were interviewing at the height of Watergate, so that had a strong influence. Finally, we have to remember that the girls actually were very concerned about issues but they did not know how to translate their concern into action. This was the first time they had been asked what their thoughts were. They talked about war, about government cheating, about race relations, and about issues relating to youth—e.g., the draft and the juvenile court. We also talked with them about the women's movement. Very often they saw only the extremes in the movement, which they didn't care for. But when we probed a little deeper we saw that they have simply accepted as their due what others fought for: equal pay for equal work, open opportunities for women, etc. So although they are not revolutionaries, they are involved, as this poem illustrates. It was written by a 16-year-old who has dropped out of school but wants very much to be a lawyer.

> You talk about the problems of the world
> And I am not allowed to speak because I am just a little girl.
> But there is something I would like to say to you, you know
> It's my world too.
> You think that you can understand more than anyone at all
> But mister, you are really short when you think you are tall.
> And I'm not allowed to give my opinions because I'm not as big as you.
> Try not to forget
> It's my world too.
> They talk about young people all the time
> But they don't think of others who are out of line
> And some problems mean nothing to you
> But while I'm living here
> It's my world too.
> What I want is the best for everyone
> Cuz thinking of yourself is not good in a long run.
> So think about what you want for me and you
> And while you are thinking, remember
> It's my world too.

7. School

School was often seen as very positive, mostly because the girls find friends there. Race discrimination hurts deeply, especially when teachers insult minority girls or show fear of them. Their anger at being treated differently flares out. "What do they think I am, an animal?" Many girls experience enjoyment in school. When we asked what they expect of school they spoke of friendship and understanding, but also of learning. Often the subjects they preferred were those we consider difficult. Exceptions were the delinquent girls who usually have been treated abominably and feel that school has nothing for them.

8. Youth Organizations

We found it rather sad that youth organizations seem to have little meaning to the girls. In general they found them childish. Perhaps the most serious finding was an indirect one: when we asked them about significant adults, two girls out of 920 named two people from youth serving organizations. The girls do not think they can talk with youth workers if they have problems. "Organizations are only for the good ones."

I read an article recently stating that nobody knows what kind of people we want to develop. If we don't know that, then I think we should really give up. Every society has to decide what kind of people it wants. To my thinking it is really quite simple. I go to the ideals of the Bill of Rights, which I did not invent: (1) an open free society based on the proposition that the purpose of government is to advance and protect human rights; (2) a representative form of democratic government which means that citizens must be encouraged to participate in their own fate and have the necessary knowledge to do so, otherwise it will not survive; (3) a society ruled by law; (4) an egalitarian non-discriminatory society with equal opportunity for everybody; (5) a pluralistic society with opportunity for groups to have a variety of life styles without harming others or feeling that one or the other style is inferior. If we combine these ideals we get a sense of direction, a sense of how to deal with our youth in the family, in schools, in youth organizations and in corrections. The time has passed for rigid, laid-out programs for young people. Most significant are the *people* who work with them. They not only must understand these youngsters but must consciously see how they themselves relate to people. They must be able to listen to and respect young people and permit their genuine participation. I felt very strongly that these young girls were asking us not only to listen to them but to convey something of the meaning of life to them. They want to talk, they want to think things through, they want absolute honesty.

The young people we talked to were very sober. We must help them feel that there is hope, that there is compassion, that joy and commitment actually are possible. So I will end with a thought from Morris West who understands the stark reality of life but also understands its beauty:

> To reject the joy of living is to insult Him who provides it.
> And who gave us the gifts of laughter along with the gift of tears.

Our young population has that gift. We squelch it far too often; we do not enhance it enough.

Interview with Dr. Konopka

Dogma and Direction

Q. How do we move between the two extremes of trying to impose ideals upon young people (making them what we think they should be) and not giving them any direction at all?

G.K. This seems to me to be one of the philosophical questions that I hope everybody can go back and discuss with the girls themselves. To think through the difference between dogma and direction is an exciting experience at almost any age. I don't expect we will ever find the complete answer. But if our ideal is a population capable of making choices on two grounds (1) consideration of other people and (2) facts, then we have to learn to look at facts, to assess them, and to develop a measuring stick for making choices. I think we can help people learn how to make choices without imposing our own styles on them. We must allow them a large number of alternatives.

Building Trust

Q. In what ways can a worker cooperatively build trust between group and leader?

G.K. First of all, you surely don't build trust with gimmicks. Kids very quickly spot phoniness. I don't learn trust in a weekend therapy session, by falling back blindfolded and being caught before I drop. Since the whole "bag" at that moment is to create trust, I assume they won't let me drop. Does that mean I can trust the next guy I meet in the community who wants to cut my throat if I disagree with him? No.

Another way some of us try to build trust is by sitting across the desk from a person saying, "You know I understand who you are and what you think, and you must trust me." It doesn't work. Trust is built slowly, through experience. When you are working with people, be honest. By that I don't mean be brutal. But be open; don't pretend the world is all good when you know it is not. When they need you, be available. It takes time to build trust.

If you are asking me how to build trust with very distrustful young people I would need an hour to discuss it. You have to undo so much. But it is not as difficult as most adults seem to think. What came out over and over in our study was this incredible yearning to have somebody to talk to.

Meeting Needs—Toward Greater Effectiveness

Q. Should every girls' organization try to meet all the needs of all girls, or are there some basic needs or concerns that all organizations should broaden their base to meet?

G.K. In my opinion no organization and no individual can ever serve all the needs of all the people. That's impossible. So it's all right sometimes to say we will just cut out a certain slice from the whole pie and, let's say, provide services for a particular neighborhood, or serve girls in a particular area of interest. What I think is dangerous, though, is separation on the basis of delinquency or race or ethnic background.

Now, are there basic needs all organizations should meet? I think so. We may not always agree on all needs and concerns but we have to know them and develop our thinking and our programs around them, based on some philosophy. I talked about this in the Bill of Rights context. For instance, if we believe people must be able to make choices, otherwise our democracy will die, then it behooves all organizations to provide experience in making choices rather than having authoritarian leaders who set the program and expect everyone to work by the book.

If we agree that self-esteem is the basis for respecting other people, then we have to provide the ingredients which enhance self-esteem: real participation in decision-making, for instance, not just asking for opinions; genuine acceptance of young people as equals, not just as pre-adults. We can translate almost every one of these basic "shoulds" or ideals, combine them with what we understand, and make them part of our programs.

So I would say all youth organizations have to fulfill some of the basic needs of human beings and serve a wide variety of young people, yet they cannot reach all of them.

Q. You mentioned earlier that the girls had quit some of the organizations when they were in junior high school. Can you elaborate on that—what they liked about some organizations and disliked about others?

G.K. Okay, what do they like? Written very big is opportunity for adventure—the real possibility to get out and do things that are different, not the tame camping or the usual kind of summer program. I don't mean necessarily running the rapids but just going somewhere else, meeting totally different people, discussing new and exciting things. Wish for excitement is very big in that age range.

I don't usually name names, but 4-H got a good press so I'll use it as a concrete example. One thing the girls liked there was the coed organization which allowed them to be with boys at some times. We found kind of a general feeling: "No, we don't want always to be with boys but we like to have the opportunity to work with them and not just to party with them." Second, they liked individualized projects—not programs where everybody has to do the same thing. They liked the feeling of doing something distinct and getting recognition for it. Third, they liked being allowed to travel. "It wasn't just going on a vacation. We did something, we exhibited something, we worked on something together, and we were somewhere else." Being involved in actual helping also is important to them, as is the kind of adult they meet. Their most negative reaction is to the adult who treats them like little kids and looks down on them.

I think all organizations could be more effective. One of my great hopes is that we will get away from the notion of compartmentalization—school is for learning, youth organizations are for fun, parents are for nurture. We have to work together and eliminate the jealousies among us. For that we need the right kind of people. Partially they have to be found, but partially they can also be developed through training. At the Center we are starting a two-year project, funded by the Lilly Endowment, Incorporated, in which we hope to train 400 significant personnel within eight youth-serving organizations plus some staff from corrections.

Reaching Troubled Adolescents

Q. Do you have any ideas on how organizations and resources can better reach troubled adolescents?

G.K. First of all, do not segregate them. Why do we call one "troubled" and another "untroubled"? I have not yet seen an adolescent who is not troubled at times. In fact, I have not seen a person who is not troubled at times, regardless of age, but in adolescence everything is worse. It's a more touchy age. Almost every experience is brand new. The ability to see failure in perspective has not yet been developed. For instance, you have fallen in love and the boy leaves you. You haven't experienced this before and you are ready to commit suicide. In contrast, I feel scared before I give a speech but I have experienced over and over that somehow it will work out. So I am anxious, but not desperate.

My answer then is: first, don't segregate; second, take the troubles seriously, but don't look on the "troubled" as a group apart; third, understand the enormous range of normalcy. In general, much of what we consider emotionally disturbed is normal.

Q. What are the alternatives to traditional ways of dealing with runaways?

G.K. Certainly they vary. Sometimes we treat runaways as offenders rather than as victims, and then things get worse and worse and worse. I think definitely this has to stop. There have been some very good places for runaways here in the Twin Cities—open places where a girl could go and stay. But some changes are taking place that worry me. The current approach seems to be "now that we have been good enough to take you in, we expect you to bare your soul. Tell us all about yourself." That's not what I call an alternative. Neighborhood houses used to offer people refuge, but few such residences exist any more. Desperately needed, I think, is a network of residences all over the country (not only in the cities) where young people can stay for a time and where they will find helping people to talk to if they wish, but only if they wish. These residences might be called youth hostels— not runaway houses or half-way houses. We who work with youth often have gold in our hands, not yet tarnished by the taste of being something bad. Why label prematurely a person in the making? Just because our young people take to the road we don't have to label them runaways.

Changing Structures That Oppress Youth

Q. What can be done politically to change the structures that oppress youth and especially female youth?

G.K. I do not think that youth is totally "oppressed." Perhaps the most important structure in need of change is the family structure where double standards still prevail. Girls in our study often complained that they were not allowed to go out in the evening but their brother was, or the boy was allowed to hike in summer with a group but the girl wasn't. And this distinction was not made on the basis of age; it was strictly boy/girl. Sexuality is not the only basis for uneven treatment, but it certainly is the strongest one.

I see changing the family structure not so much in terms of making a new structure but rather in terms of moving away from the male dominated authoritarian structure. I also see the family structure as a mirror of the political structure. That means in the old monarchies in authoritarian countries the family followed the same pattern. Most people in this country come from this kind of background where the king was at the helm and below him were the people subservient to him. Now it is odd that change in political structure does not necessarily result in change in other structures. It didn't follow in the family; frequently it didn't follow in the schools. But these are structures that need to be changed.

Another structure that definitely must be changed is the one surrounding status offenses. Boys and girls are brought before the courts because they are not going to school. Americans feel very embarrassed because our delinquency figures are so high. Naturally they are when we count every kid that plays truant as delinquent. I don't know of any other country which does that. If the status offender (the offender who has committed an act that would not be a crime for an adult) were to be taken off the courts, most girls wouldn't even be offenders. Most of the time they are in that category because of "sexual misconduct" which is not considered misconduct among the boys, even today. This will be changed and the change will come through the legal profession. Who will then take care of these girls? Who will work with them? I say it is the responsibility of people in the neighborhoods and of the youth organizations in the community.

Other structures—vocational education, for instance—need to be changed, too. But enough for now.

Reaching Young People

Q. How can we change our approach to young people so that we can reach them?

G.K. They are not so hard to reach. They want to be reached. They want to be listened to; they don't want to be talked down to; and they don't want to be constantly told that they must be exactly what someone else is. I'll finish up with two illuminating poems. The first is one by a 16-year-old girl, written after she was found in the "gutter," labeled "mentally ill," and placed in a mental hospital.

> You aren't normal you know, the fat nurse said accusing me,
> No, I don't know, I said heavily under my breath.
> She heard me though, as her neck stretched out straining to hear more.
> What's your goal in life?
> To castrate all the guys in town and marry the women.
> Not really, just playing a little game.
> She changed the subject because of her uncomfortable position
> And fixed her gaze steadily upon my poetry book.
> What's your favorite poem?
> I hear America sighing.
> Isn't it, I hear America singing?
> Not the way things are going nowadays, said I, in a flat tone.
> The psychos got up for lunch, and she stood there directing the line.
> I think she felt safer with them.

How little we know about what goes on beneath the hostility we encounter. How fast she catches our fear . . . From another 16-year-old:

> I used to be the cocoon all wrapped up
> In what I thought then was safety,
> Insulating myself from all the hurts and joys of life.
> Afraid of so much of love, strangers, of being rejected,
> Of trying new things, of being wrong, of being laughed at.
> Or of just being.
> Snuggled in my security blanket, I miss so much.
> Now I am the worm, just breaking through the cocoon
> Crawling slowly, inching my way towards the light.
> Crawling a little, a little, each day, I hope.
> Trying not to slip back a foot for every inch I gain.
> Some day I will be a butterfly, free and glorious,
> Not afraid of everything I do.

The message I get: Don't make young people feel they have to be afraid; let them be creative; try not to crush the butterfly; let them think, live, be concerned and develop.

Related Readings

Conger, John Janeway. *Adolescence and Youth*. New York: Harper and Row, 1973. Related physical development and self concept. Outward appearance and inner self-image are more closely bound together for females than for males.

Gottlieb, David, ed. *Youth in Contemporary Society*. Beverly Hills: Sage Publications, 1973. Contributors identify and analyze anticipated trends in youth behavior. Focus is on implications for programs and policies dealing with youth in the decade ahead. Includes good chapter on drugs and one on "the real generation gap."

The Mood of American Youth, 1974. Reston, Virginia: National Association of Secondary School Principals, 1974. A poll was conducted of 2,000 high school students sampled nationwide by the Gilbert Youth Research Division of Herff-Jones. Outlines the national issues of concern to youth. Reflects a determined and ambitious generation of students who are committed to their own individual goals.

National YWCA Resource Center on Woman. *Teen Women Tell About Their Needs*. New York: National Board, YWCA, 1974. Questionnaires were sent to 1,111 adolescent women and four workshops were held, to determine young women's concerns. Subject areas are: jobs, sex, recreation, drugs, child care, counseling, racism, women's changing roles. Implications for programs are evident. The project was planned and carried out under the leadership of teen women.

Part B:

Doing
Youth Ministry

Essay 13

Young Life Statement of Mission Purpose

The Young Life Board of Trustees

Some readers may question why the following Young Life statement appears in a section on doing youth ministry. The reason is that this chapter and the following essay by Jeff Johnson are companion pieces about a specific program of youth ministry—in this case, a Christian but nondenominational one.

The Young Life statement is valuable because it lays out clearly the purposes of an organization held in suspicion by some people in various denominations in the United States and Canada. Wherever I have heard Young Life criticized, people seemed more annoyed that this group had more success with the young people of a particular church than did the congregation. Yet the clearly stated goal of Young Life is to direct youth to their own local congregations. If any criticism of Young Life were to be advanced, in my judgment, it would be that their announcement of the Good News is a privatized one. That is to say that their gospel is political in the sense that it ignores conscious attention to social and political matters that affect young people and will continue to affect them for many years to come.

My hope in presenting this statement of purpose is that it may provide a sort of paradigm against which parishes, areas, or dioceses can develop their own statements of purpose in dealing with youth. The paradigm is more one of clarity than of exact purpose, as I hinted in the previous paragraph. I have found too few parishes or churches, dioceses or presbyteries or synods that have worked out a coherent approach to youth ministry.

This statement is taken from the Young Life's Board of Trustees Manual *(Colorado Springs, CO, 1985), by permission of Young Life.*

Young Life Statement of Commitment

We are committed:
- to the welfare and spiritual health of those who do this ministry, that they may do it out of a consistent and growing relationship with Christ and His Church;
- to submit to and communicate effectively the whole Gospel of our Lord Jesus Christ, as best we understand that Gospel;
- to researching and developing innovative approaches to the evangelization of young people so that the unreached, uninterested, or uncommitted youth of the world shall continue to be reached;
- to all young people wherever they may live in the world, or whatever may be their social, economic, ethnic, cultural, or racial environment;
- to seek out and welcome all those whom God directs to our ministry, male and female of all races, salaried and volunteer, with a diversity of Christian traditions linked in our common purpose, and to honor their calling and encourage the fullest expression of their gifts;
- to obey our Lord's mandate that all His people should be one, and therefore to work cooperatively within the Church of Jesus Christ around the world, so that more young people may be reached;
- to the highest standards of stewardship of all the resources placed in our trust.

Young Life in the Broad Perspective of God's Work

Young Life in the Church

Historically we have viewed Young Life as part of the church . . . in mission to the world. When Young Life goes into any area, we realize that the movement of God is already taking place there among His people, and we are joining in and enhancing that movement. God does not arrive when we arrive—He has been there!

With this in mind, we cannot ignore other believers, Christian organizations, and ministers in the area. Every effort must be made to establish healthy relationships between our staff and those leaders who share our overall objectives. Though progress may be slow and discouraging, we must not let down in our attempts to harness our contribution with others in the community of believers. Practically speaking, we wish for every staff person to seek a regular, working, praying relationship with a group of other Christian leaders and ministers.

Out of this relationship may come grand new opportunities for outreach in the community. Local congregations have resources which, when combined with ours, may serve to expand God's purposes in remarkable ways.

Their most obvious resources are volunteer leadership potential, Christian nurture opportunities, and finances. Our resources? . . . What we have learned about relating personally to young people, the approach to proclamation of the Gospel, presentation of the winsome Savior, the camping ministry, and concepts of leadership.

The Lord has laid upon us the conviction that we cannot reach the young everywhere without a broader view of how we may work with and influence local congregations. Young Life can be a model in the community—a resource for motivation, training, and encouragement—that ends up with a lot of young people reached with an incarnational approach through leaders who may call it by a different name but who are committed to those things we have learned and shared.

In summary, we affirm that:

1. All Young Life staff are to be responsible, involved members in a local church congregation. (This does not mean we must teach or give heavy time involvement but rather to worship and serve as the Lord enables.)
2. Young Life staff should seek ongoing relationships with Christian leadership in the community.
3. We are to pray and work toward mutual involvement and sharing of experiences and resources with local congregations.
4. Young people we influence for personal commitment to Christ are to be encouraged toward local worship congregations for nurture and service.
5. We recognize the existence of other Christian organizations that may even appear competitive for Christian support. We should take the initiative in our approach to these people in hopes for honest dialogue and creative fellowship and service.

Young Life and Community Agencies

As in the case of church relatedness, we see the necessity for leaders to become familiar with other helping and reconciling agencies at work in the community, and to cooperate with and learn from these agencies. This is not only for "public relations" reasons, but rather what we believe about the quality of our outreach, our limitations, and the great help these agencies can be to our ministry.

For example, too few of us understand the complexity of the problem of alcoholism—what happens to the family of the alcoholic—the unbelievable effect upon the growing youngsters in the home. There are people who have given their adult lives to dealing with this immense social problem of our day. One out of six of the young people we work with comes from a home affected by alcoholism. We have little choice as responsible, incarnational leaders. We should learn from these special agencies and establish working relationships with them.

Do we know what local resources are available to us in the fields of mental health, law enforcement, health care, drug rehabilitation, remedial and special education? It is true, the Young Life leader has a specific calling in the relational proclamation of the Gospel—all the more reason to work with the resource agencies which can help the people we are dealing with.

In summary, we affirm that:

1. We as staff and leaders in a community will take the initiative to study agencies and be in contact with them for resources beyond our own as we deal with young people. Where we find qualified agencies we will utilize their services in order that we might maintain our focus upon our primary task.

2. We have never considered ourselves experts in every personal and social problem, but we should be good students, learning and equipping ourselves for a "whole person" ministry to the young. We know that man's more obvious needs (physical, etc.) are related to the ultimate need of his relationship with God in Christ. Whenever possible, we want to minister to these obvious needs, too.

Our Ministry

Contact/Club

Young Life has as its basic ministry the establishing of unconditional relationships with adolescent young people who need Jesus Christ, and the proclamation of the Gospel to them in an informal setting. There may be situations where the traditional club ministry may not work best, but we affirm the contact/club approach as a valid Young Life strategy and calling for our day.

Young Life in any area must have trained the leaders majoring in direct relationship-building with non-Christian young people, wherever they are. In most cases this will lead to an opportunity for sharing Christ in a meeting of some kind—a meeting designed for the non-Christian.

In summary, we affirm that:

1. All Young Life outreach is to be characterized by personal contact by leaders with uncommitted young people, recognizing that many who claim church membership actually do not attend or are anti-church in attitude. We are determined to reach out to these young people wherever they are, building unconditional friendships.

2. Proclamation of the Gospel, by deed and word, be it in the small or large meeting, or individually, is to be a learning situation for non-Christians. These may follow different programmatic and cultural forms, but the test

is: What are the young people learning about Jesus Christ, and what does it mean to be committed to Him through redemptive faith?

3. Young Life leadership aspires to be in the front ranks of outreach strategy—seeking new approaches, innovation—trying by every means possible for a ministry with hard-to-reach young people.

Urban (Economically and Socially Disadvantaged) Ministries

The Lord has blessed Young Life with remarkable results in our approach to middle and upper class suburban-oriented young people. This work must continue and expand. The future is bright for reaching many of these who will take community leadership roles in years to come.

When we speak of a commitment to the city to minorities, and to the poor, we do not mean a shift of emphasis from our suburban ministry to something else more important. Some have read it this way—that Young Life is not excited and challenged anymore by its opportunities in suburbia. On the contrary, we seek by every means possible to reach suburban high school people.

We believe God is calling us to look at our communities in their entirety. We know the incarnational principles of outreach will be effective wherever applied, whether in the cities or suburbs. Like our Lord Jesus Christ, we, too, are called to go into all the world around us. It is our mission to help raise up more Christian leaders for our work among minority groups and deprived areas.

Our history in the cities has not always been encouraging. We have needed leadership and funding in these urban ministries. Failures have taught us lessons, and successes have encouraged us. We are not giving up. We must find ways to reach all sorts of young people in all kinds of living situations and cultures.

In summary, we affirm that:

1. The commitment made years ago to economically and socially disadvantaged young people is very much with us today, and we will pursue every means possible for leadership and funding.
2. In areas which include suburban people, city, and minorities, the strategy for expansion is to show commitment to all of them.
3. Since suburbia holds so much of the power and financial resource in a community, we cannot allow our friends there to go unchallenged by the needs of the city.

Camping

It is expected that any Young Life area will be involved in year-round camping ministries. We are convinced of the effectiveness of being with young people for an extended period of time in a new and different environment. Our incarnational approach thrives in these situations.

In recent years we have seen innovations to meet many objectives — stress/adventure camping, bike trips, Campaigners camps, urban plunges, etc. Some of our most creative efforts will continue in these directions.

The one week camp at a major Young Life property is for the purpose of outreach to those who need Christ, or for those who are so new in their understanding of the faith that they need to hear the Gospel carefully reviewed.

In summary, we affirm that:

1. The camping experience for urban and suburban young people is a valid and effective means for outreach and nurture.
2. Some of the camping effort is for the purpose of Christian nurture, but the Young Life emphasis in its major properties will be outreach to those who need Jesus Christ.
3. Each Young Life staff person normally will be expected to participate by bringing young people to camp from the area and having a camp staff assignment during each summer.
4. Every area will take advantage of what we have learned about camping with young people and utilize this whenever possible with adults. The purpose will be to expose them to what we do with young people and to share with them our Savior.

Junior High

Recent developmental trends among young people have caused us to lower our Young Life age to the junior high level. We find most of them quite capable of understanding and appropriating the life-changing concepts of the Gospel. Due to contemporary social pressures, some young people by the time they are in high school have already tasted enough of life to appear harder to reach, and in some cases are embittered or apathetic.

In the highly mobile urban scene, there is even more of an urgency to reach the younger ones before some of them are forced into destructive patterns associated with high density populations and limited opportunities.

We have discovered that one very effective means for outreach to junior high is through high school and college age leaders. Effective ministry has been given by these young people, under staff guidance, with positive things happening in the lives of the young leaders themselves.

In summary, we affirm that:

1. The ministry strategy in Young Life areas will include junior high age outreach.
2. In most cases the junior high program will be implemented by short-term involvement of high school or college age Christians, trained and carefully supervised in leadership responsibilities.

International

The dynamics of relational outreach to young people seem to be common to all cultures . . . people respond to unconditional friendships and genuine love, national boundaries notwithstanding.

We have made a commitment to reaching young people wherever we can. This will not require us to tool up for the task of doing it all ourselves with a traditional Young Life U.S.-style operation. Rather, we will respond to those Christian people in the world who want to establish Young Life-type concepts in their own cultures, with their own national leadership, financial autonomy and responsibility, and with their own God-given strategies for reaching young people in their land. We desire to encourage a network of God's people in the world who have a desire to reach young people who need Jesus Christ.

In summary, we affirm that:

1. We are to have a global concern for young people who have yet to hear the claims of Jesus Christ.
2. Our strategy will be either to send advisors to foreign lands for a few years helping indigenous leaders adapt our principles into their culture, or to make available our U.S. training resources to any qualified leaders from other countries.
3. We have no desire to build a world-wide Young Life organization, but rather to see young people in the world exposed to the beauty and truth of Christ because of His life-changing capacity contained in His redemptive act upon the cross in whatever cultural and organizational setting God would provide.

Christian Nurture

Though the primary thrust of Young Life is outreach to young people who are not committed to Jesus Christ, we take very seriously our role in helping new Christians to a basic understanding of personal growth and responsibility in the world. This will mean emphasis upon study of Scripture, disciplines of prayer and worship, responsibility to the church, Christian fellowship, active concern for the spiritual and physical needs of mankind, and living in obedience as disciples of Christ.

Our task is not to indefinitely follow up Young Life participants with the assumption that if we don't, nobody will. The Holy Spirit will be able to work in these lives to take them into new dimensions of Christian experience. We fail any young person if we do not expose him/her to the magnificent scope of the church around the world, and his/her responsibilities and opportunities therein.

In summary, we affirm that:
1. Young Life leaders are responsible to help committed young people understand the basic ingredients of Christian growth and responsibility and to establish teaching situations where they may receive this instruction and encouragement.
2. Our goal is to lead these to a full appreciation of the Church of Jesus Christ, the resources therein, the breadth of involvement by people in the world, and its task in sharing the Good News in word and deed.
3. We have a responsibility to stay in touch as best we can with these committed young people, following their high school days, helping them into growth situations and encouraging them in their walk with Christ. Many times this follow-up activity may be handled by a volunteer leader on the local team.
4. We recognize that the growth and development of a believer in Jesus Christ is to take place over a whole lifetime, and that Young Life has a limited time to contribute to the total process of one's growth and development. For the most part, we will have the privilege of getting them started in the adventure of living life for our Redeemer.

Rural Ministries

A host of young people are in smaller or remote communities of the U.S. As a mission we are committed to research and develop outreach specifically designed to meet their culture. Most likely this will involve training volunteers who will give themselves to this strategic task.

In summary, we affirm that:
1. Young Life must not restrict itself to the large metropolitan areas, but we must explore ways to minister to rural youth.
2. Because of financial considerations, this probably will mean training volunteers and local church leadership to do incarnational ministry with the young people of their communities. Whenever possible we stand ready to give this training.

Handicapped Ministries

Physically and mentally handicapped young people must not be overlooked in the broad spectrum of Young Life ministries. Enough experimentation has been done to validate the effectiveness of our approach to these boys and girls. Most handicapped ministries will involve some special training for staff and volunteers and unusual financial outlay for such matters as transportation of young people. It is the mission's stance that these should not be overlooked in our relational proclamation of the Gospel of Jesus Christ.

In summary, we affirm that:

1. Physically and mentally handicapped young people should be in the strategy of outreach for the mission of Young Life.
2. We must seek cooperative relationships with community agencies skilled in working with these people and able to train us for the task.
3. Our national camp properties should be equipped to handle physically handicapped young people.

Our Leadership

Personal Welfare of Staff

As staff where do we get our encouragement and refreshment? What do we do with our own personal problems and needs? Is Young Life supposed to meet our total emotional, psychological, and spiritual needs?

Young Life is an avenue of expression of the call of God upon a person's life for mission. Warm and significant relationships are often created among staff colleagues. This is only natural when people go through heavy and joyous times together in an incarnational ministry. Other staff are often the people closest to us in heart and spirit when difficult personal needs arise.

We must recognize the danger of casting too much of ourselves upon Young Life, or considering it to be our only family. This can be devastating and a great hindrance to growth. The family of Christ extends so much further. We must take advantage of those relationships beyond our mission.

In summary, we affirm that:

1. Young Life is a fellowship of staff who have special needs that can often best be met by the ministry of another staff person. We should be sensitive and available to our colleagues for this personal ministry. We also recognize that there will be many other Christians outside of Young Life making a very valuable contribution to the needs of our staff.
2. All staff should seek involvement in some commitment and accountability group, broader than the confines of Young Life, where sharing and growth can be enhanced.

Staff Training

Training must be a major emphasis in Young Life. The quality of the ministry will largely depend upon this focus.

In summary, we affirm that:

1. Each staff member is to have an assigned supervisor of his/her training who has responsibility and authority to pursue to completion a basic curriculum of staff training. Their basic curriculum is to include all of the following:

    a. Basic academic curriculum—Old Testament, New Testament, Bible Survey, Theology, Church History, Ethics and Philosophy of Religions

    b. Psychological training

    c. Practical field work training—outreach to young people, area strategies, leadership, office, fund raising, etc.

    d. Supervision under a trained Area Director during training period

    e. Urban sensitivity

    f. Evaluation of trainee, trainer, program, Area Director

    g. International philosophy of Young Life

    h. Troubled young people training

    i. Personal spiritual growth and nurture

2. The assigned supervisor is also responsible for encouraging and monitoring continued learning efforts, structured and/or personal initiative learning, for as long as the person is on staff.

3. There will also be a special training program devised for every volunteer in the work, with each of these volunteers being held accountable to an Area Director or to a Regional Director where an Area Director is not present.

Team Concept in the Area

One staff person cannot carry the weight of ministry upon his/her shoulders. We need area teams, male and female in make-up, as an expression of the Body of Christ.

Our unique, specialized ministry to the adolescent opens doors to all levels of ministry with adults. Time factors make it impossible for area staff to follow and develop each of these opportunities. A group of committed people can do it together.

Support/ministry teams are forming, sometimes around one high school, where people can use their God-given gifts. A high level of commitment to one another and to the Lord is characteristic of these teams.

In summary, we affirm that:

1. Club situations are best handled by a team of leaders. There may be a diversity of age and personality—so much the better in order to reach

the sociological groupings of the local adolescent scene. The senior leader in this situation is responsible to see that gifts are being utilized and team members communicated with and encouraged.

2. We are to involve people at all levels of the area ministry, giving them a chance to utilize gifts and to feel an integral part of the Young Life team.

3. The local committee is an integral part of any Young Life area team. This group of men and women is to be involved in prayer support, financial support, community information and promotion of Young Life, planning and evaluating (with staff) the area ministry, and in spiritual partnership with area staff.

4. Opportunities for ministry with adults will arise. Members of the team can take advantage of these. Responsible staff are to remember that these opportunities have come because of our clear focus upon young people who need Christ, not primarily upon adults. Without the ministry to the young, there most likely will be no sustained effectiveness with adults.

5. The opportunity for working with adults is not simply a secondary privilege arising out of our ministry with young people, but has also become a definite responsibility of ours. Young Life must share what we have learned with the Body of Christ at every opportunity. Working with the adult provides us the vehicle for sharing not only the beauty of the Gospel but all that God is teaching us about communicating this message to the young. This becomes one of the finest methods available for giving ourselves away.

Epilogue

We realize that this is not a complete statement of all the things Young Life believes. We have considered the more mission-oriented tasks before us. Matters of personal habits and disciplines are largely left unsaid. However, we respect the relational nature of our ministry that demands our lives be a demonstration of the Christ we represent.

Essay 14

Young Life Ministry: Room for Catholic Lay Ministers

Jeffrey Johnson

It was in 1969 that I first heard of Young Life. While supervising a CCD program in a parish near Washington, D.C., I listened to the bitter complaints of two fifteen-year-old girls. Why did they have to *attend CCD when they already attended Young Life, which was so much better? The following evening I went with them to a Young Life session. Since then I have not ceased to be impressed with the method of this ministry.*

Young Life claims to serve all Christian denominations, but in my own mind I had always inserted the word Protestant *between* Christian *and* denomination. *Jeff Johnson has shown me the place for active Catholic support of this interdenominational ministry. Writing as a Catholic professional in youth ministry, Johnson shows us, especially through his own personal story, an inside look at the origins, philosophy, and methods of Young Life. Rooting themselves in what they call* relational ministry *and the ministry of friendship with teens, Young Life ministers are traveling the route that must be followed by any successful ministry to youth. If Catholic parishes followed this single foundational aspect of Young Life ministry, they would be well on their way toward fostering a renewed ministry to young people.*

Johnson's essay raises the serious possibility of several parishes' hiring a youth minister to work with the young people of an area. Since the primary affiliation of youth is not solely with church or parish but with a more complex network of relationships that includes school, sports groups, peer friendships, jobs, and family, an area-wide ministry to youth seems sensible. Many places in the United States and Canada have experimented over the past several years with area-wide youth ministry. One of the pioneering efforts was that undertaken in the northern counties of the Diocese of Santa Rosa, California, by Fr. Don Kimball in the early 1970s.

This essay is reprinted from Resources for Youth Ministry, *ed. Michael Warren (New York: Paulist Press, 1978), pages 45–58.*

During the past six years a group of Catholic youth ministers has been using the methods of an evangelical organization called Young Life to reach young people in Saint Cloud, Minnesota. The story of our area was a familiar one—high school CCD classes that no longer attracted students, failure of a released-time program, frustrated parents, pastors, and parishes. In this context, two of us began a Young Life club in Saint Cloud, and soon I realized that the strengths of Young Life's ministry matched the needs of the Catholic Church in our area. The purpose of this article is to explain Young Life's style of youth ministry and how we have incorporated this into our local and diocesan approach to youth catechesis.

The strength of Young Life centers around the ability to evangelize, disciple, and call into ministry the high school kids who are totally uninvolved with a local church. I am convinced that this outreach and relational style of ministry can complement any program of youth catechesis, whether in a parish or a school setting. My belief comes from the fact that my first faith experiences, leadership training, and invitation into ministry came through Young Life.

Young Life began in Dallas, Texas, with the work of a young seminarian named Jim Rayburn. Jim was a deeply committed Christian who loved kids and could effectively communicate his concern for them. The time was 1940, and Jim was working with a Bible-oriented Christian group called the Miracle Book Club. He had an effective ministry going with this group but found that he naturally gravitated toward kids outside the Church. Jim began hanging around the high school in an effort to make friends with young people who were untouched by church programs. These kids soon responded to his easygoing manner and were attracted by his acceptance of and concern for them.

As Jim attempted to love them unconditionally, he won their respect and friendship. It was easy for Jim to gather these kids together for an evening of fun and music that finished with a short talk on the Christian faith. The response was tremendous. Kids heard the story of God's personal concern for them made credible by Jim's individual concern for them. Those early years were filled with summer camping trips, tent meetings, and school assemblies, but mostly with hours of hanging out with kids.

Jim soon realized the sound scriptural approach of his ministry, for just as God came into our world as a human person in order to communicate God's love, Jim was entering the high school world in the understandable form of an adult friend. As Jim saw it, he was "winning the right to be heard." The key to his success was friendship, genuine caring for young people that communicated God's concern for their individual lives.

As his ministry grew, Jim recruited fellow seminarians and other adults to help him establish the "Young Life Campaign." Young Life's style of reaching out to kids with the Christian message was radical for that time and place. Within the neutral setting of the high school world, Young Life was especially successful with kids who were uninvolved in their local churches.

In a few short years Jim's vision had spread beyond Texas as Young Life grew in numbers of clubs, staff, and support from interdenominational groups of adults. Today Young Life operates in about 125 communities in the United States and in thirteen foreign countries. About 400 full-time staff and 5,800 volunteer leaders work in 1,120 Young Life clubs. Young Life also owns properties that will serve 16,000 kids in summer programs.

The Five Cs in Operating a Young Life Area: Club, Camp, Campaigners, Contact, Committee

Club

A typical Young Life club operates in much the same way as Jim's original club did. The group gathers in the home of one of the young people for an hour on a school night. The atmosphere is informal, and lively sing-along music helps to release energy and begins to focus the group's attention. Next comes a skit of some sort, involving the kids or leaders. The leader may get three of the biggest guys in the club up front, dress them in bibs and baby hats, and have them drink Cokes from baby bottles. The skit gets the group to laugh at itself and is usually followed by announcements about a weekend camp or a special event. After some quieter, more thoughtful music is played, a short personal talk is given about Christ and the Christian message.

The club is a vehicle for meeting new kids and strengthening existing relationships and proclaiming the Gospel in an informal setting. The dynamics of the meeting – the music, the humor, and the informality – are all geared toward creating an atmosphere to present the story of Christ in an attractive and digestible form. Young Life staff describe their meetings as designed for non-Christians, that is, people who have not heard or accepted the Gospel. The club is meant as an outreach tool, not as a complete catechetical program, in the belief that a relationship with Christ is the necessary basis for learning Christian doctrines and values.

The uniqueness of the Young Life club lies in the leader's ability to present the story of Christ in a personal and understandable form. The basics of the Christian faith are covered in a year's messages in such a way that kids feel free to come and go with no pressure to accept anything. This style of presenting the faith is coupled with the belief that the Word proclaimed does convict the hearts through the work of the Holy Spirit. Ever since Jim

Rayburn's humorous yet powerful messages moved those Dallas kids, Young Life has given special attention to presenting Jesus in an attractive and identifiable way. When effective proclamation is coupled with an attractive model of the Christian lifestyle, the impact of the Christian message is significant.

Camp

As other youth organizations have found, retreats are the richest context in which kids can experience the Christian message. Young Life also uses weekend retreats and week-long camps to build new relationships with kids. The program provides quality time for friendships to develop. The local Young Life leaders are free to spend more time with their group members because other staff people run the clubs, the skits, recreation time, and meals.

Campaigners

The follow-up group to both club and camp is called Campaigners, small Christian growth groups that focus on Bible study, discussion, and prayer. Kids deepen their relationships as they learn to apply the Scriptures to their own lives and to pray conversationally. The group's effectiveness is dependent upon the leader's ability to model a credible Christian lifestyle.

Contact

From the leader's perspective, the core of his or her ministry is "contact work," the unstructured time spent in building relationships with kids. Contact work is creative loafing in the adolescent world, hanging out at the focal points in a community that attract kids—primarily the high school or extensions of the high school subculture. Contact work means spending hours at the school or at games, practices, concerts, shopping centers, and fast-food restaurants, all for the purpose of meeting and talking with kids on their turf.

Committee

From the Church and greater community's standpoint, the most important element is the core of committed adults who form the Young Life committee. These men and women are local community people who are responsible for the financial, spiritual, and moral support of total Young Life ministry in a community. They provide the budget of an area, staff salaries, camp expenses, leadership training, and so on—all from donations solicited from the community. In this way Young Life can exist in an area only as an expression of community concern for young people.

Because Young Life is not the total Church, it cannot provide a total ministry for youth. Acknowledged weaknesses include follow-up after high school, the sacramental dimension, and involvement of Young Life kids in the needs of their communities. Within the Church's total ministry to youth, Young Life sees itself as an extended arm of the local Body of Christ, offering God's love in a unique outreach of friendship.

My own involvement with Young Life began when I was a sophomore in high school and my group of friends started going to our school's club. At Young Life I heard a story of Jesus in my own language and saw this message lived out in Jack and Andy, our two club leaders. Through club, winter camp, and Campaigners, I learned that faith involved not merely attending Mass, receiving the sacraments, and being a good person, but also having a personal relationship with Christ.

During my junior year my mother was concerned that I receive some Catholic doctrine, and so I reluctantly attended my parish's CCD program. My last CCD class had been in sixth grade in preparation for Confirmation, and I found the high school classes even more boring. The difference was that now I had a personal faith and found weekly quizzes too detached from everyday life to help me grow in my faith. I am certain that I learned some facts from those classes, but they would have been meaningless without my faith experience through Young Life. It was in the boredom of those CCD classes that I first asked the question, Why can't the Catholic Church do something like Young Life?

This question was to stay with me. After graduation I attended the University of Notre Dame and there met a man named Chuck Lehman who was doing groundwork for Young Life in South Bend, Indiana. During my sophomore year he invited me to visit a meeting and soon after asked me to join him in leading the club. For the next three years I led music and learned from a leadership perspective the essentials of club and Campaigners while building relationships with high school kids.

During my senior year I learned about "Youth Leadership, Minnesota," a training program created by Young Life staff members concerned about preparing qualified leadership for the future. Youth Leadership places men and women in churches or youth agencies for field experience while they pursue graduate studies, usually in theology. The thrust of the training is relational in style and is supervised by an experienced youth minister in the trainee's community. Through the guiding friendship of Dave Phillips, Youth Leadership's director at the time, I received additional training while in the theology master's program at Saint John's University, located near Saint Cloud.

During those two years another Youth Leadership student and I began Young Life in Saint Cloud, first by introducing ourselves to school administrators and church leaders in the area. We met a few kids through Young Life contacts, invited them to a club meeting, and began building relationships. After four kids attended a Young Life camp that summer, we began a Young Life club in the fall while considering how to expand our ministry.

The question I had asked in high school CCD class was to be answered in the ministry being developed in the Saint Cloud area. The following spring we gathered the pastors of the local churches together to further explain Young Life and ask them to support the ministry in Saint Cloud. Four parishes supported me for the next two years to do the work of a Young Life staff person, and since then I have focused my work in one church while joining the Catholic diocesan staff in youth ministry.

During the last six years we have developed our leadership team by drawing from the community and from nearby colleges, and from that group has come four of the eight youth ministers in our area. All of us are using the Young Life style of ministry to some degree—club, Campaigners, weekends, team leadership—as well as doctrinal classes, liturgies, social and recreational activities. Our greatest weakness is the lack of adult leadership from our own parishes, for the majority of our forty adult leaders come from the colleges in our area. We are pleased that five of our present adult leaders have come through our Young Life clubs, but we recognize the need to sink deeper roots into the adult community of our parishes.

Our individual programs differ, but we all agree on the primary importance of contact work. We have been blessed with sympathetic school administrators who allow us to circulate freely in the high schools that we serve, only one of which is Catholic. We are further blessed with generous pastors and parishes that are freeing our time to work relationally with young people. Our experience in this predominantly Catholic area confirms what Jim Rayburn found forty years ago, namely, that life changes come from "one life touching another."

Principles of Young Life's Ministry

Friendship has been the most essential element in Young Life's style of ministry—the belief that a personal friendship is the best vehicle to share faith with a young person. Adolescence is a time of transition from childhood to adulthood, a time of profound physical, emotional, and spiritual changes, a time of identity formation. Unfortunately, this is the time when an adolescent is moving away from familiar institutions—the family, church, or neighborhood—the traditional sources for adult friends. Young people today see most adults in authority roles such as teachers, bosses, priests, police officers, and consequently, are left to their own peer relationships for guidance and friendship.

Young Life attempts to work with the sociology of the adolescent world by discovering the key focal points for kids in a community and being present there. To expect kids to come to a church program can at times go against the flow of their lives; rather we must take the initiative and bring our concern where they can hear it. Beginning with Jim Rayburn's concern for the outsiders, this outreach orientation has tuned leaders in to the needs to which they must address the Christian message.

One Young Life staff man named Don Johnson uses the following drawing to explain his approach to outreach.

Christian Ministry to Those "Without"
(Colossians 4:5)

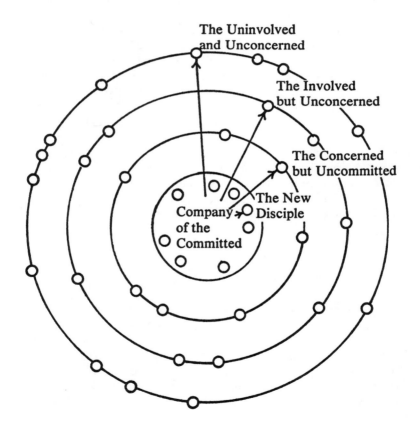

There are varying levels of relatedness to Christ and his Church, from the uninvolved and unconcerned to the "Company of the Committed," Elton Trueblood's term for the Church. Believers seek to reach out to all segments of the world in hopes of inviting them into the fullness of life in Christ. Applied to youth ministry, the varying levels of involvement look like this:

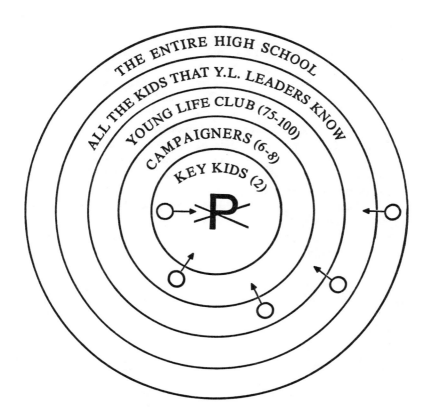

Our ministry would then be seen as an effort to invite the young people we encounter one step closer into the Christian life. When each person of a leadership team has his or her own set of relationships established in different parts of the high school world, the impact on a school can be significant.

Theologically, this ministry through friendships could be called *incarnational evangelism*, literally "bringing the good news in flesh." The most complete revelation of God came in the person of Jesus so that God's message of love could be understood by humankind. Likewise, the Church's concern for young people must find its expression in adults who are committed to sharing their faith in a personal way. As Jesus pitched his tent among us (John 1:14), so we must walk in the world of adolescents, to discover with them God's understanding and acceptance of them. We can see this lifestyle in Paul's First Letter to the Thessalonians (2:1–13), where he describes how he brought those believers to faith through his personal caring and uncompromising faith. As Young Life's president, Bill Starr, says, "There is no substitute for living life with kids," sharing their hurts and joys, successes and failures, while modeling the creative alternative of the Christian lifestyle.

Another major strength of Young Life has been its ability to present the essentials of the Gospel in clear and simple terms to young people who have failed to hear it in their churches. Part of that effectiveness comes as a result of contact work, but mostly from being simple, direct, and personal. In a club setting kids hear the basic story of Jesus told by someone truly committed to the message he or she speaks. Jim Rayburn's formula was simple yet effective, "Get their attention, tell them a Bible story, and apply it to their lives." The club's messages usually include humor and always contain stories from the leader's life that are related in such a way that kids can easily identify with the leader and then with the scriptural story (e.g., Zacchaeus as a social outcast, up a tree). Throughout the year, the messages also give kids practical applications of gospel values and definite challenges to deepening their relationship with Christ.

Young Life's presentation of the Gospel is divided into four parts: (1) the person of God, the Incarnation; (2) the need of humans for God, a relational concept of sin; (3) how Christ meets the needs of humans—the words and work of Christ; and (4) Christian commitment and lifestyle. Club leaders vary their use of this message scheme, covering the sequence in a month, a semester, or a year. The impact of the club's messages is that the young person can hear the Good News as a unified story.

Lastly, the key to any successful youth ministry is the adult leadership. Young Life has always put its best resources into training and creative development of new forms of ministry. The quality of ministry in a Young Life club or any youth ministry is directly related to the quality of the relationships and faith-life of the adult leadership. Fellowship brings forth ministry. When Christians gather to share their lives and faith and to pray together, ministry emerges as a natural expression of that fellowship. Ministry without fellowship is merely "youth work." When fellowship truly happens, young people can see a leadership team as a community of believers giving witness to Christ, a visible model of the Church in their midst.

Practical Application

1. Outreach: A Ministry of Friendships

If we believe that faith is best communicated through friendships, how does our ministry reflect that belief? Ministry to the total young person requires that we know the high school world—its atmosphere, its pressures, the heroes, the outcasts, its rhythm of life, and its needs—in order to speak God's Word within this world. This direct contact outside a "religious setting" is essential to a ministry that seeks to truly serve young people. I know that the quality of my ministry is directly affected by the number of hours that I am able to spend with kids outside of meetings; there is no substitute for contact work.

Do you know the adolescent subculture in your area? If not, take time to do some informal sociological research: Where are the kids? What are their hangouts? Who are their favorite teachers? Talk to school administrators, favorite teachers, parents, fast-food restaurant managers, police officers, Protestant youth ministers—anyone who is knowledgeable about the high school scene—and become an expert on your area. Then ask the question, Where can I spend time to build relationships with young people?

This outreach mentality moves us from being concerned only about the ones who come to our program to offering ourselves in friendship to those outside the influence of the Church. We do not have to look far in the Christian Testament to see the concern of Jesus and the early Church for outsiders.

2. Proclaiming the Good News

When do most young people (or people in general) tune out of a sermon? Usually when the talk ceases to be personal and is simply moralizing. Young people are most interested in other people's lives, what makes adults tick, and how they make their decisions. In preaching or speaking to young people we must begin with their interests—human lives—and more importantly, with our own lives and faith. Adolescents need to see transparent adult examples of faith who are willing to share their personal stories of faith and are able to express the story of God's love for them. The Scriptures are relevant to the adolescent's world, but we must do the translating, not only with a new paraphrased version but also with our lives.

The question for us then is, Have our young people truly heard the Good News of God's love for them—personally? If not, perhaps we need a new setting within which to present the message. A new combination of music, humor, and informality might open some ears to God's acceptance and love.

3. The Call into Ministry

The greatest source of leaders for Young Life is from within its own ranks, that is, the kids themselves. It is not unusual for a Young Life staff person to tell of his or her initial involvement with Young Life through first meeting a leader at school, being invited to a club, then perhaps to a weekend or week-long camp. The next steps might be a work-crew assignment, a month of volunteer work at one of the Young Life properties, then perhaps a period of leadership training during college. Finally, after graduate training, that person may be invited to join the full-time staff. Many others serve as volunteer leaders and committee members or use their experience in service to their local churches.

I believe that this is a modern model of the early Christian style of deepening involvement in the Church; namely, evangelization, discipleship, and the call into ministry. Through an outreach style of evangelization, Christian growth groups, and gradual leadership training, a totally uninvolved young person can be invited into the fullness of the Church's life. The challenge facing us is to create ways of gradually inviting young people into the ministry and leadership of the future Church.

4. Fellowship→Ministry

If true ministry is indeed based on Christian fellowship, what does that mean for our group of leaders or teachers? It means that young people will go no further or deeper than their leaders go. If leaders are not praying together it will be hard to ask the group to pray; if they cannot speak personally about their faith it will be difficult to get the kids to express their own faith. Many Young Life leaders spend as much or more time with other leaders as with their kids to ensure a spiritual depth that focuses the leadership group on God's love. This is also the best way to reproduce one's own ministry, to give away what one knows about youth ministry for the benefit of more young people. The questions for us all are: How much quality time do we spend with our leaders? What would happen if we were more involved with their lives? Perhaps we need to rewrite a few job descriptions around the needs of the relationships involved in Christian ministry. Notice how relational and spiritual the "job descriptions" were among the Apostles in the early Church.

5. Schools and Religious Education Programs

The challenge to any structured program is to include relationship-building activities within the existing curriculum, both for teachers and capable volunteers. We are emerging from a time when we taught faith intellectually by utilizing only educational vehicles to pass on the faith. If we believe that the student-teacher relationship is of prime importance in learning faith, how does that appear in our lesson plan? We know how authority can stifle relationships with young people, but do we offer some nonauthoritarian settings for our teachers?

I know of a Catholic Young Life leader teaching junior high CCD in a parish who insists on staying with the same group of kids for three years. One of his relational tools is a "secret notebook," a journal that kids write in at the end of class and pass on to Gene. During the week he replies to their questions or comments and returns the journals at the beginning of the next class, and Gene assures me that the journals are filled with some deep thoughts and feelings. This style of education tells kids that their teacher is more concerned about his or her relationship with them than with mastering a certain grade-level text. It tells them that they are important, a message our young people deeply need to hear.

Conclusion

Young Life's philosophy of ministry to the unchurched of the adolescent world speaks prophetically to our Catholic Church's efforts in youth catechesis. Our Church needs to develop the tools of outreach ministry through incarnational evangelism—solid Christian growth groups that teach and disciple believers and graduated levels of leadership involvement that call people into ministry. In shaping our youth ministry around friendships, we can invite young people into the greatest friendship available—a living relationship with Christ.

Essay 15

Adult Training Program
for Youth Ministry

Richard Costello

Richard Costello's article about training adults to work as ministers with young people is written in a concise style. Thus it could be read in a few minutes. However it deserves to be studied and pondered for the deep understanding it shows of the work of helping adults develop an intentional ministry with youth. His approach stresses the skills of listening and responding to young people in flexible, creative ways.

Costello started with adults who were more comfortable working with teens in structured situations, such as classrooms. He wanted to help them become comfortable with youth in other, more flexible, situations. He said the first task of adults working with teens is not to teach them something but to focus on them and to listen to them. He wanted the adults he was training to reverence teens at the same time they were becoming better at relating informally with them. His efforts may have been successful simply because he himself reverenced the adults he worked with and went with them step-by-step, always giving them an opportunity to voice their fears and hesitations.

At the time this edition was being published, many of the adults Costello had worked with were still actively doing ministry with youth and training the older young people in the very methods he originally used to enable their own ministry. This essay is reprinted from Resources for Youth Ministry, *ed. Michael Warren (New York: Paulist Press, 1978), pages 38–44.*

Does this sound familiar? "Interested adults *desperately* needed to help with the high school program. Please contact the rectory or the religious education office for details."

The odds are pretty good that if you walked into Any Parish, U.S.A., in September, you would find this announcement or something similar in the bulletin. Even if a parish is fortunate to get adult volunteers for its high school program this way, too often these same adults quit in frustration halfway through the year. A typical parish repeats the bulletin petitions in January.

It's true that we might produce something edible by reaching into the refrigerator, randomly pulling out five or six items, and throwing them into a covered dish in a 350 degree oven for forty-five minutes, but our chances are remote at best. Yet we apply the same haphazard recipe in recruiting adults for work in youth ministry. A general appeal for help in the parish bulletin *may* interest adults who have sensitivity toward and a facility for dealing with youth, but the odds for this are no better than the possibility that we will get a gourmet dish from our refrigerator casserole.

I think we need to take a new look at our recruitment and training of adults for youth ministry.

My experience in youth work has convinced me that the most beneficial way of recruiting adults is by personal invitation. But identifying those adults within the parish community who obviously have the ability to minister to youth is a first necessary step. I will list here some of the ways of locating these adults that I have found effective:

1. Survey the teens in your parish about the quality of their relationships with their parents. If teenagers indicate to me that they have excellent rapport with their own parents, I immediately consider these adults as good possibilities for youth ministry. It isn't always true, but usually if parents can relate well with their own teenagers they will do the same with others.

2. Ask the teens in your parish if they know any adults, possibly teachers or bosses, whom they like and feel would be good at working with youth in the parish.

3. Offer an adult education program in the parish on topics such as Understanding the Adolescent or The Faith Development of the Adolescent. Often adults with the ability to work well with youth can be identified at such meetings and discussions.

4. Contact volunteer agencies in your area to find out if there are adults successfully working in volunteer programs with young people. Many of these same adults may be parishioners, and they may be exactly the kind of adults you are looking for.

There are many other possible ways of identifying potential youth ministers for your program. It would be unfortunate if these adults are "out there" in our parishes but have never become involved because no one ever challenged them to use their gift of ministering to teens. The key, therefore, is personal contact and personal invitation.

As necessary as it is to identify the right adults for youth ministry, it is even more important to provide them with the proper training. Often the adults who volunteer in September and quit in January do so because they aren't growing themselves. Hence they feel inadequate to the task. Working with youth becomes a difficult experience for which they have not been prepared.

Because I believe that little or no preparation is the primary reason many well-intentioned adults cease working with young people, I would like to propose some guidelines for developing a realistic training program. Three basic guidelines have been helpful to me in training and working with adult volunteers.

1. Adults who wish to work with youth must be willing to try to articulate their own faith experiences. They need not be theologians, but they should be adult Christians who are struggling to understand the presence of the Lord in their own lives and who are willing to talk about their struggle. A training program should show them what it means to share their faith and how it can be done.

2. Adults who work with youth must attempt to find in one another's company a sense of Christian community and support in their ministry. Without mutual support, prayer, and a sense of community, ministry will always become a discouraging task. Training programs must help build this sense of community interdependence.

3. Adults who wish to help youth grow in an understanding of their faith must be willing to continue the same quest in their own lives.

These simple guidelines were my blueprint for designing the following training program.

The Program

The Youth Worker Training Program ran for twelve weeks. It was divided into three four-week sequences.
- Sequence 1: Personal Growth of the Youth Minister
- Sequence 2: Theological Input
- Sequence 3: Practicum in Program Planning

Sequence 1: Personal Growth of the Youth Minister

Sequence 1 was based on the belief that youth ministers cannot successfully help others to grow unless they themselves are involved in a growing process. Effective youth ministers are actively involved in growing and are prepared to take the next step in their own spiritual journey, unsettling though it may be.

Most of Sequence 1 consisted of assignments that the participants were asked to complete between the 2½-hour meetings. The majority of the meeting time was spent in sharing "homework" results and exploring together the implications. The assignments to be done in preparation for each of the four-week sessions were as follows:

Week 1

Assume that you are put in a classroom with an assortment of twenty teenagers and must remain there for twenty-four hours. Assume further that you have no books, no weapons, no pencils, paper, blackboard, or other equipment. Assume further that you are asked to communicate the message of Jesus in this situation.

What would you do? How would you begin?

How would you see yourself in that situation (e.g., as one who should control the situation to prevent damage)? What would your initial feelings be and why? What message would you be trying to make the teenagers aware of? Specifically what would you be trying to tell them? How could you judge whether that message was successfully communicated?

Now set up a time chart and try to sketch out hour by hour how you would spend this time.

Note: If you have envisioned yourself as a teacher in this situation, do it again and envision yourself as an adult participant with no investment in the property and no direct commission to be in that classroom.

Week 2

What do you think Jesus would want to say to a typical teenager today? (If you cannot imagine this, think of a teenager who lives on your block — who you know at least by first name — and imagine what Jesus would want to say to him or her.) Specifically — write it down — describe his actions, his words, his mannerisms, the tone of his voice, where the dialogue would occur.

Note: If you find this hard to do, read in the Christian Testament what Jesus said to Zacchaeus, the rich young man, and the woman taken in adultery.

Next, write down what *you* would like to say to that same teenager. Be specific.

What is the difference between your message and that of Jesus?

Is it possible to communicate the message of Jesus if you are not committed to trying to first live the message yourself?

Week 3

Map out a schedule of activities that you can engage in to make contact with teenagers and to get to feel at home with them (at least two per week, each contact a minimum of a half hour).

Write out what you can do to begin making this kind of contact. Think of your opportunities (lunch hour, social involvements, etc.); think of yourself, what you could honestly do and what would come off as phony.

After each actual contact, take time to write a paragraph on how you felt while making the contact and why you felt that way. Then write a paragraph on what you learned during the contact.

Week 4

Administer the following questionnaire, using a cassette tape recorder, to ten teenagers of various descriptions over the next week. Tell them you are taking a course on adolescents of today and want to get their opinion on a few things.
1. Do you feel that school is a good preparation for life?
2. What is the basic problem with parents today?
3. What is the most important thing in your life right now?
4. What does being a Christian mean for you?
5. If you were a teacher what would you try to do for your students?
6. What do you think about this interview?
7. What questions, if any, would you like to ask me right now?
8. Would you like to learn more about Christianity?
Note: Before you begin this project, try to guess what the teenagers would say by doing the test yourself as though you were a teenager.

After engaging in these experiments, what can you say about
• The needs of teenagers
• The questions of teenagers
• The attractive points of teenagers
• The negative points of teenagers
• What I would like to do for teenagers
• What, honestly, I feel I am capable of doing

The exercises in Sequence 1 were designed to help the adults discern the validity of their call to youth ministry.

Through the various exercises, especially as they were analyzed, discussed, and prayed over at the 2½-hour meetings, the adults were able to clarify the objectives of youth ministry and to begin to develop a working methodology for their future ministry.

Sequence 2: Theological Input

Sequence 2 was designed to offer theological input to the adults.

The topics and content for these sessions grew out of the questions and misconceptions that surfaced as a result of Sequence 1. As a leader of the training program, I had to listen carefully to the adults to discern in what areas of theology they needed the most clarification. The four-week program in Sequence 2 dealt with topics such as the Scriptures, Christology, Revelation, Grace and Sin, Development of Conscience, Ecclesiology, and so on. In some cases this four-week session was expanded when we felt that more input was needed. Along with the content of each session, the adults were supplied with resource readings that formed the basis of their preparation for each session.

Sequence 3: Practicum in Program Planning

The last four-week segment of the training program was a practicum in program planning. In this sequence the adults were asked to design a one-hour program for a group of twenty teenagers. The group leader provided the adults with resource material and suggested to them a topic or theme for the program. The adults were organized into teams, at least two adults to each team. The group leader then contacted a group of twenty teenagers who were already involved in a youth program. He explained to them that the members of his group were conducting a training program for adults interested in working with youth and that they needed their help. The youth became the pilot group that the adults worked with to test their program design.

Once the adults had run their program with the teens each week, the entire group of teens and adults held a debriefing session. The youth were asked to critique the program and offer their suggestions on what they liked, what they didn't like, and what recommendations they could make for improving the design or the manner of presenting the material.

The practicum provided the adults with an opportunity to test their program design in a realistic situation, while it gave them valuable input as to how they came across. It also allowed the teenagers an opportunity to minister to adults. Perhaps the most significant result of the practicum was that it allowed all of the participants to see clearly that they are in ministry together.

Conclusion

The three elements of the training program were designed to help adults to discern the validity of their call to ministry, to provide them with some theological updating, and to offer them a practical opportunity to plan programs.

As I indicated at the outset, however, unless the adults themselves are growing spiritually in their ministry, they will become frustrated and quit.

It seemed to me to be important, therefore, to build into each of the sessions an opportunity for spiritual growth through prayer. As the participants continued in the training program, they developed a sense of trust in one another, a trust that eventually enabled them to share their prayer with one another. The participants saw these prayer sessions not as a flourish or add-on to the program, but rather as an integral part of it. They understood that their own willingness to pray with one another and with the young people was a necessary prerequisite for growing in faith.

As the leader of the training program, I felt that it was also important to allow participants time for gathering socially. Between the first and second sequences I structured breaks that provided opportunities to simply enjoy one another's company. These social opportunities went a long way toward helping the adults develop a genuine concern and friendship for one another.

Through a personal contact in our recruitment and a well-organized training program we were able to diminish the necessity for our SOS bulletin announcements. We had discovered a core of adults who were not only willing but also able to lead youth toward fuller involvement in a community of faith.

Essay 16

Developing Youth Ministers in the Southwest

Thomas Cahalane

Many dioceses throughout North America have set up programs to train youth ministers, although these programs are much more common in the United States than in Canada. My own view is that some of these programs are better conceived, better planned, and based on a more solid theological foundation than many programs to prepare permanent deacons. However, many of these programs are relatively new and owe a debt to the people who had the vision to conceive of such training at a time when they had no models to follow.

One of the original youth ministry training programs was the one devised and described here by Rev. Thomas Cahalane of the Diocese of Tucson, Arizona. When Tom Cahalane first explained his program to me, I became eager for him to put it in writing for others. Now that it is one among many, however, I still find his original essay worth studying for the way it explains the gradual evolution of his efforts. His description may give hope to those who see problems all too clearly but who do not see results as quickly as they would like. The Tucson experience seems to teach us, "Make haste slowly; start small, start well, and watch things grow."

Note the stress on evaluation, on taking a second look, and on remapping the route that characterized this program from the beginning. These characteristics will never cease to be important in any ministry.

This essay is reprinted from Resources for Youth Ministry, *ed. Michael Warren (New York: Paulist Press, 1978), pages 158–167.*

This article encompasses the sharing of a six-year journey and the experiences and efforts of many people who providentially joined me on the way. It deals with efforts and experiences spanning the years 1970 to 1976 in the field of ministry to youth. In being appointed CYO director for the Diocese of Tucson, in May of 1970, my overwhelming feeling was one of not wanting the job. I wanted to tell the personnel board of the diocese: "If you can find someone else for this job, give it to him." However, the next communication from the board was a letter of appointment by the bishop. In hindsight, my not wanting the job basically sprang from personal lack of conviction that CYO was a viable approach to meeting the real needs of young people. Prior to this time, I had been a director of CCD high school programs and CYO programs in three different parishes over a seven-year period of time.

My basic source of energy in serving as the diocesan CYO director was a lot of frustration with the two basic approaches (CCD and CYO) of the Church to young people. In too many instances, both of these approaches resulted in groups expending much of their energies in maintaining themselves against each other, and at best they survived in a cold-war atmosphere of coexistence. This reality is unfortunately still to be found in too many parts of the country today. Generally, in looking at the staffing for youth programs, I found goodwill on the part of both the youth and the adults functioning in these groups. Adults usually were present as volunteers serving in the varied functions of teacher, moderator, chaperone, adult adviser, but in many instances, with very little training. Again through the window of hindsight, both CCD and CYO programs used heavily adult-centered leadership styles. For the young people, it was better to receive (from the adult world) than to give to each other and the adults. For the adults, it was better to be givers than receivers from youth. However, in our diocese the adult leaders of CYO and CCD gradually began to work together and to approach young people in an entirely new way because of their experience of Weekends of Christian Living. Using as they do some of the insights and techniques of humanistic psychology, these weekends helped the adults encounter one another and helped them in turn meet the young people in a new way. Through these weekends, the discovery that young people could minister to young people in significant ways was a rediscovery of the pearl of great price.

Young people sincerely desiring to commit themselves to these weekend community encounter groupings became a feeble whispering sign of a hopeful vision, which in turn has given birth to the more fully developing youth ministry vision emerging today in the Catholic Church. In this rediscovery process, ministry to young people changed focus from being heavily adult oriented to a youth orientation, properly described as youth ministry. Youth ministry is a calling to minister *by*, *with*, *from*, *to*, and *for* youth.

Leadership Formation

The challenging task confronting us at this point in youth ministry in Tucson is training and forming three basic categories of people who are being called into ministry: (1) *youth* to be peer ministers to youth, (2) *young adults* to be full-time or part-time ministers to youth, and (3) *adults* (laypersons, priests, religious) to be effective ministering persons to youth, to the degree that they are called now in full-time, part-time, volunteer, or paid categories. The key words for all these categories are "called into ministry," training, and formation. Unless there is an effort to sustain people on all these three levels, the dangers of shortsightedness will become very real. A developmental movement, from peer ministry to young adult ministry to adult ministry, calling forth gradual commitment in the individual ministering person is to be supported as the ideal, but it must be flexible and sensitive to peoples' needs. Our efforts in the Diocese of Tucson are so directed.

Leaders from the peer ministry efforts of the Search weekends, as they move into their young adult years, often express their need for a more prolonged involvement by asking the question, What is there for me now? It was somewhat on the basis of this question that two of our young adults volunteered themselves as diocesan staff in a ten-month "Project YES" (Youth Extends Service) as full-time youth ministers among four parishes of the diocese from August 1974 to May 1975. They did so for a nominal salary, but more so in response to their call into fuller ministry.

Mike Berger, one of the YES staff, saw a twofold purpose for the project, "To respond creatively to the needs of young people and to motivate the adults of each community to take a greater interest in the lives of their kids." As young people search for identity, self-esteem, and the reality of God, Berger claimed, there is a tremendous skepticism about whether institutions such as the Church can help them in that discovery process. In explaining the program, Sharon Komadina, the other YES person said, "To create any lasting youth programs, a team of adults and parents working with the parish staff and the Project YES staff is necessary. Too often priests or nuns are transferred and then the youth program falls apart. We want to work with lay adults, share insights on youth ministry, and build a program together, so that when the ten-month project ends, there will be confident, prepared lay adults to continue working with the kids." Berger added, "We hope to be in a position, after ten months, to make a more definite statement of what really is needed in youth ministry to make it effective. We are also obviously experimenting with a new form of lay ministry in the Church." Komadina and Berger are presently associate diocesan youth ministry directors, and their conclusions about Project YES are documented in a twenty-page written report, which is available from our Diocesan Youth Ministry Office. One of their conclusions reads: "Pastors must become more committed to supporting financially the training experiences for selected adults in youth ministry, for it is in encountering spiritually alive adults that youth will come to experience the true Church."

In communicating this to the leadership of the fifty-six parishes of the diocese, through priests, vicariate meetings, and *Esperanza,* our diocesan newspaper, we refocused our diocesan youth ministry direction. The rationale for our 1975 to 1976 budget noted:

> The concept involved here, successfully illustrated in YES is that of tapping a real part-time commitment from college-age kids for a definite period of time and directing it to benefit the total believing community. The fruits of the pilot Project YES should become a reality for some of the other vicariates and will invite them and challenge them to do something more for youth. Matching funds, from a core group of parishes in the vicariate, would be the main source of funding, and the Youth Ministry Office would offer one thousand dollars toward each vicariate. Individual parishes must participate with support and matching funds.

The rationale also stated:

> Youth ministry is a full-time endeavor and it requires more direct contact with youth and adults on a sustained basis—but especially in outlying areas. The Youth Ministry Office will put one thousand dollars toward the salary of the Project YES college person for each vicariate requesting such a person, provided that the requesting parishes, working as a unit, will come up with matching funds.

At the moment the desire for such a person is strong, and requests have come from many areas of the diocese. There is likewise a strong interest on the part of five or six college graduates for such a personal investment and commitment. The need exists all over the diocese and will be answered only by extended services on a full-time, live-in basis. The extension of this project will initiate "new ministries" for young people and will, I hope, bring more commitments to the people of God—the Church.

In appealing to the leadership of the parishes to seriously consider placement of full-time people willing to serve as youth ministers, we pledged ourselves, as diocesan youth ministry staff, to be a support unit in training and forming youth ministers. During that year (1974–75) we sponsored and placed four full-time people to serve among sixteen parishes. Yet our training and formation on an in-service basis was less than satisfactory because of the lack of a consistent, comprehensive approach.

Youth Ministry Certification Program Design

Our present certification program for developing youth ministers grew from our first efforts at leadership formation. Throughout 1974 to 1975 other points became clearly evident and gradually formed essential components of our certification program. It became apparent that no one should be accepted into the program unless he or she would be willing to make at least a two-year commitment to serve as a youth minister. On the assumption that the heart of ministry is a calling into special relationship with God through persons, it became evident that a lesser period of time diminishes or totally destroys consistent fidelity, so central to effective ministering presence. Again we communicated our clarified direction to parish leadership through priests, vicariate meetings, *Esperanza,* and posters, inviting young adults, twenty years of age or older, to consider a two-year commitment to youth ministry. About twenty-five people requested more information, and six of those now participate in the program. Two of those are serving out of the Youth Ministry Office in the Diocese of Phoenix, while the other four program participants minister to youth in eight parishes in the Diocese of Tucson. As part of the admittance process, each applicant had a personal interview with a staff person, provided three favorable recommendations, and undertook an evaluation of his or her level of commitment in a four-day orientation to the certification program. During orientation, two of the applicants decided they were not ready for a two-year, full-time commitment to youth ministry.

While designing the two-year program for these six participants, we discovered nine other people who wanted to grow into fuller commitment in youth ministry, but who, because of time conflicts, could not meet the requirements. So the certification program was designed with two tracks— Track 1 for beginners in youth ministry and Track 2 for people already in the field with at least one full year's experience in full-time youth ministry. At the end of the first year of the certification program the diocesan Youth Ministry Office will verify qualifying participants as knowledgeable and competent in youth ministry, but full certification as a youth minister doesn't occur until the two-year program is completed. The overall requirements of the certification program are outlined as follows:

First Year (September to May)

Performance Requirements

1. Develop a core group of adults, at least four in each parish, who have grown in responsiveness and shown sensitivity toward and an understanding of the vision of youth ministry. To avoid isolation between adult and youth leadership, establish a parish youth ministry planning board that includes the core group of adults and at least two teen leaders.

2. Work on at least two retreats—once as an observer-helper and once as part of the retreat team in a significant witnessing capacity.

3. Conduct and facilitate two or three youth ministry meetings.

4. Design three different retreat models (at least twenty-four hours each) and execute at least two of them with the youth communities with whom you share ministry.

5. Design a calendar of activities and outline the goals, the needs, and the resources by which the activities calendar will be attained during the next year. Complete this by May.

Documentation Requirements

1. Write a report by midterm evaluating the places where youth come together in your area and what efforts, if any, are being made to minister to them in their community.

2. Chart noticeable change, if any, in the young people's response to and participation in the youth ministry program.

3. Participate in an interview with a member of the parish staff (priest, religious education coordinator) for a performance evaluation.

Time Requirements

The specific time investment required by each program participant is as follows:

Track 1
Two weeks in residency orientation at Regina Cleri Center
   September 7–21

Full day-overnight sessions of in-service training and formation
   October 19–20
   November 16–17
   December 14–15
   January 25–26
   February 18–19
   March 8–9
   April 12–13
   May 3–4

Track 2
Four weekends in residency orientation at Regina Cleri Center
   October 29–31
   December 10–12
   March 4–6
   May 6–8

Overnight and Weekend Session Formats

The basic schedules of the group that meets monthly for overnights (Track 1) and the group that holds weekend sessions (Track 2) have the following components in common: Each participant (1) gives a basic update of his or her ministry experience of the past month, (2) identifies at least one problem for shared brainstorming, (3) brings a tape of a youth ministry meeting conducted since the last get-together to be critiqued by the group, and (4) submits a written book report and gives a verbal report of insights gained from reading. Then a major presentation is made by the diocesan youth ministry staff, or an outside competent person, on a topic previously requested by the group or selected by the staff. Morning and night prayers, eucharistic liturgy, and meals in common are also regular features of these scheduled get-togethers.

Second Year

Documentation Requirements

1. Develop a two-year position statement on youth ministry based on ministry experience that includes the participant's personal philosophy of youth ministry along with his or her position about levels of youth ministry, settings for youth ministry, and the needs of young people. The paper should also address these questions: Whom do you get to work with youth? What do you look for?

2. Make a tape of how the positions given in the statement have been carried out. The tape must exemplify twenty focal points from the position statement. The explanation and exposé of at least ten of the main points will be a part of the final examination.

3. Write up two case studies (preferably, the case studies should span a period of more than one year).

4. Prepare a list of resources and references used (at least sixteen, six scriptural).

The first draft of these written requirements is due in January.

Personal Growth Experience Requirements

1. Participate in twenty hours of workshop programs.
2. Participate in a seven-day retreat.

Evaluation Requirements

1. Report on perceived personal changes for the two-year period of time.
2. Keep a personal journal of experience in ministry.
3. Have your work performance evaluated by key personnel in the area.
4. Keep a personal record of the twenty hours of workshop (Where? What did you learn? How have you used it?) and the seven-day retreat experience (Where? When?).

Certification Program Evaluations

The following evaluation comments, from both Track 1 and Track 2 groups, measure in some way the success of our efforts in developing youth ministers in the Southwest:

Track 1

"I'm really glad I came, have learned a lot and grown a lot, and I know it will help me when I leave, thanks."

"This has been one of the best experiences for me. In this short two-week period, many questions and hang-ups on community were answered, Thank you Jesus."

"I thank God every day for leading me into this special ministry and for all in our youth ministry family. Blessed be God forever, Amen."

Track 2

"I appreciated the presentation outlines on styles of leadership, they will be of great help to me."

"This was a great time together; it was neat; I learned so much."

Monthly Overnights

"The overnights are a wonderful learning process for me. It's very helpful to the extent that all youth ministry 'trainees' are able to share the good, as well as the bad, with each other and to share problems. It seems that most of us are normally experiencing the same things but in different ways. By talking things out, we gain support in a beautiful way. Every month I've experienced life in different ways, and sometimes I need space and time to think and talk and sort things out. Whatever it was I needed, I received either from my fellow ministers and from the sessions by the staff. I find these overnights highly beneficial to the spiritual development of the youth minister trainee. The knowledge and guidance of the staff is fantastic. I always look forward to our monthly overnight! I treasure this time spent together in prayer, study, meals shared, discussions, planning, and play. Very special place in my life right now."

"The overnight is a time for me to get away from my area and be with people who understand and support me. The atmosphere is nonthreatening, so I feel relaxed from a lot of pressure of the job (sort of, a time of little risk). I need time to evaluate things that have happened (meetings, retreats). It is time to talk about some problems that have come up — not to solve them — but to look at the way I have handled them. It is difficult to look at the large picture when you are in the middle of it, and much easier when looking back from a distance. I don't feel quite as alone either when I see the other people struggling with similar situations. The overnight also serves as an enforcer of goals (reading, tapes, core group); I would be very inclined to just say 'I didn't have time to read,' but the team is there to 'answer to' (in a positive way)."

These comments, gleaned from a few evaluation forms at the end of each get-together, measure at this point God's blessing on us in our risk taking into the revelation of God's ministry vision.

The basic focus of our certification program could be summarized as follows: It is to help the person (1) to grow to his or her fullest potential, (2) to delve into the doing of ministry, (3) to take a look at "how" he or she is doing ministry, with real emphasis on the ongoing evaluation of "how," and (4) to share with peer ministry people "my how of doing it."

From the hit-and-miss approach during the early seventies, with basically nontrained volunteers in ministry, to youth in our parishes, we are moving slowly as a diocese to meet the larger need of trained ministers. Presently twenty-eight parishes of the Diocese of Tucson are being touched by full-time youth ministry personnel, in an areawide or parishwide approach.

Essay 17

Deciding for Oneself,
Not by Oneself

Nancy Hennessy Cooney

During a one-year period when I was directing a series of workshops on youth ministry, I asked the adults present to list and rank the ten most important needs of teens. With rare exceptions adolescent sexuality was omitted from these lists. Yet pursuing a sexuality is one of the crucial tasks of adolescence. Issues related to sexuality are never far from center stage in the lives of teens.

To a large extent, U.S. Catholics have responded to the needs of adolescent sexuality with either silence or moralizing. Some pressure groups in the U.S. Catholic Church think the matter of adolescent sexuality should be kept locked in a basement cupboard. Some parents also are rightfully anxious about possible harm that might be done to their youngsters by ill-planned and poorly implemented programs of sex education. As a result of these tensions, courageous educators like the late Bro. Hugo Hurst, CFX, have suffered much for their efforts to make a contribution to education in the area of adolescent sexual development. Other educators and catechists possessing both the interest and the ability to make a contribution to this area have taken the safer route of silence and inaction.

One person who has not taken that route is Nancy Hennessy Cooney, a specialist in adolescent catechesis from Milwaukee. She has taken care to examine the available information and the current programs of sex education for adolescents, especially those developed by religious groups. What she has found is the existence of a few excellent programs that involve parents and teens in dialogue on matters of sexuality and genitality. She is currently engaged in sharing this information with Catholics in youth ministry in hopes that they will develop new programs suitable in different contexts for different age-groups. Certainly this is an area that deserves much more attention from those ministering to youth.

In 1980 Nancy Hennessy Cooney published Sex, Sexuality, and You: A Handbook for Growing Christians, *which has been widely used in schools and programs of ministry to sexuality among people in their early teens. In 1986 she established a national ministry placement network called Minis-*

try/Match, designed to match parish needs and expectations with the skills and vision of particular persons seeking a placement in ministry.
     This essay is reprinted from Resources for Youth Ministry, *ed. Michael Warren (New York: Paulist Press, 1978), pages 179–189.*

Have you ever seen someone pull a tablecloth out from under a set of good china? A friend of the family once did that trick just as we were about to sit down to her beautifully prepared meal. I forget what we ate that night, but I will never forget the sense of awe and relief I felt after I heard the cloth snap and saw all the dishes standing upright on the polished wood.

That experience has been a help in explaining to myself and others the possibilities within a certain program in sex education for junior high youth and their parents. The program, called Deciding for Oneself, Not by Oneself, succeeds in pulling away the invisible barriers between young people and parents surrounding discussion about questions of sexuality. Questions like: How do you get VD? What is a rubber? Do boys like girls who are easy? Is it a sin to have sex before marriage? How do you know if you are queer?

Many parents wait for their youngsters' questions, although when they reflect upon their own experiences at puberty, they remember how difficult it was to confront an adult with questions. In the Deciding program, parents and youth are given the structure of a weekend workshop and the stimulus of its content to share a new experience and allow it to be the occasion for getting conversation going.

Such conversation is the goal of a weekend program conducted by a trained leader and a small group of local adult parishioners. They lead large- and small-group sessions primarily for the youth but include additional sessions for parents. Ultimately, it is the adult volunteers from the parish who act as catalysts for better parent-youth communication in the home.

On another level, the tablecloth is pulled from the problem of "doing sex education in a parish setting." Many parish leaders realize the limitations of an approach that brings a doctor, a priest, and a parent in for a couple of hours to lecture a group of youth. This structure makes it difficult for youth to raise their questions or to be challenged to look deeply at their attitudes. In the weekend program young people meet much of the time in small mixed groups of eight that are led by a man and a woman parishioner who have been trained the previous weekend. Sexuality, through them, is witnessed as something that is normal and can be talked about with nonexperts who are interested in the young people as persons and who believe in their capacity to make their own decisions.

On still another level—that of the wish, the not-yet-realized event—the tablecloth can be pulled from a vision of the Church that is concerned about sexuality only as a series of "thou shalt nots." If through this program young people and adults begin to share and grow in their appreciation that sex is good, perhaps ventures like this can multiply and show what is underneath the admonitions and accretions of history—a desire to reveal that the beauty and power of sexuality can be an expression of and a concrete sign of God's creative love.

The Deciding program was first developed by the United Methodist Church and is being reworked for use in Catholic settings. My first acquaintance with this program was in a Methodist parish in Fond du Lac, Wisconsin, as I was trained in the first stage of the five-step process. Following that, I became co-leader of a small group in a parent-youth program. After describing this experience, I will offer some observations and suggest implications for Catholics who wish to develop sound programs in sex education. Finally, I will share some of the changes that have taken place in the model as it has been piloted in the Archdiocese of Milwaukee.

The Program

The Deciding program touched the lives of youth, their parents, and a small group of adult parishioners who were the discussion leaders. When one of the pastors had gained approval from the parish leadership for starting the program, he sent a letter to the parents of the junior high youth inviting the young people to participate in five 1½-hour sessions on Christian sexuality over a weekend on the condition that the parents agreed to attend two sessions of their own. The parents and the young people were told that the course was designed to "open up a channel of communication within the home about sex." The letter explained that the course leader, Rev. Wayne Banks, director of academic procedures and associate professor of education at Perkins School of Theology, Dallas, Texas, had been on the planning team for the course in 1968 and has since led many courses throughout the country. Rev. Wayne Banks intended to give twelve hours of preliminary training for parish religious educators and youth leaders familiar with the young people. He also invited others around the state who had expressed interest in the program. I was one of the eight local people selected from the total training group to co-lead the small-group discussions. These discussions are at the heart of the youth program.

Most of the twenty-eight young people who signed up had done so at the urging of their parents. On the first evening, the attitudes of the participants ranged from hostile to uneasy. These young people were concerned that they might be embarrassed in the presence of their friends or be given a lot of moral exhortations about how to behave sexually.

Youths' Sessions

Youth Session 1

Friday night's meeting was designed to break down hostilities and begin to create a climate of trust between the young people and their adult leaders. This was accomplished by introducing the course in an enjoyable manner. We broke the ice by playing a famous-person guessing game when the participants came in. Then at supper, which was provided by parishioners, my partner, Bob, and I met our group of four girls and three boys. All of us moved into a large meeting hall decorated with pictures and symbols about love and sex, and we participated in an introductory values-clarification exercise. This exercise focused on the folly of making decisions that are not based on correct information. The whole group then viewed a filmstrip called *Learning About Sex*. It showed the importance of learning more about sexuality in the junior high years and was also used to introduce some of the topics to be covered. Small-group discussion of the filmstrip was followed by an agree-disagree sheet. The purpose of the sheet was to surface some of the course topics and to indicate something about the level of the students' maturity. A question box was available into which participants could drop their written questions. The presence of the question box not only allowed the leaders to respond to individual questions but also assured the group that questions would remain in confidence and receive honest answers. Central to the course is a climate of openness and ease in which students can raise questions that are important to them and have these questions discussed. Finally a short paperback titled *Love and Sex in Plain Language* by Eric Johnson was given to each person. This book contains both factual information on biological functioning and an emphasis on forming values that respect other persons. This session closed with all the groups forming a large circle and giving thanks to God for making sexual persons.

Youth Sessions 2 and 3

As in the first session, these two meetings moved quickly and contained minilectures, discussions, games, and questions. The purpose of the Saturday afternoon sessions was to help develop correct vocabulary and ease in discussing the male and female reproductive systems. There was much to do and the participants were free to linger over subjects of interest in the small groups. I had presumed that students who had had courses in hygiene would find these sessions repetitive. However, they quickly moved from the factual presentation to questions about the Christian perspective on sexual conduct.

Youth Session 4

The first topic discussed on Sunday afternoon was sex roles. Opinion sheets, a filmstrip, and a value-making experience were used to aid in the process of discovering what authentic masculinity and femininity mean. Through this process, the group began to see the conflicts between the culture's narrow view of sexuality and a Christian view in which preference, experience, and the acceptance of oneself as loved by Jesus Christ play a large part in the decision about the kind of person one wants to be.

Youth Session 5

Late Sunday afternoon was spent discussing relationships with young people and parents. Three skits involving the issues of pornography, the influence of the gang, and exclusive dating gave humorous portrayals of how young people and parents listen to one another. We stressed the responsibility young people have to initiate conversation with their parents and, if that failed, with adults from the church. Our discussion ended with a spontaneous prayer in which we expressed thanks for God's love, for our capacity to love, and for God's forgiveness when we fail to respect ourselves or others.

Parents' Sessions

Parent Session 1

On Saturday morning, parents were presented with the materials that had been taught to their children the night before. A telescopic introduction to the next few sessions was also given to the parents. They had a chance to meet with their child's discussion leaders and talk about how he or she was responding to the program. The aim of this meeting was to give parents the opportunity to talk about whether they felt their child reacted positively to the experience and to discuss any difficulties they foresaw. The leaders had been instructed not to betray the confidentiality of their talks with the young people. It was a time to create feelings of trust among the leaders and the parents and to give the parents the positive reassurance that they were being supported in their role, not superseded.

Parent Session 2

In the final session with the parents, the content of the youth sessions was summarized, and Rev. Wayne Banks answered questions from the parents. Small groups provided the opportunity for further discussion and the chance for parents to sample the evaluation of the program by their child's group, for example, "I see that sex is beautiful, not dirty," and "I talked to my father about these things for the first time last night." Most of the evaluations were positive and the students expressed hope about continuing this communication with their parents. Our discussion with the parents included ideas about how they might keep the door open for further communication and how the local church would be available to serve them on a formal or an informal basis.

Adult Training Sessions

The initial twelve-hour training classes included interested persons from around the state, and after this training the group of eight persons prepared for each youth session with the youth and evaluated the sessions afterward. This schedule produced pressure but helped forge us into a strong community. The group also found satisfaction in accomplishing our limited objectives. One leader said, "Sometimes I get tired of working through a process at church. Real progress often seems so far away. It was good to be trained this time and be in a structure in which I knew what was happening and could concentrate on getting to know the kids and respond to them."

Rev. Wayne Banks's training erased whatever doubts I had about my own performance in the program. Our sessions included practicing short, clear ways to answer questions. We reviewed our plans and reflected on the responses of the young people. Working with a partner assured me that I did not have to know everything, and this reassurance gave me the freedom to relax and enjoy myself. I felt that I had come a long way in my ability to communicate about sex with youth. Parish leaders had the added satisfaction of being able to offer themselves as resources to youth and parents in the future.

Some Observations and Implications for Catholics

1. **The certified leader.** The position of a certified leader in a program of Christian sexuality in the Methodist Church is not taken lightly. A person like Wayne Banks, who has great humility, charm, and a sense of humor, used a five-step process to pass on his expertise to others. A person wishing to become a certified leader in the church must
- act as a group discussion leader,
- be responsible for organizing a program in a local parish,
- assist the trained leader in giving a course,
- design a program on his or her own, and
- lead a program under observation.

The leader must be able to make the many hours of adult preparation and evaluation challenging and productive. He or she needs to be a living example of a Christian who has integrated his or her sexuality, and must also be a serious educator able to operate within a behavioristic mode. Sessions are tightly structured, and clear directions of how to proceed are provided to ease leaders and students in awkward moments and to help them overcome feelings of insecurity. Banks once said to the adult leaders, "My concern is primarily for the young people. If I disagree with one of you in front of them it is because I believe you are wrong. I count on you to be willing to accept such correction for their sakes."

2. Parent-youth-pastoral support. Both parent and youth groups were encouraged to keep communication going. Going home at night was essential to the program because much informal conversation was carried on in the home environment. The adult leaders from the parish were presented to the young people as normal people who were willing and able to talk openly.

3. Religious content. The religious content per se came predominantly from the answers to the questions raised by the young people. For example, when they asked about the sinfulness of intercourse outside of marriage, the leaders gave a full and positive Christian perspective. But the real religious content came from adults witnessing to their belief that sex is a joyful gift from God. For Catholics, a natural conclusion of this conviction would be to end the course with a celebration of the Eucharist. This liturgy could be a strong demonstration of the unity formed over the weekend.

4. Adult education. Catholics have had available a great deal of theological background accompanying any change or new development in the Church. In the area of sexuality, too, it would be well for parents and adult leaders to study some of the current writing on the Church's teaching about sex in order to update their knowledge and review their own understanding of the subject. They might also seek opportunities to explore their attitudes on the subject.

5. The text. Catholics need to search out a different student book than the one described above by Eric Johnson. Official Catholic thought on topics such as abortion, birth control, and homosexuality differs from Johnson's and would need to be presented along with, or in place of, the more secular view.

Subsequent Developments

1. A pilot program in a Catholic parish. Since my initial experience of the program I have worked with a team in Milwaukee, and we have successfully conducted a pilot at Saint Rita's Catholic Church, Racine, Wisconsin. A certified Methodist leader, Rev. Bob Hays, worked with Mrs. Raejean Kanter and me on the presentation of the adapted model. Full support from the parish education committee and the pastoral team helped make the weekend program important in the parish. Senior high youth volunteered to baby-sit so parishioners could be free for training and program weekends. (They had one condition—that a program be created for them, also!) Parishioners responsible for food, recreation, and organization also attended some of the training sessions and increased the number of parish people willing to be available for future conversations with parents and youth. A liturgy celebrating the beauty of creation and sexuality ended the youth program and brought parents, youth, leaders, and support team members around the Lord's table. The joy and enthusiasm with which people celebrated the liturgy was a reminder to me that once the questions of young people are met openly, the youth are free to enter into other dimensions of church life without reservation.

2. Expert critique. Last fall Mrs. Kanter and I presented the model to a group of eighteen persons with backgrounds in sex education, theology, education, and parenting. They made a number of recommendations that helped shape the training process of Catholic leaders. They also recommended that every parish interested in our program have three evening sessions of adult education before conducting the weekend program for the young people. If the parish community is to be a resource in this area, they reasoned, the adults in the parish community must first meet on the level of their own needs, then concentrate on the youth. The format of the three evening sessions could be a shortened version of the process described below called the Awareness weekend for program leaders.

3. Training program leaders. In March 1977 we completed the first stage in a process that will culminate in certification of leaders for the Christian sexuality program. It was called the Awareness weekend. Here is the outline sent to the fifteen invited participants:

> The aim of the weekend is to evaluate our own attitudes toward sexuality including the Church's tradition on it. Participants will have a chance to come to grips with whether or not they feel ready to continue with practical training in the weekend model.

Saturday

9:00 a.m.–12:30 p.m. *Sexuality, American Style: Decisions and Consequences.* This session aims to help participants situate themselves along a continuum of values held in our pluralistic society. We will review some major elements shaping American consciousness in sexuality. We will have an opportunity to experience "desensitizing" and also ask whether it is a useful tool for coming to a deeper understanding of attitudes.

12:45–1:45 p.m. Lunch

2:00–4:30 p.m. *Understanding the Catholic Tradition Concerning Sexuality.* The reality of human sexuality is often isolated from the totality of human, Christian life. What is our relationship to our Catholic Christian tradition regarding sexuality?

5:00–6:00 p.m. *Liturgy.* Planned by three group members and introduced by the film about prenatal development *The First Days of Life.*

6:00–8:00 p.m. Social hour and dinner

8:00–10:00 p.m. *The Future of Sexuality and Sex Education.* A time to loosen imaginations and freely explore: Where is it all going? What are the limits? Who sets the limits? What are our hopes and fears for our children, grandchildren, ourselves?

Sunday

9:00–11:00 a.m. *Catholic Guidelines for Sexuality.* A chance to reflect upon an approach taken by a committee from the Catholic Theological Society of America in their book *Human Sexuality: New Directions in American Catholic Thought* (New York: Paulist Press, 1977). We will also test the usefulness of the principles and values outlined there by applying them to a concrete dilemma.

11:30 a.m. Evaluation of the weekend

12:00 m. Close

We encouraged people to get to know one another through the small-group sessions, the work projects (preparing food and liturgy), and the social times so that they could decide whom they would like to work with on the program weekends. We decided that a team of two or three (married, single, and celibate) would better image the diversity of lifestyles in the Catholic Church. This was also a practical decision. Since the "first-generation" leaders do not have as much experience as we will eventually require, we want them to have as much support as they need. Further, we believe that young people and adults need to be exposed to team ministry—a role they can and must play in the Church of the present and the future.

Although the full training process is not yet complete, we have a good idea of the steps that are necessary:

a. Private conversation with Mrs. Kanter or me about the person's interests and abilities

b. Participation in an Awareness weekend to refresh ideas and attitudes and to meet possible teammates

c. Specific preparation in how to use the model, how to train parish leaders, how to run the parent-youth program, how to deal with specific questions, and how to share leadership

d. Experience as a small-group leader on a weekend

e. Experience as a team member for the program leadership

f. An interview with the coordinators (Mrs. Kanter and me) to discuss our evaluation of the person's progress and to explore further background that might be needed

g. Experience as a team member who initiates new persons into sharing the leadership for the program

h. After observation and conversation, written recognition by the Office of Religious Education that the person is qualified to be on a team for the Christian sexuality program

As we experience the process with the "first generation" we will revise this outline. The coming year will present more opportunities to learn the best way of training. There is a waiting list of parishes that wish to have the program, although we did not use formal publicity. The fifteen leaders who have completed the Awareness weekend will begin to function as program leaders and discussion leaders for the small groups. Meantime, we will conduct other Awareness weekends to surface others willing to serve youth in this special way.

Some say one weekend for a junior high youth is not much. This is true in the light of the many needs Christians have concerning sexuality. But it is a beginning—the kind that elicits joy and gratitude from those involved. Perhaps the people who are touched by this program can be witnesses of the special presence and insights that Christians bring when they accept, share, and celebrate their belief in the totality of the human person. Perhaps these young people and adults will strike observers today with the same amazement as did the early Christians when outsiders remarked, "See how these Christians love one another."

Essay 18

Radio: A Ministry to Feelings

Don Kimball

Fr. Don Kimball's work of reaching out to youth through the medium of radio has attracted a good bit of attention among Catholics in youth ministry. Many people have expressed admiration for his low-key, yet moving, broadcasts entitled "Reflection: Music with a Message." Few people, however, have considered the possibility of starting a radio ministry to youth in their area. They reason that they have neither Don Kimball's talent for spontaneity nor his contacts in the local radio industry.

In hopes of encouraging many more persons to use radio as a means of communicating with youth, Father Kimball has contributed a lively account of his own experience in radio, together with some practical how-to suggestions for those wishing to get started. His account suggests that getting into this ministry is easier, and that more opportunities are available, than many would suspect.

This essay is reprinted from Resources for Youth Ministry, *ed. Michael Warren (New York: Paulist Press, 1978), pages 237–244.*

The Disc Jockey

Disc jockeys are the freaks of the media midway. They are also the single most influential, persuasive and powerful force in the vast world of communication.

Sorry, editorial writers. Sorry, network newsmen. Sorry, Johnny, Dick, David, and Merv. Sorry *Newsweek* and *Time*. Sorry, *New York Times*. Sorry, Madison Avenue. Sorry, record companies. Sorry, syndicated columnists. Sorry, A.P. and U.P.I. All of you may have the more important roles in communications, but that little pipsqueaky rock jock on some obscure 5,000 watter can move and shake his audience, baby, like you wouldn't believe.

The love relationship between disc jockeys and their audience is frightening to behold. Other communicators often . . . most of the time, really, have a certain love and hate relationship with their audience. "I stay half mad with Walter Cronkite all the time, but I watch him anyway." "Sure, I read the editorials . . . I don't agree with all of them, believe me . . . but I read 'em anyway." And so on and so forth.

But not disc jockeys. You love 'em or hate 'em, and listen only to the ones you like. No one listens to radio out of hate. Radio is a love object. It's a friend, an auditory security blanket, in the home and car. It's hard to be alone with the radio on.

And the objects of your affection come in a variety as wide as the range of their salaries . . . from $300 a month to $300,000 a year. All of them have an overriding characteristic . . . they need to be heard, based on the firm belief that you want to hear what they have to say. Newspaper columnists have this same strange belief. Everybody out there in Audience, U.S.A., wants to know how we think, feel, and react. Please don't tell us you don't!

Disc jockeys . . . be they record spinners, talk showers, rip and readers, etc., all seek a "thing." They seek their niche in their ego tripping, super competitive world that will set them apart from the other on-the-air personalities. Some find their "thing" is their voice. Some have a natural wit. Some get by on style. Some rely on production and gimmicks and scripted schtick. Some rely on phones and the audience. But all have a power that is unequalled in the world of communication!*

I am a Catholic priest, working part time in a parish, plus the youth ministry coordinator for the Diocese of Santa Rosa, California, and I am a disc jockey.

Ten years ago, these ministries would have rarely interlocked. There were occasionally priests who "worked with youth," but youth ministry, as we know it today, has become a new model for a perennial need. I don't know why all these roles in one person should blow people's minds, but as I reflect on it, the whole thing blew *my* mind as I tried to adjust to the challenge each role offered.

Becoming a priest was a big role change for me eight years ago. Spiritually, I became a "marked man," living my life in a fishbowl. Moving to a diocesan office has forced me to stop the criticism and start the action. However, the biggest change for me has been the disc jockey bit.

In one sense, I am not a disc jockey, that is, a paid, full-time employee of a radio station. In another sense, I am. I do a weekly rock-music show that requires the skills and awareness of a professional. But it didn't start that way.

It all began six years ago in Eureka, California, during my first assignment as an associate pastor. The local radio station, up for license renewal, needed to show the Federal Communications Commission (FCC) that it was fulfilling its promised public service commitment and needed a locally produced show, so I was contacted through another priest ("You work with teenagers; you can do it"). Fortunately, the music format at the station was

---

*From Bob Talbert's column, 4 August 1971, in the *Detroit Free Press.* Reprinted with permission of the author.

rock music, and after some terrifying doubts, I agreed to do the show provided I could use their music. A week later, never having even seen the inside of a radio station before, I went on the air—"live"—with "Reflection: Music with a Message," a program that was to run several years on Sunday evenings at nine.

In the beginning, I didn't know a turntable from a cart-machine. I just designed a thirty-minute show from the available music each week, then went to the station and did it. The disc jockey on duty ran all the equipment while I was allowed to operate one switch: number four, the microphone. Listening to tapes that copied my first broadcasts off the air was scary. (Listening *now* to those early tapes is *really* scary, beyond my coping ability.) I was projecting my voice, as in pulpit, instead of lying back, as in friendship. That needed work. On top of that, within three weeks I had exhausted my knowledge of rock music and had used up all the songs I really knew. So I started spending hours—late hours—at the station, listening to songs, making notes. I began preparing my show *at* the station, taking advantage of all the records there. Gradually, the disc jockeys and other employees started dropping into the production room where I was working to chat and tell jokes and stories. We came to discover each other as people, and then things really took off. The disc jockeys began to teach me some of their broadcast tricks; then I was invited to join their DJ basketball team, and then there were the Christmas parties, the office parties, the benefits, the remote broadcasts. I was making it in *their* world, and I knew it.

Within a year I was running all the controls on the air (having received my license from the FCC) and was picking the themes for my shows from relationships and feelings instead of from abstract theology. I had learned by now that most music focuses on relationships: people coming together, people falling away from each other, people alone. These were the areas in which Jesus ministered; why not a priest? I had a hook into something important here and didn't want to let go. People needed healing in their relationships, in their feelings. I could speak to that, and the music would be the message.

Rock music, I discovered, is effective more for its beat and cadence than for its words. Not only could I give the listeners a message; I could give them *momentum.* Pacing the show became important: open fast, use fast-moving songs in the beginning of the show; locate the listener in the feeling area; don't put two slow-paced songs back to back (that loses momentum); keep the blockbuster, big-message songs in the middle of the show, then pivot on the "problem" and move toward hopeful options; tie it together in the middle with a personal experience shared over instrumental music; play up-tempo, hopeful songs going out at the end of the show; and never let the music stop!

Compared to television, radio is much more effective in reaching teenagers. Their radios are always on at home, in cars, at parks and beaches, at school, even in the classrooms (watch for those earplugs!).

Production of a radio show is ten times easier than a TV show. I've worked with television too, and I know! In radio, the image is created *internally* by the listener, making the impact more personal. Most people listen to the radio while alone or with one other person, so I become an intimate friend, one side of a vital dialogue. If people's greatest need is to be cared for, then radio is a great place to do ministry. Television doesn't quite have the same credibility or the same intimacy.

I am no longer stationed in Eureka. A year ago I was transferred to Santa Rosa, so I needed a new base from which to broadcast. Through the San Francisco Archdiocesan Communications Center I entered the radio world at a whole new level: radio station KFRC, the biggest radio market in the Bay Area; it has huge reach, top ratings, and the best equipment, with engineers who really know how to operate the equipment. Live broadcasting is out of the question for this kind of a show in this kind of market. Also, only the engineers touch the equipment. And public service time is from 2:00 to 7:00 Sunday mornings. I was assigned to 6:15 a.m., and later the station decided also to run the show at 2:45 a.m.; so now it runs twice on Sunday mornings. When the operations manager at KFRC told me they were going to run the show a second time on Sunday I thought, "Wow! noon, or late evening." Then he told me, "2:45 in the morning," and I must have winced because he grinned and cracked, "Well, do you want to be popular or do you want to minister?" I felt like one of the sons of Zebedee.

So now this humble son journeys each week into San Francisco (fifty-five miles from Santa Rosa), coming into the station on Wednesday afternoon around two o'clock. I work for two hours in the disc jockey office, listening to current songs, hot albums, and also "oldie-moldie-goldie" hits from the past. As I plow through the music available to me (and there is tons!), I work up a list of "possible" songs, including the introduction ("intro") time and running-length of each. Within an hour and a half, I have twenty to thirty titles listed. Then I gaze over the list and look for relational "events." Songs start clicking together, and I draw up a "laysheet," listing in sequence the songs I will play in the show. It is unreal how different songs snuggle up to one another according to a relational theme.

Did I say "theme"? Right! Because it is only at this point—as I'm walking my play-sheet to the Xerox machine to copy it for my engineer—that I select the title theme for the show. I don't start with a theme and then build a show around it. The theme comes from the music. The activity inside the music suggests the relational areas that I will deal with that week. I've seen too many people do violence to a song by trying to bend it to say something it really isn't saying. The people listening *know* the songs, and they know when the meaning is twisted.

Since the format of the show is designed to minister to feelings, I move into those areas to do some healing. I'm no psychologist, and I don't pretend to be. Instead, I become a journeyman joining the listeners in *their* world, sharing some of my hurts and growth experiences, sending some care, understanding, and hope. This vulnerable approach is somewhat hard to handle with my friendly engineer peering at me through the glass. I pray the Lord never gives me a "crowd-shot" apparition of my whole listening audience (about 100,000). The thought of whispering "soft-heavies" into the hearts of all those people is a little overwhelming for this music minister.

Like a conversation with someone, "Reflection" has an integrated theme, but usually parts of the show hit the hardest. So it is important not to pour it on too heavily. The listener needs room to move and respond, some space to supply the real feelings inside. I become a sharing friend and a fellow listener, not an expert. I am not telling my listener friend how to correct or reform. Instead, I offer an ear; I become transparent myself, melting into the music, the mood, the struggle, the doubts, the healing. I am with that person because Jesus is. When people have a friend, there is hope. And when there is hope, there is always a solution: *their* solution, not mine.

That's why I don't use a script. I ad-lib the whole show and share only what is going on inside me. In the beginning, I wrote out what I wanted to say; then later, I just outlined what I wanted to talk about. Now, I pretty well know what I'm going to deal with, and the rest happens when I open my mouth. I operate with the confidence that spontaneity is God's gift to me and with the security that, if I blow a talk-up, we can stop the tape and edit. So I become free to fall into the music and share what is going through me. I find now that while I am recording, I am praying. Feedback on the show tells me that the listeners are praying too, praying the music, praying the feelings, celebrating the healing.

I don't think most adults realize how powerful music and the media world are yet. Media have an unseen audience with unmeasurable results. Media are still generally regarded as "the enemy." I remember in my first years of the seminary that we were not allowed to listen to radio or watch television. I agree that some of the music and messages of the media world are destructive. A lot of the content, though, is excellent. And most of it is at least neutral, waiting to be used by the right person. A weapon is simply a tool in the hands of the wrong person. Media are tools of communication that loving, Christian people can use for ministry. If we abdicate this opportunity, then we have no business blasting the media for the junk they have to broadcast. Who is responsible for the Good News in this world? We are! Not station managers.

Media people are first of all *people* themselves. They are looking for some meaning to their lives, as well as the listeners, viewers, and readers they serve. If they see something good, they will offer their public service time to share it with others. I've listened to many a public service director *beg* for some quality programming. Only now does there seem to be some small interest here and there in getting into media with some solid ministry.

I share this article as a story because it happened as a story. It happened because of relationships. It happened because I responded to something that fell in my lap. I didn't seek it, but was called to it. I didn't discover my gifts for this until I needed those gifts.

If people ask me how to get into radio, I tell them to start in the small markets first: build relationships with media people, share your dream. Chances are they will be willing to help design formats and teach skills. There is more than one format; in fact, there are millions of designs and formats that could be used, as many as people's creative minds can invent. Teenagers themselves could design shows from their own awareness of their music and their perception of God, other people, and themselves. How about taping rap sessions and then playing the best chunks back, punctuated by appropriate music selections? Many stations are playing shows with just that format right now. Sometimes Catholic disc jockeys at radio stations will work with teenagers in producing a weekly show. Believe it or not, even non-Catholic disc jockeys and program directors are willing to help! Some might even become – gasp! – friends.

Once you are into radio, there are a lot of residual benefits. It is usually very easy to produce sound tracks for slide shows by using the same skills that go into producing a radio show. Then one can shoot slides of the youth group or retreats and create some wild happenings. One person I know records a sound track focusing on retreat growth experiences, then brings a camera to the retreat and takes slides of everyone on the retreat on Friday night, rushing them to an overnight photo developer. Sunday morning at the Mass of Celebration: zap, a slide show, customized to that group.

Good slide shows, especially in small media markets, can be produced for television. We did this several times in Eureka. In addition, I produced over twenty-five slide-meditations that a local TV station in Eureka broadcast for its sign-ons, one every morning. I found that when I did favors like that for radio and TV stations, they did favors for me and the programs I was working with.

There is much more to the media than I have discussed in this article. But no one can really understand fully what I have already shared until they open up to a call to ministry and realize that the Lord is working through each of us to renew God's people. If the opportunity is there, then it is a call, an invitation.

All ministers are scared to death of what will happen next because we know how quickly God moves sometimes and how our lives are changed by the way God moves. I know that fear and the excitement that has been in my life ever since that first Sunday night over six years ago when I went on the air with: "This is 'Reflection: Music with a Message.' I'm Father Don Kimball. And this week: *Panic Button!*"

Part C:

Envisioning the Future of Youth Ministry

Essay 19

The Future of Youth Ministry in Canada

Michael Warren

In the spring of 1985, Canada held its first national convention on youth ministry, coordinated by the Canadian Bishops Conference. Invited as the keynoter and facilitator, I considered the event to be of special significance for its possibilities in renewing ministry to young people in Canada.

I include here the text of that keynote address in the hope that it will be of interest not only to Canadians but also to persons in the United States. The essay tries to reformulate some guiding principles for youth ministry in general. Readers will see that these principles are in the direction of greater concern for justice and peace. I am proposing a vision that, unfortunately, has not characterized ministry with youth in North America. In my view, the youth ministry revolution, which started in the early 1970s (many of the persons whose essays are included in this book helped launch it), has hardly begun. It will not have even begun to approach its maturity until it pays the appropriate attention to the issues of social justice and peace.

Today we begin a gathering with no precise precedent in the Roman Catholic Church in Canada. This is the first national convocation to deal explicitly with the topic of youth ministry. Obviously what is new here is not that the Catholic Church in Canada is for the first time discovering the question of the pastoral care of youth. Canadian Catholics have a long history of concern for their young people. What may be new, however, are the angles from which we approach our care for the young. In this conference we use two key phrases that deserve special attention: *the option for youth,* the title of our conference; and *youth ministry,* the topic that brings us here.

Puebla's Preferential Options

Many of you know that the Third General Conference of Latin American Bishops that met in 1979 in Puebla, Mexico, set out as one of its guiding norms for pastoral action what is called "the preferential option for the poor."[1] These bishops did not call the Church to be concerned exclusively with the poor. But in a world of growing economic inequities, they publicly committed themselves to choose sides and align themselves in a special way with the concerns and needs of the poor, the powerless, the victims of society.

Puebla's preferential option for the poor has become so well known that it now guides pastoral priorities worldwide. Far less well known, however, is that Puebla set for the Church in Latin America not one but two pastoral preferential options. The second one was the option for youth, which has been adopted as the title for our conference.[2] What is the meaning of "the preferential option for youth"?

In a world so used to manipulative ways of controlling people, of deceiving them, and of manipulating their assent, cynics might claim that the option for youth is a sleight-of-mouth wordplay designed to keep young people in the club called the Church. However, Puebla's option for youth is not a strategy to deceive youth or to control them. Rather it comes from a radical vision of the possibilities of young people in society and in the Church. Where do these possibilities come from? In Puebla's vision, they come from the special tendencies of youth. Young people tend toward a "non-conformity that calls everything into question" and toward "a spirit of risk that leads to radical commitments and situations." In this vision, youth possess "a creative capacity [for] new responses to a changing world, which they hope to keep on improving as a sign of hope."[3]

Puebla's affirmations of youth are not so common as one might hope them to be. Some societies see young people as in a period of preparation for a future role but as lacking any significant present role. This period, one of subservience, is spent in institutional structures over which they have little control and in which they have almost no voice. We can all ask ourselves where our own visions of youth stand in relation to the following vision of Puebla:

> [Youth's] strongest and most personal aspiration is freedom, emancipated from all outside tutelage. They are a sign of joy and happiness. They are . . . sensitive to social problems. They demand authenticity and simplicity, and they rebelliously reject a society invaded by all sorts of hypocrisy and anti-values. This dynamism then makes them capable of renewing cultures that otherwise would grow decrepit.[4]

Note the importance of this last sentence. Here we find not the dynamism that is dangerous because it is disruptive or intolerable because it questions taken-for-granted procedures. Nor do we find the dynamism that is simply annoying because it tends to think of alternative ways. As presented by Puebla, youth's dynamism is a creative one, capable of renewing cultures. The preferential option for youth means that because young people possess a treasure of creative restlessness, we cannot afford to do without them.

If society cannot afford to lose the enriching dynamism of youth, neither, according to Puebla, can the Church. Puebla never even hints that young people will be the Church of tomorrow. Its conviction is that youth are the Church of today.[5] It presumes a reality called the "young church," given as a life-giving leaven to the community.

> The Church sees in young people an enormous force for renewal, a symbol of the Church itself. This it does, not for tactical reasons but by virtue of its own vocation. For it is called to constant self-renovation, that is to say, to repeated rejuvenation. . . .[6]
>
> Some young people are very disturbed over social issues, but they are repressed by the systems of government. They look to the Church as a space for freedom, as a place where they can express themselves without being manipulated and engage in social and political protest.[7]

Before this option of the Church for youth will become clear to the young, however, some problems must be overcome. One of these problems has to do with how they perceive the Church.

Often the option is put completely backward, at least as far as it is perceived by young people. What the Church is concerned about, some of them are convinced, is not any true option for them but rather their option for the Church. They sometimes hear the Church saying to them, "You opt for us, and then we might opt for you. And when you reach middle age, you might even have some say." One of the most serious problems with Confirmation today may be that many young people are faced with a decision about their option for the Church before they ever come to see the Church's option for them.

However, the genuine option for youth (what was intended by the bishops at Puebla) is an openhanded, loving commitment of the Church to young people as the dwelling place of God and as the locus where the Spirit of Jesus is coming to new vitality. The simple truth is that the Church does not possess the option for youth by merely proclaiming that it does. The option for youth is only real when the Church lives it out. Young people know this, and they will not be fooled.

For example, the Roman Catholic Church in Canada cannot expect a full pastoral strategy for youth to be carried out by the schools. The Catholic school is not the Church. In actual fact it is as much under state control as it is under church control, though not all Canadian Catholics may want to admit this fact. The school is not the place for the coming together of the freely assembled community; the local parish is. Some young people may actively resist any pastoral care reaching them through the school because of what the school symbolizes for them. Could it be that for some native Canadian youth in the far north the school might represent most clearly the place where white social structures and the dominance of the south enter their lives?

It might be comfortable and neat if the school were able to meet all the religious needs of young people, but then such a strategy would not be the option for youth as I have described it. It would be a terrible mistake for the Church, under the guise of a commitment to youth, to use the school as a way of not having to take young people seriously in the parish community. In such a case, the option for youth would become the evasion of youth. As a phrase, *the option for youth,* obviously has a nice ring to it. But as a serious guide for pastoral work with the young, it offers some difficult challenges to the Canadian Church.

Development of Youth Ministry

There is another phrase we are using this week, and it provides the topic we have gathered to consider—*youth ministry*. Recently I asked myself why, in the past fifteen years in the United States and more recently in Australia, New Zealand, and Ireland, the area of youth ministry has become such a vital part of the Church's life? I suspect that something has become increasingly clear to the Church about young people and about its relationship to young people. The Church has come to see that it is but one agency in a complex network of agencies seeking to influence the young. Television, film, music, and advertising are all influencing the minds and hearts of the young, who are also influenced by the latent violence of a world poised for nuclear annihilation. Against all these influences, the Church has been relying on the counterinfluences of family, Sunday Eucharist, and the Catholic school.

Even in Ireland, where every child receives at least ten years of daily religious instruction in state schools and where the Church prides itself on family stability, there is a growing realization that the influence of the media is overriding that of worship, family, and school. The Irish bishops are now preparing a pastoral letter on youth ministry, to give direction to a renewed and better-integrated pastoral work with youth. I know from conversations with Catholic Canadians over the past several years that many of them believe, as do their fellow Catholics in Ireland, that there needs to be an integrated ministry to youth.

In the English-speaking world, youth ministry first received the most attention in the United States. It arose there initially as a concern for youth in their out-of-school time.[8] This is how the emphasis on youth ministry came about. In the United States no more than 20 percent of young people of high school age ever attended Catholic high schools for the nourishment of their religious faith. The rest attended what were called *religious instruction classes* once a week. These classes, of course, did not constitute the whole of the Church's work with youth. There was also Sunday Eucharist, as well as parish sports and social activities sponsored by the parish Catholic Youth Organization (CYO). For a long time this arrangement seemed to work.

About 1970, however, growing numbers of Catholic young people simply refused to show up for these religion classes. In truth, large numbers had never attended the classes, but when the numbers dwindled to the zero point, truly perceptive people began to catch on. Apparently youth were resisting the once-a-week indoctrination in religious abstractions. Some pastoral thinkers suspected that young people were in fact correct: these sessions were not an appropriate way of leading persons to insight into the meaning of the Gospel. There needed to be a better-balanced pastoral strategy for the young than could be offered by sports programs on the one hand and by classroom instruction on the other.

I stress here that youth ministry in the United States began out of concern for young people who did not attend Catholic high schools. This ministry did not rest on the assumptions that are appropriate in schools, but it sought to deal with how learning occurs in truly "de-schooled" ways. Stressing this difference in no way demeans the work of schools or the assumptions of schools, but it does highlight a distinctive quality of youth ministry. In schools young people do not assemble out of full choice. They are assembled partly by the state, and if any young persons refuse to assemble there, the state will begin to interfere in their lives.

Youth ministry, however, does not deal with already assembled groups of youth. Those who come together in youth ministry do so freely, out of choice. A special rhythm can be detected in the way youth ministry gathers the young. The tone is set, not by directives, communiqués, or "oughts," but by welcome, hospitality, sharing, and celebration. In youth ministry there is almost no institutional power. Whatever power does exist rests on personal credibility and on bonds of affection. I claim that this feature has helped the Church in the United States to better understand the nature of adult catechesis and even the true nature of worship, which has been subverted by the notion of the Sunday obligation presented as an obligation external to the self.

One can pick up this rhythm of youth ministry quite clearly in the programs that have replaced the once-a-week instructional sessions. These are the various weekends of Christian living, such as Teens Encounter Christ (TEC), Search, or COR. Young people do not come to these weekends to fulfill some religious requirement, for example, for graduation. They come because they want to, often because a friend invited them or encouraged them to sign up. In the weekends I am most familiar with, there is an attempt early in the program to assess whether anyone is present under duress. Why? Because these weekends center their activities in celebration, whereas duress always subverts celebration.

The once-a-week religious instruction class, however, tended to bring in its participants under clear notes of duress. Most who came had to come. There were penalties for not showing up or for coming late. Adults policed the corridors in order to keep the damage down, as well as to keep the students in their proper classrooms. In some places the atmosphere was not that of a school but of a detention center.

I do not wish to give the impression that these weekends of Christian living are the whole of youth ministry. I use them as an example of the rhythm of invitation and response that is so central to youth ministry.

Aspects of Youth Ministry

Actually four aspects are involved in youth ministry, and understanding them might help the Church in Canada develop a broad but integrated ministry to youth.

1. The first aspect is the *ministry of the Word,* a ministry to the meanings that bind any community together. Community is fostered by common understandings, and when these understandings cease to be common to all in a group, the unity of the group begins to disintegrate. In the early Church the ministry of the Word had a special place, and those who had a gift for this ministry were given special recognition in the community. Of the several forms of the ministry of the Word, the two most important to youth ministry are evangelization and catechesis. I have written extensively about the nature and practice of both evangelization and catechesis.

What I want to note here is a simple but very important aspect of catechesis, namely its nature of being occasional but lifelong. Yet in far too many places, catechesis is practiced in exactly the opposite way, as continuous but terminal. It starts when a child is seven and continues every fall and spring semester until the child becomes old enough to say, "No more"—often on the occasion of Confirmation. At that point catechesis terminates. In a Church where lifelong catechesis is the exception, it is no wonder such stress is placed on laying out every nuance of Christian faith before the age of twelve. Some of you know that this is not just a problem affecting the young. Some priests think their own catechesis ended or should have ended when they left the seminary; thus they are very much like the confirmand who says on the day of Confirmation, "Never again."

2. The second aspect of ministry is the *ministry of worship.* When members of a group understand something wonderful, they tend to want to celebrate this understanding: Two people we love now love one another; let us celebrate it. Someone has found a job or had a child or found a home or gotten out of the hospital; let us celebrate it. Although one could sometimes get the impression that worship is the only ministry that concerns the Church, in youth ministry it is one among a number of aspects of ministry. Worship is not in isolation from catechesis and other aspects of ministry but in concert with them.

3. The third aspect of ministry is the *ministry of guidance and counsel,* which includes education. The epistles of the Christian Testament give witness to the importance of guidance and counsel in the early Church. Indeed in today's ministry to youth, guidance and counsel have a similar importance. Some young people come to the Church seeking not religious assistance but simply the guidance and counsel of wise persons. That is a very appropriate way of coming under the loving service that ministry is meant to be. Note, however, that I have included education here under guidance and counsel. In doing so I have separated it from the ministry of the Word. I want to stress that the Church may have a ministry of education even when there is no explicit religious teaching involved.

4. The fourth aspect of ministry is the *ministry of healing.* This category is added to highlight the need for the Church to pay attention to social ills and systemic evil and to work at healing brokenness and evil at the societal and global levels. Some ministers who work with youth want to limit their healing to the personal level of guidance and counsel. The personal level is not enough. I claim that the young are as much harmed by the systems of evil (e.g., the arms race and the militarization of our society) as they are by their own personal or familial hurts or fears.

In some countries youth ministry is serving to remind the wider Church of the need to attend to a broader range of ministries, and there youth ministry is in the forefront of the renewal of ministry in general. Even further, in the United States youth ministry is one aspect of a revolution bringing laypersons into parish ministry. There are now many hundreds of laypersons doing youth ministry full-time in U.S. parishes, the majority under the age of thirty. Most of them have entered ministry after an apprenticeship of leading their peers in various youth programs, especially in weekends of Christian living. As one might expect, there are problems in this situation, difficulties regarding salaries and job protection; proper formation for the role, especially theological formation; and reliance on support from diocesan structures while functioning as a layperson in ministry in a clerical, male-dominated Church.[9]

Five Steps of Pastoral Methodology

The main focus of our gathering here, however, is not just youth ministry but youth ministry in Canada. My own suspicion is that youth ministry in Canada promises to be headed in a sound direction, simply because the most important principles to guide it have already been enunciated—not in the United States, Australia, or Ireland, but in Canada itself. The writings of the Canadian bishops and of the pope in his visit to Canada last year contain all the clues needed for a healthy youth ministry.

I am aware that setting forth principles and putting them into practice are two different matters. Setting forth principles is fairly easy; the practice of these principles is much more difficult. This problem notwithstanding, I propose that youth ministry be guided by the five steps of pastoral methodology proposed by the Canadian bishops in their 1984 pastoral statement "Ethical Choices and Political Challenges."[10] These five steps, quoted from the documents, seem to me to be profoundly sound guides for youth ministry. The bishops have not claimed that this methodology is all that the Church does; neither will it be all of youth ministry. Still it defines the angle from which we look at the task. Let us examine each of these steps.

Step 1: Being present with and listening to the experiences of the poor, the marginalized, the oppressed in society

What a wonderful (though certainly not comfortable) starting place this is for those directing youth ministry. When youth ministry is done among the middle and upper classes (and in the United States at least, most of the parishes hiring youth ministers are from those strata), too easily it can lean toward following the cultural values of those economic classes, rather than the values of the Gospel. The middle and upper classes can tend to be first of all interested in themselves, in their self-affirmation, their self-approbation, and their self-advancement.

If the first priority of the middle and upper classes tends to be their own comfort, then of course the last thing they want is to be challenged or disturbed. Actually, they will not tolerate it. They pay well to have life kept on an even keel and to have those who do not fit screened out: minorities with their minority ideas and also the unscrubbed, the unkempt, or the unscented.[11]

If youth ministry in Canada is based on the bishops' methodology of being present to and with the poor, it can hardly be limited to the middle-class rereading of the Gospel. Actually, youth ministry everywhere ought to be based on this methodology, both in a basic sense and in an extended sense.

In its first, basic sense, this methodology gives preferential attention to those most marginalized, those most at the edge, those most poor. Who are these among Canadian young people? First of all, they may be the youth of the Indians among the native peoples.[12] For example, the death rate from motor vehicle accidents for all Canada in 1974 was 26.9 per 100,000. But in 1976 for Canadian Indians it was 60.5 per 100,000, two and one-half times the rate for the others. For the group aged five to fourteen, violent deaths among Indians are now three times the national rate, and for the group aged fifteen to forty-four, the rate is four to five times the national rate.

In 1978, the suicide rate for all Canada among those aged fifteen to twenty-four was just under 20 per 100,000, a very high rate, higher than the rates in Australia and the United States and identical to the rate in West Germany.[13] However, in that same year, the suicide rate for Canadian Indians aged fifteen to twenty-four was 130 per 100,000. Could there be an error in the statistics? After years of checking suicide statistics, I have never seen anywhere a rate that high.

In many countries the most marginalized people are the gays. They are the only group who are treated as were the lepers of Jesus' day, the untouchables banned from ordinary society. Consider the terror experienced by a young person who at fifteen or sixteen realizes that his or her primary sexual attraction is not to the opposite sex but to the same sex. At a time when most of their peers are experiencing their sexuality as a great gift, these young people, because of an unjust social stigma, may view their sexuality as a curse.

Another group deserving preferential attention under this methodology are those economically at the bottom, who as a group get the poorest educations and the most unstable jobs. When the Church is on the side (and also *at* the side) of these young people, the Church becomes especially believable to all young people.

Any youth ministers who adopt this first step and try to defend it among the middle class will, I predict, find there a strong tendency to transform the notion of oppression into the notion of middle-class oppression; that is, oppression will be defined and reduced to whatever injustices middle class people judge themselves to suffer. I am not denying that in a world readied for nuclear devastation all young people, regardless of economic status, can realistically count themselves oppressed. But I am warning that middle-class people want to define oppression in terms of whatever rights or opportunities they are being denied. In the face of this tendency, let youth ministers remember that primary attention, according to the bishops of Canada, should go to the poor and the marginalized, the deprived in society.

In a second and extended sense, this methodology will work to help middle- and upper-class young people attend to the experiences of the poor and the marginalized. Not all youth workers will find it easy to undertake this methodology with privileged youth, partly because they will resist it and partly because it will not be popular with status-conscious parents. Yet few things relativize the actual, but not fully disastrous, pains of well-off young people as much as encountering the real, disastrous, despair-inducing pains of the marginalized. Someone told me recently that all conversion to social justice comes from meeting the victims of injustice. I know that such has been true for me personally, and I presume it would also be true for young people.

Step 2: Developing a critical analysis of the economic, political, and social structures that cause human suffering

Any of you who have worked with young people know that the practice of this second step will not be easy. Young people are influenced as much as we all are by the illusions of a society that defines *human person* as *consumer*.[14] Notice, not as gardener, not as caretaker or steward, not as artist, not as lover or gift giver, but as *consumer,* a term that conjures up images of the stomach or the furnace.

Most of the young people I meet through my teaching have their sights already clearly set, not on the contributions they might one day make to the common good but on the range and quality of purchasable goods with which they will judge the success of their lives. However, the problem is not just this consumerist orientation. The deeper problem is that the young people do not see this orientation as a problem. Many of them have a mind-set that pits one person against another in the scramble to get "mine." So the task of encouraging critical analysis in the face of such a mind-set will not be easy.

What is significant here is that the bishops are telling us that analysis is the task. Today many persons working with young people in the name of the Church are not facing this task. Actually they are unable to face it, because they themselves have not been paying attention to economic, political, and social structures that cause human suffering. When they do occasionally speak of these matters, their speech is filled with code words and clichés that show they have paid more attention to the sports pages, the comics, and the sales in their newspapers than to the news. My fear is that such persons, whose skills of critical analysis have never been developed, will end up ladling out to youth huge, sticky gobs of religious comfort. Such comfort in one way or another encourages young people to regard themselves as their own special pets.[15]

Developing a sense of political, economic, and social structures demands of anyone at any age a certain amount of what Rollo May calls *perceptual courage*.[16] It is not easy for young people to look at human suffering and examine the structures that cause it. But we trivialize the potential of youth by encouraging them to live in a narcissistic world of self-interest. Speaking in Canada in 1984, a leading thinker about youth issues warned people to look at themselves and all society with critical eyes:

Begin your task by looking critically at yourselves and then at the society in which you live. . . .

Every day the media and the example of people around you present certain models of life. Very often these show selfishness winning over generosity. Today I invite you to look at *another model of humanity.* [17]

Those are the words of Pope John Paul II. Of all those speaking about youth and to youth today, he speaks the truth most clearly. In his 1985 World Day of Peace message to young people, he wrote:

The effective promotion of peace demands that we should not limit ourselves to deploring the negative effects of the present situation of crisis, conflict and injustice. What we are really required to do is to destroy the roots that cause these effects. Such ultimate causes are to be found especially in the ideologies that have dominated our century and continue to do so, manifesting themselves in political, economic and social systems. [18]

Here John Paul is offering youth not whipped cream but red meat. He is challenging them to pay attention to social structures.

Step 3: Making judgments in the light of gospel principles and the social teaching of the Church concerning social values and priorities

I wonder how many young people have heard the social teachings of the Church. Do they know that in the early Church, a person could not serve in the military and be a Christian at the same time? Are they aware that the Church is (and has been for years) calling for a redistribution of wealth, not as part of a Communist manifesto but as part of discipleship? Have they heard that "the basic rights of working people take priority over the maximization of profits and the accumulation of machines"? Are they familiar with the principle that "in a given economic order, the needs of the poor take priority over the wants of the rich," or that "in effect the participation of the marginalized takes precedence over an order that excludes them"? These last three quotes are taken from the pastoral letter of the Canadian bishops we have been referring to, *Ethical Choices and Political Challenges.* [19]

Are we ever going to get around to designing weekends of Christian living that get at these Gospel-based principles? Our COR, Search, and TEC weekends, as now structured, do not get at these matters, not even after twenty years of experience. [20] I am not suggesting we cancel every effort we have made with youth in order to deal with justice. But I am suggesting that to work with young people year in and year out and never get to these matters of justice is to shortchange youth on the Gospel and to trivialize their energies. No, it is more; it is to betray both the Gospel and the young.

Step 4: Stimulating creative thought and action regarding alternative visions and models for social and economic development

We live in a time when our lives are continually being imagined and reimagined for us by teams of quasi-hidden elites. Who are these persons imagining our lives for us? They are the scriptwriters of "Dallas", "Dynasty", and other depictions of what human life could be. Have you noticed how many movie ads in this week's newspapers depict a man with a gun in his hand? Those who create these images are imagining our lives for us, however subtly. How do they imagine the lives of women? Look at another series of movie ads, and you will see that to be a woman and to be alone is to be a potential victim. And how do they imagine young people? They imagine the time of youth as one of crass vulgarity, manipulative lust, and careless destructiveness. They imagine youth not at its best but at its least.

Part of the task of youth ministry is to help the young envision the world in new ways, to help them dream alternate dreams, to help them imagine their lives lived to the rhythms of Jesus rather than to those of mean-spirited men and women on "Dallas". Again, Pope John Paul II spoke to youth about this in 1984 in Canada, at Memorial University in Saint John's, Newfoundland.

> Every day the media and the example of people around you present certain models of life. Very often these show selfishness winning over generosity. Today I invite you to look at *another model of humanity.* . . .
>
> Begin by doing something concrete in your own situation. Do not look too far afield. Begin now where you work or study, in your youth groups, in your family circle, in your parish.

Then he said something that made the alternate model very concrete for those young people who heard him.

> Never allow anyone among your acquaintances to be deprived of his or her rights, or put down by others because he or she is not of your social milieu, or your color, or does not speak your language or share your faith. Refuse to build barriers between yourselves and older people.[21]

So the vision the pope offers youth is that of unity in the Spirit of God. In our society that unity is very much a countercultural vision. Increasingly in the future youth ministry that is worth anything will be countercultural. It will help young people to critique; to judge from a stance of commitment to one's fellow human beings; then to say no to junk, to lies, to what separates one person from the other, to what militarizes, and to whatever imperils the future of the race.

To be any good, youth ministry must encourage young people to boo, to give the big boo to those things that should be publicly booed. The capacity to boo is the potential to judge, to find that something does not measure up, and then to call for it to be rejected. My position here is similar to that of the pope when he spoke to young people at the Olympic Stadium in Montreal:

> In times of darkness, do not seek an escape. Have the courage to resist the dealers in deception who make capital of your hunger for happiness. . . . Have the courage not to take the easy path; have the courage to reverse direction if you have taken it. And know how to lend a helping hand to those of your companions who are haunted by despair when the darkness of the world is too cruel to them.[22]

Step 5: Acting in solidarity with popular groups in their struggles to transform economic, political, and social structures that cause social and economic injustices

With the fifth step we can see that the bishops' five steps contain the basic formula for Christian action outlined by Cardinal Cardijn for his Young Christian Worker and Young Christian Student groups: *See, judge, and act.*[23] Take note that this formula has been used in youth work for more than fifty years. But over the past twenty years, in the United States at least, it has been put aside for less radical, more upbeat, and easier-to-implement strategies. In their five steps, however, your own bishops now essentially are proposing Cardinal Cardijn's *see, judge, and act* as fundamental in working for justice.[24]

The fifth step of the bishops' pastoral methodology is especially about action. A brief caution is needed here. Some people judge that young people are not capable of significant action, and so they propose to them action that is safe and trivial—most often in the form of raising money. The energy, the attention, and the skill of young people are orchestrated into activities that are in solidarity with popular groups or causes. But these activities are often not in solidarity with the struggles of people to transform economic, political, and social structures. The role of young people then is reduced to one of generating funds to be spent by older persons to solve such and such a problem.

For example, in Australia two years ago a group of young people rode power mowers a thousand miles from Cairns down to Sydney to raise money for cancer research. The trip took enormous energy and many weeks of time on the part of the young. I wondered if these young people realized the relationship between cancer and nuclear power; I wondered whether, in those thousand miles of travel, they ever once reflected on the fact that their nation is one of the world's leading exporters of uranium. Could their energies have been better focused on this aspect of the problem instead of on raising money to cure cancer? In proposing action to youth, then, it is not enough for the cause to be significant; the action must also be significant.

Action to transform unjust social structures is an issue for youth ministry that needs a great deal of further attention. It is a key step in any educational aspect of our ministry with youth. If we divorce our educational work from action and, at the same time, live our lives with the young in middle-class parishes, our young people may never get to see the works of justice or to meet those who have risked all to do the works of justice. (They may see the Church engaged in education, but unfortunately young people tend not to name education as a work of justice.) They need to see the Church at the side of the poor and to see themselves as part of the caring body of the Church.

As Pope John Paul II told the young people in Newfoundland:

> Be present also in . . . situations [of injustice], because there your voice is needed and you will contribute and learn. Give your enthusiastic support to those local groups which are seeking to build a more human world, and then broaden your horizons and work with the joyful energy of youth to share with the hungry and with young people who have received less than you.[25]

Conclusion

We are assembled at this national convention to work out what the preferential option for youth will look like in the Canadian Church. I encourage all of you not to flinch from hard questions or even from proposing new directions. Behind all I have said here, and also behind the bishops' pastoral from which I have quoted, is a concern broader than the concern for youth. It is a concern for the sort of Church we are to be in its local embodiments.

I would like to conclude by asking you what would happen if we proposed to youth a true catechesis of signs. The catechesis of signs was the most seminal and ancient character of catechesis. Suppose in talking with youth about the Church, we stopped telling them what the Church is supposed to be and stopped claiming that these ideals *are* what the local church in fact really is when there is clear evidence to the contrary.

In other words, suppose we stopped asking youth to believe in the Church and instead asked them to examine the lived belief of the Church. Suppose we encouraged in young people an active search for signs of the lived Gospel among groups of people. Suppose we said to them something like this: "Go find the group of disciples of Jesus who most follow his way of siding with the victims. Find the ones whose lifestyle exhibits nonviolent love, patterns of sharing and compassion, and a concern for the future of this world of ours that is given us as a sign of God's love. Find those who have risked something to follow Jesus' way, and ask them if you can walk along with them while doing the works of justice and peace. Don't worry about what denomination they are with, just join their life."

If we proposed such a catechesis to youth, would they pick your parish? Would they pick a parish in your diocese? Would they pick a Roman Catholic parish at all? This is the question I leave with Canadian youth ministry as it faces the future of its options.

Notes

1. Third General Conference of Latin American Bishops, *Evangelization at Present and in the Future in Latin America: Conclusion* (Washington, DC: National Conference of Catholic Bishops, 1979).

2. Ibid., nos. 166–1205.

3. Ibid., no. 1168.

4. Ibid.

5. A stimulating series of reflections on the young church has been done by Micheal Liostún under the title "The Emerging Church," in the four 1983 issues of *Resource* magazine, published in Dublin by the Young Christian Workers.

6. Latin American Bishops, *Evangelization,* no. 1178.

7. Ibid., no. 1180.

8. This brief history has been more fully elaborated in Michael Warren, *Youth and the Future of the Church: Ministry with Youth and Young Adults* (Minneapolis: Winston-Seabury, 1982), pp. 1–26.

9. For an inkling of these problems, see Thomas P. Walters, *DRE: Issues and Concerns for the 80's* (Washington, DC: National Conference of Diocesan Directors of Religious Education, 1983).

10. Canadian Conference of Catholic Bishops, *Ethical Choices and Political Challenges: Ethical Reflections on the Future of Canada's Socio-Economic Order* (Ottawa: Canadian Conference of Catholic Bishops, 1984), p. 2.

11. Here I am paraphrasing sections from Robert Coles and G. A. White, "The Religion of the Privileged Ones," *Cross Currents* 31, no. 1 (1981): 1–14.

12. Except where indicated, the statistics that follow are from two sources: Minister for Indian and Northern Affairs, *Indian Conditions: A Survey* (Ottawa, 1980); and Health and Welfare Canada, Medical Services Branch, 1978–1981, *Annual Review.*

13. See Minister of State for Youth, *Youth/Jeunesse: A New Statistical Perspective on Youth in Canada* (Hull, Quebec: Public Affairs Branch, 1984), pp. 134 (Data Set 52) and 136 (Data Set 53). The extensive data in this document, which covers almost all aspects of youth in Canada, deserve the close attention of all people concerned with youth.

14. See Dorothee Soelle, "The Need for Liberation in a Consumerist Society," in Brian Mahan and L. Dale Richesin, eds., *The Challenge of Liberation Theology* (New York: Orbis Books, 1981), pp. 4–16.

15. Making oneself one's own pet is the direct opposite of prophetic concern, according to Canadian philosopher Donald Evans. See his *Struggle and Fulfillment* (New York: Collins, 1979), pp. 143–145. Also see Gregory Baum, "Theology Questions Psychiatry," *The Ecumenist* 20, no. 4 (May–June 1982): 55–59.

16. Rollo May, *The Courage to Create* (New York: Bantam, 1976), p. 8.

17. John Paul II, "Speech to Youth, Memorial University, Saint John's, Newfoundland, 12 September 1984," *Canadian Catholic Review* 2, no. 9 (October 1984): 346.

18. John Paul II, "Youth, Builders of the Twenty-first Century," *Origins* 14, no. 30 (10 January 1985): 493.

19. Canadian Bishops, *Ethical Choices,* pp. 5–6.

20. For an extended critique, see Michael Warren, "Youth Ministry: Further Dimensions of the Weekend Retreat," *Origins* 14, no. 6 (21 June 1984): 90–96.

21. See note 17 above.

22. John Paul II, "Talk to Youth, Olympic Stadium, Montreal, 11 September 1984," *Canadian Catholic Review* 2, no. 9 (October 1984): 341.

23. Cardinal Cardijn started the first Young Christian Worker groups in Belgium in 1912 and worked actively for more than fifty years.

24. See Michéal Liostún, *A Movement for Young Workers* (Dublin: Resource magazine, no date, but probably 1982).

25. See note 17 above.

Index

A

abortion, 155
accidents, 73
adaptation, principle of,
17–18, 140
adolescents: and catechesis,
65–67; and the Catholic
Church, 201, 229, 235, 240;
characteristics of, 49,
185–186, 228–229; and
congregations, 18–19, 37,
83–86, 114–115, 132,
148–149, 150; development
of, and religion curriculums,
121; experimental
commitments of, 81–86;
expressivity of, 32–33; and
faith, 119–120, 147–149; faith
development of, 47; and
feelings of statuslessness, 132;
junior high, 174–175; needs
of, 19–20, 99–101, 117–118,
138, 161–163, 165, 171–172,
208, 221; and negativity, 43;
and "searching faith," 48;
self-images of, 59, 147, 150,
153, 162; and service, 49–50,
58–60; and sex education,
209–217; and social justice,
60, 69 n.10; struggles of,
72–74, 75–77; study of
female, 151–165; view
religion as moral standard,
74, 148. *See also*
adult–adolescent relationships;
young people
adult-adolescent relationships,
37, 86–90, 118, 150,
159–160, 165, 192; building
trust in, 161; and community-
centered programs, 107–108;
in CYO and CCD, 200; and
fieldwork, 93; importance of,
16, 19; motives and methods
for developing successful,
144–146; myths about,
155–157; and Young Life,
174–175, 181. *See also*
adults; adolescents; parents;
youth ministers
adult education, 90, 193, 214
adults: faith development of,
106–107, 116, 194; and faith
sharing, 113, 134, 187–188,
189; leadership training of,
91, 115, 192–198; as models
of Christian lifestyle, 87, 95,
188; relationships among,
106–107, 190; young, 19–20,
50, 60, 67, 201; and Young
Life camping, 174; Young
Life ministry to, 179. *See
also* adult–adolescent
relationships; parents; youth
ministers
age-segregation, 89
alcohol and drugs, 158, 171
alienation, 115
atmosphere of friendship,
107–108, 118, 140, 182
Australia, 239
authoritarianism, 156, 164,
191

F

faith, 133–134, 148, 184; crisis of, 119–120, 124, 142, 150; expressed in liturgy, 34; motivates youth leaders, 144; in relation to catechesis and evangelization, 15; seeking language, 140; service as outgrowth of, 58, 109; sharing of, 113, 120, 141, 194

faith development, 56–57, 130–131, 190; of adolescents, 33, 64–67, 119–120, 147–149; of adults, 106–107, 116, 194; considered in curriculum planning, 123; on retreats, 35, 138; and wedge model, 43–53; Young Life encourages, 175–176

families, 73, 150, 154, 155–156, 164, 171, 230. *See also* parents

fellowship, 188, 190

fellowship groups, 97, 106–107. *See also* core groups

fieldwork, 92–94, 184

financing youth ministry, 183–184, 201–202

Five Cries of Youth, 74, 108, 143–150

follow-up, 46, 133, 141, 175–176

4-H (youth group), 162

freedom, personal, 57, 68 n.7, 134, 140, 231–232

friendship, 29, 185

fundamentalists, 78–79, 80

G

Gallup, George, Jr., 49

generation gap, myth of, 155

goals: of adolescent girls, 153–154; importance of, in program planning, 116–117; setting, for retreats, 142

God, 25–27, 148, 149

Gospel, the, 25–28, 237; and communitarian witness, 15–17, 133–134; and culture, 17–19, 22, 24–27, 234, 235; effect of, on Christians, 58, 130, 131; service as response to, 49; and Young Life, 172–173, 188. *See also* evangelization

grace, 131

grade school catechesis, 64–65

Gray, Donald, 113

Greeley, Andrew, 13

H

handicapped ministries, 177

homosexuality, 157, 235

Hope, Scott, 77

Huck, Gabe, 39 n.5

I

identity formation, 75–82

impressive-expressive continuum, 31–32

Incarnation, the, 18, 188

incest, 154

India, 18

Indians, Canadian, 235

indigenization, principle of, 17–19, 22
institutions, delinquency, 156–157
interdenominational youth ministry, 96, 169–179, 180–191
intergenerational friendships. *See* adult-adolescent relationships; mentor relationships
international ministry, Young Life, 175
interpretation, process of, 75–81
Ireland, 230

J

Jesus Christ, 18, 113, 148, 187–188; and the gospel message, 25–27; identifies with victims, 22, 24, 189; ministry of, 14, 51–52; as model, 119, 140. *See also* Christ-centeredness
John Paul II, 22–23, 236–237, 238, 239, 240
journal-writing, 191
junior high school, 174–175, 209–217
justice and peace, 49–50, 227–240

K

kerussein, 15
kerygma, 45, 46
Kimball, Don, 43, 68 n.3, 180

L

laity: in parish ministry, 93–96, 233; and Young Life, 180–191; on youth retreats, 142
language: and identity formation, 76–81; in ministry, 108, 145; and principle of adaptation, 140; religious, in youth groups, 98–99; in youth liturgies, 18
Latin America, 228–229
laypeople. *See* laity
leadership: adolescents seek role in parish, 86, 115; in congregations, 132; of retreat directors, 139; style of, in CCD and CYO, 200
leadership training, 95–97, 137, 146, 162–163, 192–198, 199–207; selecting volunteers for, 115; for sexuality program, 213–214, 215–217; shortcomings of seminary, 91–94; and wedge model, 50–51; Young Life, 178, 184–185, 188, 190; for young people, 14, 109
Levinson, Daniel, 88–89
liberal churches: threats to, 84
liberation and evangelization, 27–29
Liégé, Piere-André, 15
Liégé's Evangelization School, 15
listening, importance of, 33, 140, 145, 192
liturgy, 16, 18, 21, 22, 30–39, 214, 215, 230, 231
loneliness, 155, 157
Lonergan, Bernard, 39 n.3
love, 29

Luckmann, Thomas, 132–133
Lyman Coleman–type group
programs, 108

M

McKenna, John, 34
Maguire, Daniel, 29
mainline churches, patterns of
interpretation in, 78–81
marriage, 153, 154
Marriage Encounter, 142
Marthaler, Berard, 69 n.8
Mass. *See* Eucharist
matturein, 15
May, Rollo, 236
media, influence of, 23, 24–25,
220, 222, 230, 238
mentor relationships, 86–90
ministry: call into, 190;
community support of, 54–55,
55–56; development of
models of, encouraged, 97;
elements of successful,
144–146; laypersons in,
93–96, 233; models of, 186,
187; principles of, 14–19,
138–142, 185–188; radio,
218–223; to young adults,
19–20. *See also* peer
ministry; youth ministry
ministry of friendship, 43, 45,
108, 109–110, 144–146. *See
also* relational ministry
ministry of guidance and
counsel, 233
ministry of healing, 233
ministry of the Word, 22, 232.
See also liturgy
ministry of worship. *See*
worship
missionaries, 14–15

mission of youth ministry, 150
model programs: adolescent
sexuality, 209–217; leadership
training, 194–197; youth
ministry certification,
202–207
models, use of, 42
"moment of recognition,"
46–47, 48, 57. *See also*
conversion
motivation of youth leaders,
144
music ministry, 218–223
mutuality, 150

N

Nebreda, Alfonso, 15
needs of adolescents, 19–20,
99–101, 117–118, 138,
161–163, 165, 171–172, 208,
221
Nelson, Ellis, 95
Ng, David, 82
Niebuhr, H. Richard, 76
North America, 22, 27, 62

O

orchestras, 97
ordained ministry, 91–96, 201

P

parents, 135–136, 142; and
adolescent girls, 155–156; and
alcohol and drug abuse, 158;
and children discuss sexuality,
209–217; resist youth ministry
methodology, 235; role of, in
youth ministry, 56–57; as
volunteer pool, 193
parish catechetical programs,
104–111

Acknowledgments (*continued*)

Essay 4, "Youth Ministry: Reflections and Directions" by Tom Zanzig on pages 41–70, is a revised reprint from *PACE* 11 (Winona, MN: Saint Mary's Press, 1980–81), Special Supplement. Used by permission of the publisher.

Essay 8, "Developing Religion Curriculums in Catholic High Schools" by Tom Zanzig on pages 121–136, is reprinted from *Ministry Management* 6, no. 3. (Winona, MN: Saint Mary's Press, 1986), by permission of the publisher.

Essay 11, "Effective Ministry to Youth" on pages 143–150, is excerpted from *Five Cries of Youth* by Merton P. Strommen. Copyright © 1974 by Merton P. Strommen. Reprinted by permission of Harper & Row, Publishers, Inc.

Essay 12, "Adolescent Girls: A Two-Year Study" by Gisela Konopka on pages 151–166, is reprinted from *Center Quarterly Focus* (Minneapolis: University of Minnesota's Center for Youth Development and Research, Fall 1975), pages 1–8. Used by permission of the author.

Essay 13, "Young Life Statement of Mission Purpose," ratified on 26 April 1986 by the Young Life Board of Trustees, on pages 169–179, is taken from *Young Life's Board of Trustees Manual* (Colorado Springs, CO: 1985). Used by permission of Young Life.